DA

P9-AOK-292

DUKE UNIVERSITY PUBLICATIONS

LONDON

AND THE

NATIONAL GOVERNMENT, 1721-1742

LONDON

AND THE

NATIONAL GOVERNMENT, 1721-1742

A Study of City Politics and the
Walpole Administration

BY

ALFRED JAMES HENDERSON

DURHAM, NORTH CAROLINA

DUKE UNIVERSITY PRESS

1945

PRINTED IN THE UNITED STATES OF AMERICA
BY THE SEEMAN PRINTERY, INC., DURHAM, N. C.

To

Mother and Dad

PREFACE

ALTHOUGH studies have been made in the social and economic history of eighteenth-century London,[1] there has been no careful examination of the political history of the City. Sharpe gives the eighteenth century a proportionate place in his *London and the Kingdom*.[2] Since he covers some fourteen centuries, however, his work is of necessity rather general in scope and treats with detail only particular phases and events. Sidney and Beatrice Webb, in a chapter on the City of London in their exhaustive study of English local government,[3] give an excellent picture of the machinery of the City government in the eighteenth century but touch only briefly the political history.

My purpose has been to make a careful study of London politics during the administration of Sir Robert Walpole, a time peculiarly adapted for such a study, since in this period of twenty-one years the national government was under the continuous leadership of one man. I have attempted to show on the one hand the participation of the Londoners in national affairs and their influence on the policies of the administration, and on the other the effect of the national situation on London politics—noting at the same time the participation of various members of the ministry and the Opposition in the local City elections and their activities in "creating" a public opinion in London.

My obligations to those who already have made studies of various sorts in this period are numerous. I am grateful to the

[1] Sir Walter Besant, *London in the Eighteenth Century* (London, 1903); Edwin B. Chancellor, *The Eighteenth Century in London: An Account of Its Social Life and Arts* (London, 1920); and Dorothy M. George, *London Life in the Eighteenth Century* (New York, 1925).

[2] Reginald R. Sharpe, *London and the Kingdom* (3 vols., London, 1894-1895).

[3] Sidney and Beatrice Webb, *English Local Government from the Revolution to the Municipal Corporations Act: The Manor and the Borough*, Part II (London, 1908), pp. 569-692.

staffs of the Duke University Library, of the Library of Congress, of the Yale University Library, of the Library of the University of Toronto, of the City of London Guildhall Library and the Record Office of the Corporation, of the British Museum, of the Public Record Office, and of the Institute of Historical Research of the University of London, for their assistance and co-operation.

I am deeply obligated to Professor William Thomas Laprade, who suggested the subject to me and who gave generous and kindly assistance and advice during the preparation of this study.

I appreciate especially the inspiration and constant encouragement of my wife, Elizabeth Aldridge Henderson.

A. J. H.

CONTENTS

[ix]

LONDON

AND THE

NATIONAL GOVERNMENT, 1721-1742

CHAPTER I

The National Administration and the City in 1721

London's Importance in National Affairs

Since the early days of England's history, the City of London has held an important position in the national life. A survey of all the recorded instances in which it has participated in the affairs of the kingdom would be, according to one writer, "the history of England as seen from the windows of the Guildhall."[1] London gained early recognition in Roman and Saxon times. Norman William treated it with marked favor. Stephen obtained the throne largely through its influence. It helped to wrest Magna Charta from King John. It had a hand in the deposing of Edward II, Richard II, and Henry VI and in the elevation of Edward IV and Richard III. It supplied the men and money by which Edward III and Henry V conquered France, and contributed twenty ships to the fleet that defeated the Armada of Spain. It had its part in the settlement of Northern Ireland and in the colonization of Virginia. It supported Parliament against Charles I and turned the tide of the Civil War when the City trainbands raised the siege of Gloucester. It received back the second Charles, speeded his brother James on his way, and welcomed the Prince of Orange. It warmly accepted the first George and for over two centuries has given loyal support to his successors.

The friendship—or enmity—of the City, therefore, has always been of prime importance to the ruling powers of the nation, and those at the helm have done well to court its favor.[2] Robert Walpole, who became chief minister in 1721, was to be

---

[1] W. J. Loftie, *London* ("Historic Towns Series," London, 1887), p. 192.

[2] "Have none . . . read in the Debates of Parliament, That the Weight of England is in the People; That this weight has sunk Ministers of State in almost all Ages; and the Conduct of the Citizens of London has generally turned the Scale?" (*Champion*, Dec. 1, 1739.)

no exception. Although of the landed gentry himself, he recognized the importance to the nation of the development of the commerce and trade of the City and was sympathetic with those who were engaged therein. His abilities and interests along financial lines promised him an entrée to the commercial-minded Londoners, which should have made him the most popular of chief ministers. But in 1721 there was dissension in the City. Says one writer: "London was distraught; its leaders in factions were at each other's throats. Walpole's knack at figures, his ability to talk of money as a practical man gave him a way there most politicians lacked. But divisions among themselves made the citizens a source of weakness instead of strength."[3]

To the Hanoverian king, George I, Londoners all manifested an outward loyalty, and the majority accepted him in good faith. There were many, however, who could not forget the days of Queen Anne and still centered their affection on the Church of England. There were many, also, who thought more than wistfully of the "king across the water." Even those who gladly gave allegiance to George I could not agree in their support of his ministers. And the South Sea episode of 1720 had tended to increase the animosities. All this was manifested in the unrest among the populace, in the usually far from peaceful conduct of the wardmote and Common Hall elections, in the rivalry between the Court of Aldermen and the Court of Common Council, and in the suspicion and opposition raised at any governmental interference with the City's commerce and trade. Walpole thus began his administration faced by an herculean task—the uniting of a disunited citizenry.

In this task he was to have little success, and the history of his twenty-one years of power in its relationship with the City of London was a history of almost constant opposition by the majority of the citizens. Moreover, Walpole's appeal to the merchants, which should have insured him their hearty support, failed to bring a favorable reaction; and London's clamor in 1721 at the Quarantine measures, the outcry in 1733 against

[3] W. T. Laprade, *Public Opinion and Politics in Eighteenth Century England* (New York, 1936), pp. 253-254.

the Excise Bill, and the tumult over the Spanish War in 1738-1739 were to be blamed, wholly or partly, on the opposition of the commercial interests. All this struggle, however, in the spring of 1721, was far ahead. Although unrest was everywhere apparent among the citizens, hope still ran high that London would welcome the new administration.

ROBERT WALPOLE AND HIS RISE TO POWER

Officially Robert Walpole took over the seals of office of First Lord of the Treasury and Chancellor of the Exchequer, involving also the leadership of the ministry, during the first week in April,[4] but he had already been exercising the functions of these offices for a month or more.[5] It was a momentous step in the career of the ambitious Norfolk squire, who had begun his parliamentary life twenty years earlier as a member from the family borough of Castle Rising.[6]

Walpole's rise had been rapid. His personal abilities and talents, his family connections, and his activities in the House

[4] The actual date varies. Abel Boyer, in his *Political State of Great Britain* (London, 1711-1740), XXI (1721), 449, gives April 1; William Coxe, in the first volume of his *Memoirs of the Life and Administration of Sir Robert Walpole, Earl of Orford* (London, 1798), gives it as April 2 on page 159, and as April 3 on page 730; the *Historical Register*, London, VI (1721), 113, implies either the first or second; and the *Daily Courant*, April 5, 1721, reports it as of the previous day, April 4.

[5] Sir John Vanbrugh to the Earl of Carlisle, Feb. 7, 1721, *The Complete Works of Sir John Vanbrugh*, ed. Bonamy Dobrée and Geoffrey Webb (London, 1928), IV, 128; and the Historical Manuscripts Commission, Fifteenth Report, Appendix, Part VI, *The Manuscripts of the Earl of Carlisle, Preserved at Castle Howard* (hereinafter cited as H.M.C., *Carlisle MSS*) (London, 1897), p. 29. See also the Fifteenth Report, *The Manuscripts of J. M. L. S. Clements, Esq.*, in *Report on Manuscripts in Various Collections* (hereinafter cited as H.M.C., *Clements MSS*), VIII, 300.

[6] The standard biography of Walpole is the three-volume work of William Coxe, *Memoirs of the Life and Administration of Sir Robert Walpole* (London, 1798). The second and third volumes contain letters and other documents which give valuable contemporary information about Walpole and affairs of the period. A. C. Ewald, *Sir Robert Walpole: A Political Biography* (London, 1878), is based largely on Coxe's materials, as are the shorter works of Edward Jenks, *Walpole: A Study in Politics* (London, 1894), and John Morley, *Walpole* (London, 1896). F. S. Oliver, *The Endless Adventure* (London, 1930), has used the life of the chief minister as the central theme of his philosophizing on politics. The most recent study, using materials not available to Coxe and the nineteenth-century writers who followed him, is that of G. R. Sterling Taylor, *Robert Walpole: And His Age* (London, 1931).

of Commons, all attracted to him the attention of those in high places. He had received rewards from his friends and punishments from his enemies. Through the former he was appointed to the offices of Secretary at War in 1708 and Treasurer of the Navy in 1710. By the latter he was confined for six months in the Tower. With the coming of George I to the throne he had climbed to higher places. Under his brother-in-law, Viscount Townshend,[7] as chief minister, he had been made Paymaster of the Forces in September, 1714, and then First Lord of the Treasury and Chancellor of the Exchequer in October, 1715. Dissension, however, had arisen in the ministry. There was a divergence of opinion over foreign policy. George I wanted war in the interest of Hanover, and Lord Stanhope,[8] the second Secretary of State, was willing to aid him. Townshend wanted peace in the interest of England. The result was that Stanhope, with George I, won, and in April, 1717, Walpole followed Townshend out of office. For three years he sat on the benches of the opposition to the ministry of Lord Stanhope and Lord Sunderland.[9] Then came reconciliation in

[7] Charles Townshend (1674-1738), second Viscount Townshend, succeeded to the peerage in 1687. In 1707 he became a privy councillor and served as Secretary of State for the Northern Department in 1714-1716 and in 1721-1730, retiring from the government in that latter year and devoting himself to agriculture. His first wife was Elizabeth, daughter of Thomas Pelham and sister of the Duke of Newcastle; his second was Dorothy, sister of Robert Walpole. See J. M. Rigg, "Charles Townshend, second Viscount Townshend," *Dictionary of National Biography* (hereinafter cited as *D. N. B.*) (London, 1899), LVII, 109-117.

[8] James Stanhope (1673-1721), first Earl Stanhope, entered Parliament in 1701. He served in the army under Marlborough and rose to the rank of brigadier general. He was made British minister to Spain in 1706, and became commander of the British forces there in 1708. He served as Secretary of the Southern Department, 1714-1716; as First Lord of the Treasury and Chancellor of the Exchequer, 1717-1718; and as Secretary of State for the Northern Department, 1718-1721. He was raised to the peerage in 1718. See Colonel E. M. Lloyd, "James Stanhope, first Earl Stanhope," *D. N. B.*, LIV, 14-19, and Basil Williams, *Stanhope: A Study in Eighteenth Century Diplomacy* (London, 1932).

[9] Charles Spencer (1674-1722), third Earl of Sunderland, entered Parliament in 1695. Upon the death of his father in 1702 he took his seat in the House of Lords. He served as Secretary of State for the Southern Department, 1706-1710; Lord Lieutenant of Ireland, 1714-1716; as Lord President of the Council and Secretary of State for the Northern Department, 1717-1718; and as First Lord of the Treasury and Lord President of the Council, 1718-1721. His first wife, Lady Arabella Cavendish, daughter of the second

the spring of 1720 and appointment to the office of Paymaster of the Forces. It was a subordinate post for the former First Lord and Chancellor of the Exchequer, but from it he moved within a year to the topmost place.

This opportunity came when the national situation was maturative. In foreign affairs things had just been made fairly quiet. For several years England had carried on a policy based on a desire for peace in the interest of her trade, and on the whole it had been successful. In the north England's connection with Hanover had drawn her into the hostilities in which Sweden, Denmark, Prussia, and Russia were involved, but peace had finally been brought about, and England had signed the Treaty of Stockholm in January, 1720.[10] In the Southern Department mutual treaties for aid against their enemies had been made with Austria and France in 1716; and in the next year England had signed a treaty with France and the Netherlands, which became known as the Triple Alliance. Joined by the Emperor in 1718, it had become the Quadruple Alliance, also defensive in character, but formed with the design of restraining the extravagant pretensions of Spain. Spain, however, had resisted. War, a short one, then followed, and the Spaniards were defeated on land and sea. In February, 1720, Philip V joined the Quadruple Alliance, and Europe embarked on a period of peace which was to last for twelve years.[11]

In domestic affairs, on the other hand, the situation was far less settled. The year 1720 had seen the bursting of the South

Duke of Newcastle, died three years after their marriage; in 1700 he married Lady Anne Churchill, daughter of the Duke of Marlborough. See G. Le G. Nargate, "Charles Spencer, third Earl of Sunderland," *D. N. B.*, LIII, 343-349.

[10] See James F. Chance, *George I and the Northern War: A Study of British-Hanoverian Policy in the North of Europe, 1709-1721* (London, 1909).

[11] For the foreign situation at this time see the *Cambridge Modern History*, VI ("The Eighteenth Century") (New York, 1909), pp. 21-39; I. S. Leadam, *History of England, from the Accession of Anne to the Death of George II, 1702-1760* (London, 1909), pp. 272-287; Sir Richard Lodge, *Great Britain and Prussia in the Eighteenth Century* (Oxford, 1923), pp. 7-16; *British Diplomatic Instructions, 1689-1789*, Volume II, *France, 1689-1721*, ed. L. G. Wickham Legg (London, 1925), pp. xxiii-xxxviii.

Sea Bubble,[12] with a resulting decline in public credit and an accompanying rise of a tide of bitterness and hatred against the South Sea Company's directors and, though not to the same extreme, against the national administration. "The consternation is inexpressible, the rage beyond expression, and the case so desperate that I doe nott see any plan or scheme as much as thought of, for averting the blow," wrote Thomas Brodrick to his brother, the Lord Chancellor of Ireland, in September.[13] Walpole, however, when Parliament reconvened in December, had a plan to present which was finally approved by both Houses after a long struggle.[14] This plan, while doing some good and for a time keeping up the stocks, as Walpole himself asserted, nevertheless was not so successful as had been hoped and proved "to be a mere Palliative, which had rather inflamed than alienated the Distemper," as William Shippen, Walpole's "honest" opponent, pointed out in April.[15] Further measures would have to be taken before public credit could be restored.

During the winter attention was also given to the punishment of those responsible for the disaster, and the popular sentiment was strongly in favor of immediate retribution. In this Walpole agreed, but he saw the risks in allowing men's passions to run away with their reason.[16] The government was in danger. Charges of receiving stock as bribes were brought against Lord Sunderland (£50,000), James Craggs,

[12] For accounts see Coxe, *Sir Robert Walpole*, I, 126 ff.; Norris A. Briscoe, *The Economic Policy of Robert Walpole* (New York, 1907), pp. 41 ff.; William R. Scott, *The Constitution and Finance of English, Scottish, and Irish Joint-Stock Companies to 1720* (Cambridge, 1911), III, 288-360; Lewis Melville, *The South Sea Bubble* (London, 1921).

[13] Coxe, *Sir Robert Walpole*, II, 190 (Midleton Papers, Sept. 13, 1720).

[14] This was the famous Ingraftment Scheme. By it the public contracts with the South Sea Company were to be preserved inviolate; nine millions of its stock was to be ingrafted into the Bank of England; a similar amount, under like conditions, was to be ingrafted into the East India Company; whilst the remainder (some twenty millions) was to be left to the South Sea Company. The responsibility being thus divided, it was felt that public confidence would again be established and the South Sea Company be given a chance to get on its feet. See copy of this proposal sent by Walpole to the King, in Coxe, *Sir Robert Walpole*, II, 197-201. The idea was good, but it was not carried through, and the act passed in this session was superseded by another in the next.

[15] Boyer, *Political State*, XXI, 443-445.

[16] Coxe, *Sir Robert Walpole*, I, 140, 151.

Sr.[17] (£30,000), John Aislabie[18] (£22,000), Charles Stanhope[19] (£10,000), and others for varying amounts. The situation was serious for the Sunderland-Stanhope ministry. Walpole, fortunately, had been among the opposition when the South Sea Bill had been passed in Parliament in March, 1720; and since he had been given only a minor post in the government in April, and was moreover at his Houghton estate throughout the summer while the South Sea scandal was at its height, he "had scarcely taken any part in public transactions, and did not share with the administration the general odium."[20] Yet it called for all of his skill and influence to prevent its complete ruin.

A kindly fate, however, assumed a part of the burden of his task and helped to clear the stage for him as chief actor. Lord Stanhope, apparently guiltless in the South Sea affair, was seized with a "rush of blood to his head" while defending his administration in the House of Lords (February 4, 1721) and died the next day.[21] On February 16 James Craggs the younger,[22] the second Secretary of State, died of smallpox.[23] Exactly a month later the elder Craggs, the Postmaster-General, just the day before his case was to be presented to the

[17] James Craggs (1656-1721), the elder, began his parliamentary career in 1702. He held minor offices in Anne's reign, through the patronage of the Duke of Marlborough, and became Postmaster-General with Lord Cornwallis in 1715 (D. N. B., XII, 439-440).

[18] John Aislabie (1670-1742) entered Parliament in 1695. He was in the Admiralty Office from 1710 and was appointed Treasurer of the Navy in 1714. He became Chancellor of the Exchequer in 1718 (D. N. B., I, 203-205).

[19] Charles Stanhope (1673-1760) was Undersecretary of the Southern Department, 1714-1717, and Secretary of the Treasury, 1720-1721. Charged with illegal dealing in South Sea stock, he was acquitted by only three votes (D. N. B., LIV, 40).

[20] Coxe, Sir Robert Walpole, I, 138.

[21] Weekly Journal, or Saturday's Post, Feb. 11, 1721; H. M. C., Clements MSS, p. 229 (Arthur Onslow to John Molesworth, Feb. 4, 1721); Boyer, Political State, XXI, 182.

[22] James Craggs (1686-1721), the younger, entered Parliament in 1713. He was appointed Secretary at War in 1717, and took over the office of Secretary of State for the Southern Department in 1718 (D. N. B., XII, 440-441).

[23] Boyer, Political State, XXI, 183; H. M. C., Fifteenth Report, The Manuscripts of His Grace the Duke of Portland, Preserved at Welbeck Abbey (hereinafter cited as H. M. C., Portland MSS), V, 614 (Edward Harley to the Earl of Oxford, Feb. 17, 1721).

Commons, committed suicide.[24]   John Aislabie, who had resigned as Chancellor of the Exchequer on January 23, was
convicted of promoting the South Sea to his personal profit
and on March 8 was expelled from the House and committed
to the Tower.[25]   Finally, Lord Sunderland, although formally
acquitted by Parliament for his connection with the South Sea,
could not remain in office, and on April 1, 1721, resigned as
First Lord of the Treasury.[26]

Thus the stage was set for a new leader of George I's ministry, and Robert Walpole took over that principal role.   With
him were his brother-in-law, Viscount Townshend, as Secretary
of State for the Northern Department, and the young Lord
Carteret[27] as Secretary of State for the Southern Department.
Lord Macclesfield[28] continued as Lord Chancellor, and the
Duke of Argyll[29] remained as Lord Steward.   Lord Carleton[30]
was made Lord President of the Council, and Lord Corn-

[24] Boyer, *Political State*, XXI, 312; H. M. C., *Portland MSS*, V, 619
(Edward Harley to Abigail Harley, March 19, 1721); H. M. C., Fourteenth
Report, *The Manuscripts of the Earl of Onslow* (hereinafter cited as H. M. C.,
Onslow MSS), p. 511.

[25] Boyer, *Political State*, XXI, 95, 308-312; Coxe, *Sir Robert Walpole*,
II, 210 (Midleton Papers).

[26] *Applebee's Original Weekly Journal*, April 8, 1721; Boyer, *Political
State*, XXI, 318, 449.

[27] John Carteret (1690-1763), Earl Granville, succeeded his father as
Baron Carteret in 1695, and took his seat in the House of Lords in 1711.
Made envoy to Sweden in 1719, he had been very active in the negotiations
which led to peace in Northern Europe (*D. N. B.*, IX, 210-215).   See Archibald Ballantyne, *Lord Carteret: A Political Biography, 1690-1763* (London,
1887); W. B. Pemberton, *Carteret: The Brilliant Failure of the Eighteenth
Century* (London, 1936); Basil Williams, *Carteret and Newcastle* (Cambridge, 1943).

[28] Sir Thomas Parker (1666?-1732), first Earl of Macclesfield, became a
barrister of the Inner Temple in 1691, and entered Parliament in 1705.   He
was appointed Lord Chief Justice in 1710, raised to the peerage as Baron
Macclesfield in 1716, and made Lord Chancellor in 1718 (*D. N. B.*, XLIII,
278-282).

[29] John Campbell, second Duke of Argyll and Duke of Grenwich, served
with distinction in the wars in Flanders and Spain.   He had been largely responsible for crushing the Jacobite Rebellion in 1715.   In disfavor in 1716,
he had been restored in 1719 and made Lord Steward of the Household
(*D. N. B.*, VIII, 369-373).

[30] Henry Boyle (d. 1725), Lord Carleton, entered Parliament in 1689.
He was Chancellor of the Exchequer in 1701-1708 and Secretary of State for
the Northern Department, 1708-1710.   He was raised to the peerage in 1714
(*D. N. B.*, VI, 110).

wallis[31] the Paymaster of the Forces, while Galfridus Walpole[32] and Edward Carteret[33] became Postmasters-General. Horatio Walpole[34] was made a Secretary of the Treasury, and on the board sat Henry Pelham,[35] Sir Charles Turner, George Baillie, and Richard Edgecombe. Lord Sunderland was content with the office of Groom of the Stole, and the Duke of Newcastle[36] continued as Lord Chamberlain. Others of the ministry included Charles Stanhope, William Pulteney,[37] the Duke of Grafton,[38] the Duke of Kingston,[39] and the Earl of Berkeley.[40]

It is in its relations with this administration, beginning with Robert Walpole's appointment as First Lord and Chancellor in April, 1721, and continuing until his resignation in February, 1742, that the course of local politics in the City of London will be considered in this volume.

[31] Charles Cornwallis (d. 1722), first Earl Cornwallis.

[32] Galfridus Walpole (1684-1726), a younger brother of Sir Robert.

[33] Edward Carteret, uncle to Lord Carteret.

[34] Horatio (or Horace) Walpole (1678-1757), first Baron Walpole of Wolterton, was a younger brother of Sir Robert. He entered Parliament in 1702, and remained a member for fifty-four years. He is best known for his diplomatic activities at The Hague and at Paris during his brother's administration. See William Coxe, *Memoirs of Horatio, Lord Walpole, 1678-1757* (London, 1820).

[35] Henry Pelham (1695?-1754), brother of the Duke of Newcastle, entered Parliament in 1717, and was a consistent supporter of Walpole (*D. N. B.*, XLIV, 244-247).

[36] Sir Thomas Pelham-Holles (1693-1768), first Duke of Newcastle-upon-Tyne and of Newcastle-under-Lyme. Upon the marriage of his brother-in-law Viscount Townshend with Dorothy Walpole, in 1713, he had been brought into close relations with Robert Walpole; but his own marriage, in 1717, with Lady Henrietta, daughter of the Earl of Godolphin and granddaughter of the Duke of Marlborough, connected him with Lord Sunderland, whom he had supported in the schism of 1717. He had then been made Lord Chamberlain of the Household (*D. N. B.*, XLIV, 257-261). See Stebelton H. Nulle, *Thomas Pelham-Holles, Duke of Newcastle: His Early Political Career, 1693-1724* (Philadelphia, 1931).

[37] Sir William Pulteney (1684-1764), Earl of Bath, had entered Parliament in 1705. He became Secretary at War in 1714, and had concurred with Walpole in resigning office in 1717. His failure to receive a major office in 1721 contributed to his going into opposition in 1725 (*D. N. B.*, XLVII, 28-35).

[38] Charles Fitzroy (1683-1757), second Duke of Grafton, was Lord Lieutenant of Ireland.

[39] Sir Evelyn Pierrepont (1665-1726), first Duke of Kingston, was Keeper of the Privy Seal.

[40] James Berkeley (1680-1736), third Earl of Berkeley, was First Lord of the Admiralty.

The City of London in 1721

What was the London of 1721? No sprawling metropolis of seven hundred square miles such as now spreads itself on both sides of the winding River Thames from Hampton Court to the Plumstead Marshes and boasts a population of over eight millions of people. The City of London then, with its twenty-six wards, was not much more than the present "City"—the famous "Square Mile"—and contained only about 160,000 inhabitants.[41] Outside the wards, however, to the north and east, were the liberties, or suburbs, over which the City had jurisdiction, filled with an ever-growing population. To the west, beyond Temple Bar and connected by Holborn and the Strand, was the separate though contiguous City of Westminster. To the south, across the Thames by London Bridge, was the borough of Southwark. Beyond, on all sides, stretched the fields and woods; Lambeth, Chelsea, Knightsbridge, Hammersmith, Kensington, Paddington, Tottenham Court, Islington, Bethnal Green, Stepney, Hackney, and Greenwich were still independent market towns and villages. Already, however, Greater London was spreading out to them and would engulf them within the century.[42]

London in 1721, though small in comparison with its twentieth-century counterpart, was a city of wealth and power. One of its contemporaries called it "the fairest and most opulent City at this Day in all Europe, perhaps of the whole World."[43] Another termed it "the largest in Extent, the fairest built, the

[41] Exact figures for the City in 1721 are not available. Sidney and Beatrice Webb, *English Local Government: The Manor and the Borough*, Part II, p. 617 n., give the estimated population in 1725 as 150,000. Dorothy George, *London Life in the XVIII Century*, p. 329, gives it as 208,300 in 1700 and 144,000 in 1750, showing the effect of the trend towards the suburbs after the end of the seventeenth century.

[42] John Chamberlayne, *Magna Britannia Notitia; or the Present State of Great Britain* (London, 1718), p. 203, estimated the population of the metropolitan area as 695,076. William Maitland, *The History and Survey of London, from the Foundation to the Present Time* (London, 1756), II, 744, estimated it as 725,903 in 1732. The population of England and Wales in 1720, according to C. G. Robertson, *England under the Hanoverians* (London, 1911), p. 336, was approximately five and one-half millions, which shows that almost 13 per cent of the English people were centered in and near the City.

[43] Chamberlayne, *Magna Britannia Notitia*, p. 281.

most populace, and best inhabited."[44] Maitland re-echoed both,
calling London "the most populous and opulent City and Emporium upon Earth."[45] Defoe, marveling at its growth, ex-
claimed: "How much farther it may spread, who knows? New
Squares, and new Streets rising up every Day to such a Prodigy
of Buildings, that nothing in the World does, or ever did,
equal it."[46] It was governed as a municipal corporation. Its
constitution had been formed and developed through seven centuries; upheld and maintained by a vast number of charters,
acts of parliament, and local promulgations. The ancient "Corporation of the Mayor and Commonalty and Citizens of London," with its headquarters at the historic Guildhall of the
City, had become a powerful organization, wielding vast and
not altogether definite powers; exercising complete jurisdiction
over its own territories, and even over parts of the adjacent
counties; regulating and taxing the Port of London and holding
authority over the River Thames from the Medway to Staines
Bridge; enjoying a monopoly of the markets in the country
round about within a circuit of seven miles; and levying coal
duties over a radius of twelve miles. Its income was enormous
and its patronage large.[47]

London, therefore, could easily claim the premier position
among municipalities throughout the kingdom. The City's
wealth, position, and size were readily recognizable. Its close
contact with the Court and Westminster were strategic and
advantageous. It was to be reckoned with in national affairs.
Furthermore, London was not without privileges. Its chief
magistrate, the Lord Mayor, was virtually the King's Lieutenant. At certain times he was summoned to meetings of the
Privy Council, and regularly he was officially notified of important public events. The Corporation, by its Court of Alder-

[44] Robert Seymour, *A Survey of the Cities of London and Westminster,
Borough of Southwark, and Parts Adjacent* (London, 1734), I, 3.

[45] Maitland, *History of London*, II, 713.

[46] Daniel Defoe, *A Tour thro' the Whole Island of Great Britain*, ed.
G. D. H. Cole, reprinting of the first edition, 1724-1726 (London, 1927),
I, 316.

[47] Cf. S. and B. Webb, *English Local Government*, pp. 571-572; "The
Decline and Fall of the Corporation of London," *Frazer's Magazine*, XLIX,
15.

men and Court of Common Council, had the right of access to the Throne. By the Sheriff's appearance at the Bar of the House of Commons London could make a formal statement of its own or the country's grievances. Four representatives regularly sat for it in Parliament, and through them and the Londoners who sat for other constituencies the City had a real voice in the consideration of affairs of national interest or matters of local concern. The citizens, moreover, were never lax in making themselves heard when occasion demanded, and at those times they seemed to assume for themselves the right to speak for the rest of the people of the kingdom.[48]

How London Was Governed

In 1721 as today, the chief dignitary in London was the Lord Mayor. He was the representative of all its wealth and opulence and the presiding officer of the many and varied "courts"—judicial, legislative, and executive in character— which formed the framework of the Corporation and carried on its business. Of these, four were of primary importance: namely, the Court of Aldermen, the Court of Common Council, the Court of Common Hall, and, meeting separately in each of the twenty-six wards, a Court of Wardmote. To assist the Lord Mayor, two Sheriffs were elected annually. There were also the Recorder, or legal adviser, the Chamberlain, or treasurer, the Town Clerk, and a host of lesser officers. Popular election, for England of that day, played a real part in the selection of all these, yet only a minority of the City's popula-

---

[48] For a detailed study of the Corporation of the City of London, its development, and its government in the eighteenth century, the reader is referred to the chapter on "The City of London," in S. and B. Webb, *English Local Government: The Manor and the Borough* (Part II, pp. 569-685); Seymour, *Survey of London;* Maitland, *History of London; City Liberties: or, the Rights and Privileges of Freemen, Being a Concise Abridgement of all the Laws, Charters, By-Laws, and Customs of London, down to This Time* (London, 1732); Henry A. Merewether, *History of the Boroughs and Municipal Corporations of the United Kingdom* (London, 1835); George Norton, *Commentaries on the History, Constitution, and Chartered Franchises of the City of London* (London, 1839); Alexander Pulling, *Practical Treatise on the Laws, Customs and Regulations of the City of London* (London, 1842); Walter de Gray Birch, *The Historical Charters and Constitutional Documents of the City of London* (London, 1887); and Reginald R. Sharpe, *London and the Kingdom* (London, 1894).

tion could claim the full privileges of the franchise. The great majority of the inhabitants had little to say in the government which regulated their lives and ordered their ways.

An understanding of a study of London politics almost necessitates a knowledge of the City's government. It would be best, therefore, to consider briefly its various parts as they existed in 1721, beginning with the groups which exercised the franchise.

Of these groups there seem to have been three grades (the members of which had to satisfy a property qualification requirement): namely, the ordinary householder and ratepayer, the freeman, and the liveryman. The first was permitted full political activity only in the meetings of his precinct, a division of the ward averaging about one hundred houses and some six or seven hundred inhabitants. He might attend part of the session of the Court of Wardmote, in which the business of his ward was discussed, and he might even hold a minor ward office. He could vote at the annual election of the ward Clerk, the ward Beadle, and the ward Constable, and also for the ward Inquest Jury.[49] Beyond that he could not go.

The greater privileges of the franchise belonged to the second group—the twelve or fifteen thousand householders who had acquired the freedom of the City.[50] For those who carried on trade there, this was a necessity, a sort of license. By it the freeman gained important privileges. It exempted him from payment of certain tolls on goods, qualified him for certain charities, and insured him from the clutches of the "press gang." Moreover, it permitted him to take a larger part in

---

[49] The duties of the Inquest Jury were to supervise the delinquencies of the ward, inspect the weights and measures of the shopkeepers, report nuisances in the streets (pavements not kept clean and in repair, lanterns not hung out on moonless nights, etc.), and make collections for the poor. Membership gave some prestige in the ward. See Webb, *English Local Government*, pp. 594 ff.

[50] Admission to the freedom, or privileges, of one or more of the eighty-odd companies or gilds in London was gained by birth, apprenticeship, gift, or by purchase, plus the payment of stipulated fees. The freeman of a company could then become a freeman of the City by payment of a further fee. This was £2.6.8 until 1729, when an additional "redemption fee" of £25 was imposed, which was raised to £50 in 1737. See Webb, *English Local Government*, p. 584 n.; *Gentleman's Magazine*, VII (1737), 763.

ward affairs and at the sessions of the Court of Wardmote. A freeman could be elected to the Inquest Jury. He could vote and be voted for at the annual election of common councilmen. And whenever an alderman died, it was the freemen who chose his successor.

Not all the freemen had the right to vote for the higher officers of the Corporation. This was limited to the seven or eight thousand who had been admitted to the Livery of the Company of which they were free,[51] and as such they were subject to summons to appear periodically at the Guildhall and there form the Court of Common Hall.[52] In 1721 this court did not have a great significance in the governing of the City. It could discuss any matter that concerned the Corporation if it wished to, but at this period the liverymen rarely asserted this privilege. Their main functions were annually on Michaelmas Day (September 29) to select and nominate the two aldermen from whom the Court of Aldermen would choose the Lord Mayor, and on Midsummer Day (June 24) to elect the two Sheriffs for London (who together acted as Sheriff of Middlesex)[53] from among the aldermen and freemen eligible. Annually also they elected the four Auditors of the Corporation accounts, and the four Ale-conners. When vacancies occurred, they filled the offices of Chamberlain and Bridgemaster; and when a parliament was dissolved, the liverymen returned the four members who would represent the City in the next.[54]

[51] Being allowed the right to wear the livery of a company depended on that company's regulations, but generally it was obtained by the payment of an additional fee, which varied from £2.13.4 for the Mercers' Company to £25 for the Drapers', Haberdashers', and Vintners'. See Seymour, *Survey of London*, II, 337 ff. For further study of the companies of London, see William Herbert, *The History of the Twelve Great Livery Companies of London* (London, 1837); William C. Hazlitt, *The Livery Companies of the City of London* (London, 1892); and George Unwin, *The Gilds and Companies of London* (London, 1925). There are numerous histories of the separate bodies.

[52] The "Meeting of the Mayor, Aldermen, and Liverymen of the several Companies of the City of London in Common Hall assembled" grew out of an ancient folk-mote of the citizens which met at Paul's Cross and there deliberated upon affairs generally affecting the City. See Webb, *English Local Government*, p. 616 n.

[53] The office of Sheriff of Middlesex had been granted by King John to the citizens of London in the twelfth century, and for more than six hundred years it continued to be held jointly by the two sheriffs in office in the City.

[54] At the elections candidates were introduced or named from the Hustings,

The executive and legislative part of the government was vested in the Lord Mayor, the Court of Aldermen, and the Court of Common Council. In the last-named sat the common councilmen elected each St. Thomas's Day (December 21) by the freemen ratepayers of each ward. Varying in number from four for Bassishaw Ward to sixteen for Farringdon Ward Without, they totaled in 1721 some two hundred and thirty-four men.[55] They were usually good average citizens, wealth and social position not being prerequisite; and the majority were retail shopkeepers or craftsmen, with a few apothecaries, surgeons, attorneys, and men of similar occupations.[56] Sitting with them at their meetings as members were also the Lord Mayor and the twenty-five other aldermen.[57] The sessions of the Court of Common Council were conducted with a dignity of ceremonial not without similarity to the proceedings of the House of Commons, and petitions and bills were heard and discussed with all the keenness of the larger body. Select and

---

a raised platform at the upper end of the Guildhall. The sheriffs in charge would then call for a show of hands for the candidates. If the vote was close, or upon demand, a poll was taken, the books being kept open for three days, and the liverymen coming individually to record their votes. In case of dispute, a scrutiny might be demanded, upon which the names of the voters were checked with lists of the liverymen furnished by each of the livery companies. Winning candidates were declared to be elected by the sheriffs from the Hustings.

[55] The division of the City into wards is of unknown antiquity. Their names and the number of Common Councilmen for each in 1721 were: Aldgate (6), Aldersgate (8), Bassishaw (4), Billingsgate (10), Bishopsgate (14), Bread Street (12), Bridge Within (15), Bridge Without (the borough of Southwark across the Thames) (none), Broad Street (10), Candlewick, (8), Castle Baynard (10), Cheap (12), Coleman Street (6), Cordwainer Street (8), Cornhill (6), Cripplegate (Within and Without) (12), Dowgate (8), Farringdon Within (15), Farringdon Without (16), Langbourn (10), Lime Street (4), Portsoken (15), Queenhithe (6), Tower Street (12), Vintry (9), and Walbrook (8).

[56] In 1739 a printed list of the Common Councilmen in which their occupations were given, showed that the Council then included 26 haberdashers and linen drapers, 14 druggists and apothecaries, 6 bakers and confectioners, 8 carpenters, cabinetmakers, masons, and bricklayers, 2 cheesemongers, 2 costermongers, 5 grocers, 4 colourmen, 5 vintners, 3 plumbers, 7 coopers, and about 70 other tradesmen and artificers. Also there were 4 bankers, 7 attorneys, 3 distillers, 1 brewer, 1 broker, 7 surgeons, 1 goldsmith, and 6 merchants. See the *Daily Gazetteer*, March 2, 1739.

[57] The formal title of this court was "The Lord Mayor, Aldermen, and Commons of the City of London in Common Council assembled."

standing committees, however, carried on the main business, which included the levying of taxes, the awarding of contracts, and the managing of the property of the Corporation. The Council had control of the revenues, enacted measures for the good government of the City, regulated the conduct of the various gild companies, served as a voice for the opinions of the citizens, and gave counsel and suggestions to the Lord Mayor and the Court of Aldermen. Nevertheless, it was essentially legislative in its functions, and "Acts of Common Council" were left for enforcement to the Lord Mayor, the Sheriffs, the various aldermen in the several wards, and the other officers of the Corporation.

The aldermen, besides sitting in the Court of Common Council, where they exerted no small influence, had a court of their own where they wielded important powers and prerogatives in their own right. Elected by the freemen ratepayers in each ward as vacancies occurred, they held office for life. They were as a group men of wealth and position in the City, older in years and more conservative in their opinions than their brethren of the Common Council. As individuals they governed their wards. As a group they acted as the executive body of the Corporation. The Court of Aldermen was a court of record. It maintained its right to control the membership of the Corporation. It judged the validity of all elections, from that of Lord Mayor of the City to that of Scavenger of a ward, and it claimed the privilege of "admitting" all candidates to office. It appointed the Recorder and a host of minor City servants. Individually, its members, or most of them, were justices of the peace, and served as such in their respective wards.[58] Collectively, they not only acted as a court of justice (really a court of appeals), but also exercised control over all of the various subsidiary tribunals in the City. Moreover, they governed the prisons and hospitals there, adminis-

[58] By a charter in 1608, the mayor, the recorder, and the aldermen who had passed the chair were confirmed as justices of the peace. The charter of 1638 added the three senior aldermen next the chair, and that of 1692 added six more who had served as sheriff. This left only five or six who had not qualified. In 1742 a further charter conferred the privilege on all the aldermen. See Birch, *Historical Charters*, pp. 290-294.

tered the poor and other funds, and had charge of all public buildings. In fact, the Court of Aldermen not only considered itself the supreme executive of the City government, but even claimed a veto power over the legislative acts of the Court of Common Council. In this its claim was strengthened by the City Elections Act, which Parliament passed in 1725,[59] but the struggle over the validity of the claim colored City politics during the whole first half of the eighteenth century.

Finally, at the head of the Corporation was "the Right Honourable the Lord Mayor," chosen annually by the Court of Aldermen from the two candidates submitted by the livery-men assembled in Common Hall on Michaelmas Day.[60] Inaugurated with great ceremony and pageantry on the Lord Mayor's Day (October 29), he continued for his whole year in office a glamorous and busy figure. As head of the executive authority in the City he exerted powers short only of royalty, and in the City he held rank only below his sovereign. His public engagements were many and varied, his entertainments lavish and costly, and no one, Englishman or foreigner, was too distinguished to accept his hospitality. Thus passed away a great part of his time—and also his wealth, for the fees and salary he received from the Corporation had invariably to be supplemented by thousands of pounds of his own in order to keep up the splendor of his office. Upon being called he appeared at meetings of the King's Privy Council, and at all times was in contact with the ministry. His ordinary civic duties were equally numerous. Daily he sat as judge of his own court, attended committees and corporate meetings, or summoned and presided over one or the other courts of justice and administration which ordered the Corporation, administered the laws, and governed the life of the City.

The "City Fathers"

In the spring of 1721 the Lord Mayor of London was Sir John Fryer. He had served as alderman of Queenhithe Ward

[59] See pp. 99 ff., below.
[60] By custom these had come to be the two senior aldermen who had served the office of sheriff, but not yet that of mayor.

since 1710, and held the office of sheriff in 1715-1716. A staunch supporter of the national government, he had been made a baronet by George I in 1714. Assisting him as Sheriffs of London and Middlesex were Sir George Caswell, a leading goldsmith,[61] and Sir William Billers, an eminent merchant in the City. They were both common councilmen for their wards (Langbourn and Cordwainer Street). The City Recorder was Sir William Thompson, who had served in that office since 1714, and would hold it until his death in 1739. The City Chamberlain was Sir Thomas Harrison. Each man was a loyal supporter of his Majesty's government, and had received knighthood in recognition of his services.

In the Court of Aldermen sat the chief officers of the twenty-six wards. Conservative in character, they nevertheless had decided political opinions. In 1721 they were divided over the conduct of national affairs: some stood strongly behind the policies of the incoming Walpole administration; others in opposition. Of the aldermen holding office in April, eighteen showed by their votes on measures reflecting their attitude toward the ministry that they belonged to the former group. Eight aldermen consistently belonged to the latter.[62] This alignment, however, was never static, and throughout the twenty-one years of the Walpole administration it varied upon each occasion of voting and was affected by each new aldermanic election. Thus it will be observed in the course of the period the majorities for the ministry gradually changed to majorities against it, a situation reflecting the changing attitude of the City Fathers toward the administration and toward Walpole himself. In some cases, of which the Excise scheme of 1733 is

[61] On March 10, Caswell, who sat in the House of Commons for Leominster, was expelled from the House and committed to the Tower for his connection with the South Sea frauds, being "Guilty of Corrupt, Infamous, and Dangerous Practise, highly reflecting on the Honour and Justice of Parliament, and Destructive to the Interest of his Majesty's Government." He was a partner in the Sword Blade Company, which was ordered to pay back a quarter of a million pounds of its profits. See Boyer, *Political State*, XXI, 313-316.

[62] Observed from the recorded votes in the Manuscript Repertories of the Court of Aldermen, preserved at the London Guildhall, Vols. 125-146 (Nov., 1720-Oct., 1742).

probably best known, this opposition was shown markedly. By 1742, when Walpole's administration had come to an end, only twelve of the twenty-six aldermen in the court might still be considered as his supporters, and some of those it may be said had not always been loyal.

In April, 1721, as has been stated, there were eighteen aldermen to whom Walpole could look for support in the City. Sir Thomas Abney, Fishmonger, elected from Vintry Ward in 1692, was the senior alderman of the City, and since 1716 had represented the ward of Bridge Without.[63] He had served as sheriff in 1693-1694 and as Lord Mayor in 1700-1701. Sir Gilbert Heathcote, Vintner, elected from Walbrook Ward in 1702, had served the office of sheriff in 1701-1702 and that of Lord Mayor in 1710-1711. A former member for London, he sat in the present Parliament for Helston. Sir Samuel Stainer, Draper, elected from Aldgate Ward in 1705, had served as sheriff in 1705-1706 and as Lord Mayor in 1713-1714. Sir William Humphreys, Ironmonger, who was elected from Cheap Ward in 1707, had been sheriff in 1704-1705 and Lord Mayor in 1714-1715. He sat in the present Parliament for Marlborough. Sir Charles Peers, Salter, was elected from Tower Ward in 1708, and had served the office of sheriff in 1707-1708 and that of Lord Mayor in 1715-1716. Sir John Ward, Merchant-Taylor, elected from Candlewick Ward in 1709, had served as sheriff in 1715-1716 and as Lord Mayor in 1718-1719. He was one of the four London members sitting in Parliament. Sir George Thorold, Ironmonger, was elected from Cordwainer Street Ward in 1709. He had served as sheriff in 1710-1711 and as Lord Mayor in 1719-1720. Sir John Fryer, Pewterer, was elected from Queenhithe Ward in 1710. He had been sheriff in 1715-1716, and was the present Lord Mayor. Sir Gerard Conyers, Salter, was elected from Broad Street Ward in 1711. He had served as

[63] The Ward of Bridge Without (the borough of Southwark) was not in the City proper, and the alderman in office had in comparison with his brother aldermen considerably fewer duties. Therefore, by provision of an Act of Common Council in 1711 (MS Journals of the Court of Common Council, preserved at the Guildhall, Journal 55, Folio 261), the ward was usually claimed by the senior alderman of the City, who held it as a sinecure until his death. He was known as the "Father of the City."

sheriff in 1716-1717. Sir Thomas Scawen, Fishmonger, was elected from Cornhill Ward in 1712. He was another of the four London members of Parliament. Sir Peter Delmé, Fishmonger, was elected from Langbourn Ward in 1712. He had served as sheriff in 1717-1718. Sir Francis Forbes, Haberdasher, was elected from Dowgate Ward in 1713. He had served as sheriff in 1713-1714. Sir John Eyles, Haberdasher, was elected from Vintry Ward in 1716. He had served as sheriff in 1719-1720, and now sat in Parliament for Chippenham. Edward Beecher, Draper, was elected from Bishopsgate Ward in 1718. Sir Harcourt Master, Haberdasher, was elected from Coleman Street Ward in 1718 and was chosen sheriff in the same year. Robert Baylis, Grocer, was elected from Bread Street Ward in 1719. Robert Heysham, Draper, was elected from Billingsgate Ward in 1720. He also sat in Parliament as a member for the City. Sir Randolph Knipe, Clothworker, was elected from Bassishaw Ward in January, 1721. He had served as sheriff in 1714-1715.

These aldermen belonged to the majority group. There were eight who belonged to the group usually opposing the ministry. Sir Samuel Garrard, Grocer, was elected from Aldersgate Ward in 1702. He had served as sheriff in 1702-1703 and as Lord Mayor in 1709-1710. Sir Robert Beachcroft, Clothworker, was elected from Lime Street Ward in 1703. He had served as sheriff in 1700-1701 and as Lord Mayor in 1711-1712. Sir William Lewen, Haberdasher, was elected from Castle Baynard Ward in 1708. He had served as sheriff in 1712-1713 and as Lord Mayor in 1717-1718. Sir William Stewart, Barber-Surgeon, was elected from Cripplegate Ward in 1711. He had served as sheriff in 1711-1712, and was the next candidate for the mayoralty, being the senior alderman next the chair. Sir George Merttins, Clockmaker, was elected from Bridge Ward Within in 1712. Sir Robert Child, Goldsmith, was elected from Farringdon Ward Without. He sat in Parliament for Essex. Richard Brocas, Grocer, was elected from Farringdon Ward Within in February, 1721. Humphrey Parsons, Waxchandler, was elected from Portsoken Ward in March, 1721.

These twenty-six men formed the executive body of the City's government, and their attitude for or against the national government often decided the City's recorded attitude toward the ministry in power. This did not necessarily always coincide with the attitude of the citizens as a whole, which was more nearly expressed by the members of the larger and less conservative body, the Court of Common Council. Composed of men who were still active among their fellow citizens in the wards and who were subject to annual elections, the common councilmen were probably more nearly representative of the opinions of the City's population. And throughout the period of Walpole's administration the common councilmen were regularly in opposition to his policies. As has been stated, the influence of the aldermen sitting in the Common Council was so great that the recorded attitude of the Common Council was not always the attitude of the citizens. At the annual elections of the common councilmen in the wards, however, uninfluenced then by any aldermanic veto, the citizens could show their stand, and generally did so, the "Tory" party—as the newspapers and contemporary writers termed the opposition group—regularly triumphing over the "Whigs" in the earlier years, and the "Country" party over the "Court" in the later years. Because of the large number of councilmen, two hundred and thirty-four, it is unnecessary to list them here, since individually they played minor parts in comparison with the individual aldermen. Nor did they vary as much in their attitudes. Only as a group were they important, and as a group their relationship with the national administration will be noted.

Probably the most direct link between the City and Parliament was provided by the London representatives who sat in the House of Commons. Although the City could and did on occasion give them instructions, its members possessed a great deal of independence and conducted themselves in this period as they saw fit, "neither awed by the tyranny of control, nor influenced by the incitement of corruption."[64] In 1721 the

[64] Thomas H. B. Oldfield, *The Representative History of Great Britain and Ireland . . . from the Earliest Period* (London, 1876), I, 384.

same four members sat in Parliament who had been chosen in the general election of 1715: namely, Sir John Ward, Sir Thomas Scawen, and Robert Heysham, all aldermen and already mentioned, and Peter Godfrey, a commoner. Throughout this first parliament of George I they had been loyal to the new Hanoverian king. It should be noticed, however, that all four had voted with the opposition against the Septennial Bill,[65] and that while Walpole himself was in opposition to the Stanhope-Sunderland ministry, both Heysham and Godfrey had voted with him against the Peerage Bill.[66] It is interesting also to note that three of the four representatives were aldermen, the majority therefore reflecting the viewpoint of that group. In fact, members of the Court of Aldermen monopolized the City's representation throughout the whole period of Walpole's administration.

This preponderance of the aldermen was also seen among the other members of Parliament who were citizens of London. Officially they sat for other towns or boroughs; nevertheless, they spoke for the City. These included Sir Gilbert Heathcote, who sat for Helston; Sir William Humphreys, for Marlborough; and Sir Robert Child, for Essex. The other City members were Sir William Thompson, the City Recorder, who sat for Ipswich; Sir George Caswell, one of the sheriffs, who sat for Leominster; and Sir Nathaniel Gould, a Russia merchant, who sat for Shoreham.

Thus the City, by a number of its influential citizens, was well represented in the legislative assembly of the nation. It could there make itself heard on questions of national importance and could find ready champions on matters of its own interest and welfare.

[65] By an act passed in 1694 the life of a parliament had been fixed at three years. In 1716, following upon the Jacobite Rebellion, and in order to insure the maintenance of the Whigs in power, a new act was passed by Parliament increasing its duration to seven years. The end, therefore, of the first parliament of George I, elected in the spring of 1715, would not come until the spring of 1722.

[66] A bill to limit the House of Lords, after the creation of six new peers, to its existing numbers, with the future creation of new peers only upon the extinction of the old. Scotland was to have twenty-five hereditary peers. This bill would have tended to crystallize the House of Lords into a fixed and closed body.

CHAPTER II

The First Year of the Walpole Administration

RECOVERY FROM THE SOUTH SEA CRISIS

ALMOST immediately after Walpole had attained to high office and had begun his long period of administration London raised its voice in the affairs of the nation. England in the spring of 1721 had not yet recovered from the financial crisis of the year before, and despite the determined efforts of the new chief minister during the winter the country was still distraught, with trade and credit at a low ebb. It was imperative that Parliament do more than debate the problem. The country called for action, and London became its leading spokesman. On April 3 the City formally petitioned the Commons to take immediate steps and enact measures to relieve the prevailing distresses.[1]

London well remembered the South Sea fraud, and the activities of the winter months had not softened the temper of public opinion. Pamphleteers and writers in the press[2] had

[1] *Journals of the House of Commons*, XIX, 502.
[2] At the time Walpole took office most of the newspapers were in opposition to the government. Chief of these was Nathaniel Mist's *Weekly Journal, or Saturday's Post,* and its publisher was subject to constant prosecution for his libels of the king and his ministers. *Applebee's Original Weekly Journal* was more moderate in tone, but the *London Journal* was filled with articles by Thomas Gordon and John Trenchard demanding justice for the South Sea victims (late in 1722, however, this journal was to be purchased by supporters of the government and used thereafter in the ministerial interest, Gordon and Trenchard going over to the *British Journal*). Read's *Weekly Journal and British Gazetteer* and the *Whitehall Evening Post* represented the Whig interest; and of the two most popular dailies, the *Daily Courant* was Whig and the *Daily Post* was Tory. See C. B. Realey, *Early Opposition to Robert Walpole* (Philadelphia, 1931), pp. 61, 94-95, 147; H. R. Fox Bourne, *English Newspapers: Chapters in the History of Journalism* (London, 1887), I, 105 ff.; C. B. Realey, "The London Journal and Its Authors, 1720-1723," *Bulletin of the University of Kansas Humanistic Studies*, V, No. 3; David H. Stevens, *Party Politics in English Journalism, 1702-1742* (Menasha, Wis., 1916), pp. 104 ff.

kept alive the unrest and the desire for vengeance on the promoters. The mob had taken up the cry and had "shouted in the Streets, King George for ever; down with the Directors, and the like."[3] Bonfires had been made on the day that Aislabie was sent to the Tower.[4] There was nothing but "Calamity," reported one observer, "the people in rage, fury, and povertie without doors; and carrying on their particular views and interests within; without any regard to the publick good."[5] Suicides had been frequent (all blamed on the South Sea), and both the public and private "Bedlams or Mad-Houses, as they are call'd" were filled to overflowing.[6] The recent stockjobbing was even charged with destroying "conjugal Kindnesses, making Family Breaches, and raising Civil Wars between Men and their Wives."[7] Nevertheless, all did not despair, contemporaries noticing that "during the Time of general Complaint, the Town finds Money to support four Play-Houses,"[8] and that they "are more crowded than for twenty Years past, . . . the Nobility, Gentry, and Commonality going thither to divert the Memory of the fatal Breaches in their Fortunes at the South-Sea House."[9]

Throughout the winter the stocks continued to fall. South Sea was down to 200 on the first of January and to 136 on the first of April. Bank of England stock, on the same dates, had fallen from 146 to 128. Stock of the East India Company was selling for 170 at the beginning of the year and for 139 three months later. That of the African Company had dropped from 48 to 34.[10] Business on the Exchange was almost at a standstill.[11] Foreign trade had suffered severely, and on Feb-

[3] Applebee's Original Weekly Journal, Jan. 28, 1721.

[4] Coxe, Sir Robert Walpole, II, 212 (Midleton Papers).

[5] Culloden Papers: Comprising an Extensive and Interesting Correspondence . . . in the Possession of Duncan Forbes of Culloden, ed. H. R. Duff (hereinafter cited as Culloden Papers) (London, 1815), p. 73 (Lord Belkhaven to Duncan Forbes, March 18, 1721).

[6] For examples of many references in the newspapers, see the London Journal, Jan. 14, 1721; or Applebee's Original Weekly Journal, Jan. 28, 1721.

[7] Applebee's Original Weekly Journal, Feb. 4, 1721.

[8] Post-Boy, Jan. 7, 1721.   [9] London Journal, Dec. 17, 1720.

[10] Daily Courant, Jan. 2 and April 3, 1721.

[11] H. M. C., Portland MSS, V, 620 (Edward Harley, Jr., to Abigail Harley, April 20, 1721).

ruary 4 a writer in the *London Journal* lamented the number of "foreign Bills on Merchants of this City, protested for Non-payment."[12] The public credit was low. Something constructive, therefore, must precede vengeance. According to one contributor to *Applebee's Journal*, those who thirsted for redress had lost sight of the main object. The important thing was, he wrote, "to reestablish Publick Credit, and renew the Correspondence which Mankind had formerly with one another"; but he added: "Honesty and fair Trading must be restor'd before Credit will come to us again."[13]

In this all of England was concerned, but London most of all. The City had been the scene of the stockjobbing activities, her citizens had been the most numerous losers, and her trade and commerce were now most affected by the fall of stocks and the loss of public credit. It was natural for her to complain, and her position entitled her to be heard.

On Saturday, April 1, the Lord Mayor, Aldermen, and Common Councilmen "in Common Council assembled" heard and approved a petition reported by a committee consisting of Aldermen Garrard and Brocas, and Common Councilmen Robinson, Alsop,[14] Morgan, Young, Barber,[15] and Monk, and ordered it to be presented to the Parliament then sitting at Westminster.[16] On the following Monday Sheriff Billers, accompanied by Aldermen Garrard and Brocas dressed in their scarlet gowns, appeared at the door of St. Stephen's; and when called in, presented the petition at the Bar of the House of Commons, where, after they had withdrawn, it was read.[17]

The petitioners, it was revealed, lamented not only the sad situation of the City of London, but also the "General Decay of Trade Manufactures and of Publick Creditt" arising from the mismanagement and avarice of the South Sea promoters.

[12] *London Journal,* Feb. 4, 1721.

[13] "T. B." in *Applebee's Original Weekly Journal,* March 7, 1721.

[14] Robert Alsop, Haberdasher, elected alderman of Queenhithe Ward in 1726.

[15] John Barber, Stationer, elected alderman of Castle Baynard Ward in 1722, and Lord Mayor in 1732.

[16] Journals of the Court of Common Council, 57, f. 85.

[17] *British Gazetteer,* April 8, 1721; *Journals of the House of Commons,* XIX, 502; *Historical Register,* VI, 113.

They thanked the House for its efforts "to releive the unhappy Sufferers by compelling the Offenders to make Restitucõn," and likewise its "continued Applicacõn to lay open this whole Scene of Guilt" despite the opposition of those who would protect the persons guilty. But, recognizing the need of lessening the "Load of the Publick Debts" and expressing great concern that "the Paiment of a great Summe towards them" which had been expected from the success of the South Sea scheme had now been rendered difficult if not impossible, they pointed out that the failure of the South Sea scheme hung as a cloud over the South Sea Company and not only threatened its destruction, but the public credit as well. The City Fathers, therefore, urged that "serious Consideracõn" be given immediately to bring "releif" to the situation (they humbly refrained from suggesting the method) in order "that Trade may flourish, public Creditt be restor'd, and Justice done to an injured People."[18]

This urging from the metropolis, coupled with similar petitions which were sent during the succeeding weeks from cities, towns and counties throughout the land,[19] had considerable effect.[20] The Commons, made even more sensible of the seriousness of the situation, renewed with considerable success their efforts to ease it. The details of their efforts may be read elsewhere; from the viewpoint of London and national affairs the results are far more important. These, in brief, were two: the passing of the South Sea Directors Act and the act to restore the public credit.

It was hoped that by confiscating the estates of the South Sea directors[21] and others responsible for the fraud enough might be obtained to recompense the sufferers. As much as

[18] Journals of the Court of Common Council, 57, ff. 85-85b.

[19] *British Gazetteer*, April 8, 1721. For the contents of a great many of these, see William Cobbett, *Parliamentary History of England, from the Norman Conquest, in 1066, to the Year 1803* (London, 1806-1820), VII, 761-780.

[20] H. M. C., *Clements MSS*, p. 309 (Arthur Onslow to John Molesworth, May 6, 1721).

[21] It is well to note that among them were many leading merchants of the City, including Sir John Blunt, Sir Jacob Sawbridge, Edward Gibbon (grandfather of the historian), Sir John Lambert, Sir John Fellows, Sir Lambert Blackwell, Sir Theodore Janssen, and Alderman Sir Harcourt Master.

eight or ten millions had been mentioned.[22]   When, however, on April 17, the committee appointed to inquire into the values of the estates reported, the sum total available appeared to be only two million pounds.[23]   After considerable debating and haggling, three hundred and fifty thousand of this amount was granted the directors for their maintenance, and only the remainder, by the bill which was passed on July 25, was ordered to be applied to the liabilities of the company.[24]

The state of the public credit demanded greater consideration. Bitter debates marked the proceedings, and a complete settlement had not been made when Parliament was prorogued on July 29. Three days earlier, however, the Commons presented a series of resolutions to the King which, after Parliament had been recalled on July 31, resulted in a bill "for making several provisions to restore the Public Credit."[25] On August 3 opposition was manifested from outside. A crowd of several hundred men and women, small holders of long- and short-term annuities who had converted their shares of the public debt into South Sea stock, entered the lobby of the House of Commons and thrust petitions into the hands of the members demanding "Justice to the Annuitants, who lent their money on Parliamentary Security."[26] On the floor of the House they were championed by one of the City's members, Sir John Ward,

[22] H. M. C., *Clements MSS*, p. 309.

[23] £2,014,123.16.7¼ to be exact. See *Journals of the House of Commons*, XIX, 513.

[24] 7 Geo. I, c. 28. *Journals of the House of Commons*, XIX, 513 ff.; Cobbett, *Parliamentary History*, VII, 780 ff.

[25] Cobbett, *Parliamentary History*, VII, 895-902.

[26] To finance the wars of Marlborough, and for other purposes, the government had borrowed money at rates of interest varying from 6¼ to 8 per cent. In 1719 the Treasury was still paying the same high rates to the holders of the annuities, although capital in the money market was available at 4 or 5 per cent. It was to remedy this situation that Parliament, in the spring of 1720, accepted the proposal of the South Sea Company to fund the whole national debt and convert the annuities into South Sea stock. In order to pay for the privilege, and to make a profit, the South Sea Company, however, resorted to stockjobbing. The holders of the public debt were readily induced to exchange their annuities for shares in the Company, but the prospects of profit were made so golden that the prices rocketed, only to fall with a crash in the autumn when the bubble burst. Those who had formerly held high-interest-bearing annuities now held South Sea stock of greatly depreciated value, and they wanted redress.

who at the same time presented a petition from a group whose members had more considerable holdings of the public debt, a group headed by Sir Thomas Abney, the senior alderman of London, and Sir Gilbert Heathcote, also a leading City Father. Sir John urged that the petitioners be heard. Walpole, however, speaking for the ministry, advised against it, saying that the members of the House had already approved of the provisions made for the annuitants, and they could not be changed. A motion to hear the petitioners was then voted down. The people outside, meanwhile, becoming turbulent and unruly, the Speaker, after ordering the attendance of the justices of the peace of Westminster, directed the lobbies to be cleared. The petitioners refused to go despite the attendance of five or six constables on the four justices called. It was necessary to read the Riot Act[27] twice before the crowd resentfully left the building.[28]

Some opposition also continued indoors, but the bill received clear majorities at each of the readings, and on August 10 it received the approval of the King.[29] It discharged the South Sea Company from payment of more than four millions it had agreed the year before to pay for the privilege of increasing its stock; it canceled (effective in June, 1722) two millions of the debt owed to the company by the government; it made provisions for the relief of those holding irredeemable annuities, and those who had borrowed on the stock in 1720; and it provided for the legalizing of all contracts and the suspension of all lawsuits.[30]

Although by no means to the satisfaction of everyone, these measures did prove extremely successful in restoring English public credit and settling the unrest in London and throughout

[27] The Riot Act, passed in the spring of 1716, provided that if twelve or more persons were unlawfully assembled to the disturbance of the peace, and did not disperse when commanded by a justice to do so by proclamation, and continued together for an hour afterwards, they should be guilty of felony without benefit of clergy.

[28] Boyer, *Political State*, XXII, 96-97, 149-160; Cobbett, *Parliamentary History*, VII, 903-910.

[29] *Journals of the House of Lords*, XXI, 590; Cobbett, *Parliamentary History*, VII, 910-911.

[30] 7 George I, sess. 2, c. 1. Cf. Briscoe, *Economic Policy of Robert Walpole*, p. 54.

the kingdom. Some revisions were necessary of course, in the next session of Parliament, and various provisions had to be made during the following years to put the South Sea Company again on a firm financial footing. But, for settling the fears of 1721, the measures that were passed proved surprisingly adequate. In his speech on August 10, proroguing Parliament for the summer months, the King observed that "Public Credit" was already beginning to recover and that he had the greatest hopes that it would be entirely restored when all the provisions made by Parliament should be put into execution.[31] The hopes of the ministry, so expressed, were fulfilled; and within a relatively few months English finance was again on solid ground, and the panic had passed.[32] Nevertheless, public opinion, ever slower to forgive than to condemn, was not ready to look with favor on the Walpole administration or its efforts.

The King, however, had gained the approval of the populace, and on two occasions during the spring of 1721—the birth of a son to the Prince and Princess of Wales on April 18 and the birthday of George I on May 28—the loyalty of the City to the Hanoverian dynasty was displayed. "The birth of the young Prince has been the only thing that has happened this good while, to please the people," wrote a correspondent of Lord Carlisle[33] on April 18.[34] That same day the Lord Mayor and Court of Aldermen, as "faithful and dutiful Subjects," tendered their congratulations to his Majesty upon the increase of the royal progeny and expressed their hopes for the continued health and happiness of the King.[35] Pleased, the latter received them cordially and thanked them for their "Zeal and Affection." Both birthdays gave opportunity for popular celebrations, and were marked by the customary "Bonfires, Illuminations, and the Ringing of Bells, and other publick Demonstrations of Joy" throughout London and Westminster.[36]

[31] *Journals of the House of Lords*, XXI, 591.
[32] Briscoe, *Economic Policy of Robert Walpole*, p. 49.
[33] Charles Howard (1674-1738), third Earl of Carlisle.
[34] H. M. C., *Carlisle MSS*, p. 33 (Lady Lechmere).
[35] Repertories of the Court of Aldermen, 125, f. 250b.
[36] Boyer, *Political State*, XXI, 432-434, 562.

SOME LOCAL LONDON ELECTIONS

The subject of local politics was brought to the attention of the London citizens on May 27 upon the death of Alderman Sir Robert Beachcroft, of Lime Street Ward. Sir Robert had served the City for eighteen years, had held its highest office as Lord Mayor in 1712, had received knighthood from Queen Anne, and was known as a confirmed "Tory."[37] To elect his successor, a wardmote was held on May 30; and Sir Lancelot Skinner, Clothworker, who had served as Deputy, was unanimously chosen alderman of the ward.[38] Alderman Skinner was to prove to be a loyal supporter of Walpole, and that minister's majority in the Court of Aldermen was thus increased to twelve.[39] This was pleasing to the administration according to a report sent to the Duke of Newcastle a few weeks later: "In the City there was a good Election made of an Alderman in the Room of a bad one, which has added to the Majority in that Court, and we are upon the whole as easy as I believe any great Place is."[40]

On Midsummer Day, Saturday, June 24, "came on" the annual election of sheriffs. At the Common Hall gathering, ten candidates appeared on the Hustings; but Sir George Merttins and Edward Beecher, both aldermen said to be supported by the "Tories," were declared to have the majority on the show of hands. Contesting the count, Alderman Robert Baylis and James Colebrook, supported by the "Whigs," then demanded a poll, which was granted.[41] On the following Monday the voting was heavy, but the next morning Baylis and Colebrook gave up the poll, "seeing no probability of carrying it," and Merttins and Beecher were declared duly elected sheriffs of London and the County of Middlesex.[42] "The

[37] *Post-Boy*, May 30, 1721.
[38] Boyer, *Political State*, XXI, 566; *Historical Register*, VI, Chronological Diary, p. 24.
[39] The numbers of aldermen for and against the administration were changed from 18 and 8 by this election to 19 and 7, this being the largest majority Walpole was able to muster during his term of twenty-one years.
[40] From Lord Norwich, July 17, 1721, British Museum Additional Manuscripts (hereinafter cited as Add. MSS), 32686, f. 174.
[41] *Post-Boy*, June 26, 1721; *Daily Courant*, June 26, 1721.
[42] *Applebee's Original Weekly Journal*, July 1, 1721: Boyer, *Political State*, XXI, 669. On the poll the numbers for each were: Merttins, 1,869; Beecher, 1,856; Baylis, 1,381; and Colebrook, 1,369.

Whigs have lost their cause in the City," announced a writer in Applebee's antiadministration *Journal,* and added: "The Election was declared for the two loyal Aldermen, who, on all Occasions, have testify'd their Zeal for the Interest of their Country in Church and State."[43]   In this the court party seemingly did not fare so well.   Nevertheless, the newspaper writer must have been carried away by his own zeal, for Alderman Beecher at least proved loyal to Walpole's government, and he was knighted by George I in the following year.[44]

During the summer months, when London remained unsettled and the political factions continued very much wrought up, the opposition forces did not lose any ground.   On September 29, at the election of the Lord Mayor, Sir William Stewart, of Cripplegate Ward, the senior alderman next the chair, was "unanimously" chosen for the following year.[45]   On October 6 the death of Sir Robert Child, also a "Tory," brought on an election for a new alderman for Farringdon Ward Without.[46]   At the wardmote, held a few days later, Francis Child, brother of the late alderman, was opposed by Sir John Tash, but won the election by "a very great Majority."[47]   The new alderman, who succeeded as head of the banking firm of Child & Company upon the death of his brother, also followed in his brother's political footsteps.   Thus the minority vote in the Court of Aldermen was maintained.   It is interesting to note, considering the partisanship usually shown at these and other City elections, that the newspaper account states that "the Wardmote return'd Thanks to his Lordship [the "Whig" Sir John Fryer] for his impartial Justice in the Management of the said Election."[48]   This was not always the custom.

THE STRUGGLE OVER THE QUARANTINE ACT

Following the summer recess, the last session of George I's first parliament opened on October 19.   Lord Mahon, in the next century, termed it "a very short and unimportant

[43] July 1, 1721.   [44] *Historical Register,* VII, 26.
[45] *Daily Courant,* Sept. 30, 1721; Boyer, *Political State,* XXII, 328.
[46] *London Journal,* Oct. 7, 1721.
[47] *Post-Boy,* Oct. 12, 1721; Boyer, *Political State,* XXII, 440.
[48] *Post-Boy,* Oct. 12, 1721.

Session."[49] For the Londoners, however, it was a very disturbing one. In the King's Speech were included suggestions
toward two important economic moves: the reduction of duties
on imports and exports and the development of the production
of naval stores in the American colonies.[50] These were essentially Walpole's own ideas and were proposed for the country's
good. At the same time it was a move toward gaining the
good will of the commercial interests. To London, therefore,
the bills were of primary concern. Nevertheless, in the passage of the necessary measures through Parliament the City
seems to have taken little or no direct action, for no legislation
or discussion involving them is to be found in the Journals or
Repertories of the Corporation. But there can be no doubt
that the City men in the House of Commons took part in the
debates there and informed Parliament of the attitude of London on these matters. Moreover, we know that Sir Nathaniel
Gould and Robert Heysham were on the committee ordered
to prepare the bill for the revision of the customs duties;[51]
and Sir Gilbert Heathcote, on November 17, not only spoke
warmly against relying on Russia for England's naval stores
but made the motion for bringing in the bill to encourage their
importation from the English plantations in America.[52] Exactly
what effect these men had on the passage of these bills, or how
much influence they exerted on these economic policies of the
administration, cannot definitely be stated, but the acts passed[53]
seem to have been completely to their satisfaction.

What did arouse the City's opposition followed from a
third matter mentioned in the King's Speech, namely, a request
that proper precautions be taken against the bringing in of the

[49] Lord Mahon (Philip Henry Stanhope), *A History of England, from
the Peace of Utrecht to the Peace of Versailles, 1713-1783* (London, 1856),
II, 26.

[50] *Journals of the House of Commons*, XIX, 645-646.

[51] *Ibid.*, XXII, 693.

[52] Boyer, *Political State*, XXII, 515-516; Cobbett, *Parliamentary History*,
VII, 928.

[53] 8 Geo. I, c. 12 and c. 15 ("An Act for giving further encouragement
for the importation of naval stores, and for other purposes herein mentioned":
and "An Act . . . for taking off several duties on merchandizes exported; and
for reducing the duties upon beaver-skins, pepper, mace, cloves and nutmegs
imported, etc.").

plague then raging in France.[54]   Briefly stated, the situation was this.   In the previous January, an act to prevent such an occurrence *had* been passed, ordering incoming ships to perform a forty-day quarantine and giving the government powers to combat the contagion if it should get a foothold in England.[55] At that time this act seemed entirely adequate to cope with the situation.   By October, however, as was suggested in the King's Speech, additional precautions were necessary.   In November, therefore, a bill was introduced in the Commons to prohibit for the period of one year, as his Majesty saw fit, all commerce with countries infected with the plague.   Here the fun began.   The bill passed the Commons, but in the midst of the debates in the House of Lords there was an interruption. The minority in opposition to the Walpole administration took the opportunity to call for a reconsideration of the Quarantine Act passed previously, at the same time making charges that the powers granted in that act savored of a scheme to set up a military despotism and were thus dangerous to the liberties of a free people.   The alarm spread outdoors.   London became stirred up and the citizens thoroughly aroused, at first being fearful only for their commerce and trade, then taking up the full cry to deplore the alleged insidious attempts to deprive them of their rights and privileges.

In order to get the complete story, it is really necessary to consider the situation from the year 1720.   Since the spring of that year the plague had raged terribly in France, especially around Marseilles and Aix, and the English newspapers were filled with accounts telling of its horrors.   In the autumn an effort was made to prevent its spread to England, and the Lords Justices made proclamation that all ships coming from the Mediterranean or coasts of France should remain in quarantine for forty days before unloading their cargoes.[56]   This was partially effective, and a month later an observer noticed nearly fifty merchant ships performing quarantine at Sheerness near the mouth of the Thames.[57]   Parliament then took up the

---

[54] *Journals of the House of Commons*, XIX, 646.
[55] 7 Geo. I, c. 3.
[56] *London Gazette*, Oct. 29, 1720.   [57] *British Gazetteer*, Dec. 3, 1720.

matter, and on January 25, 1721, an act was passed repealing all the quarantine laws then in force and giving new and more adequate rules concerning how all ships, persons, and goods, coming into Great Britain from places infected should perform quarantine. These rules were to prevent the introduction of the plague. If, notwithstanding, the plague should be introduced and become dangerous in the kingdom, the act also contained clauses giving his Majesty's government certain arbitrary powers whereby the plague might be controlled and prevented from spreading. This was the Act and these were the clauses which were to be the center of the dispute a year later. Specifically, these clauses empowered the government to provide proper places (lazarets or pesthouses) in which to confine infected persons or those obliged to perform quarantine, and prescribed the use of force and even the death penalty for those who failed to comply with the law; it also gave his Majesty power to cause lines or trenches, properly guarded, to be set up about infected places, towns, or cities, to prevent the passing in or out of persons or goods—again prescribing the death penalty for those who disobeyed.[58]

On February 4, 1721, the Quarantine Act was made effective by proclamation,[59] and at once orders were given to officers of all the seaports of the kingdom "to take especial Care" that the new laws be put into execution.[60] In London attention was also directed to the more immediate dangers, and the Grand Jury of the City made presentments against the extremely unsanitary conditions throughout the metropolis. It protested "the ill Repair of the Pavements" and "the throwing of Dust, Ashes, and other filthy Soil" into the streets, lanes, and passages of the City as well as the dumping out of waste matter from the slaughterhouses, and allowing the blood of slaughtered animals to run out, to stagnate and breed disease. In fact, the disposal in public places of all "Filth, Dung, or Soil,

[58] For the text of the obnoxious clauses see 7 Geo. I, c. 3; Boyer, *Political State*, XXII, 640-641; or the *Statutes at Large, from Magna Charta to the End of the Eleventh Parliament of Great Britain, Anno 1861* (Cambridge, 1762-1869), XIV, 301-302.

[59] *London Gazette*, Feb. 11, 1721.

[60] *Weekly Journal, or Saturday's Post*, Feb. 4, 1721.

which may occasion any Infection" was severely condemned.[61]

These efforts to prevent the plague from coming into England were well received, and the Quarantine Act apparently aroused no opposition from the general public. A great many of the merchants, however, affected by the severe restrictions imposed on them, expressed strong disapproval. Many of them (especially those dealing in perishable goods) in order to prevent the ruin of their trade tried by all means to get around the new laws, and during the spring months managed to bring in quantities of goods from abroad without performing quarantine. To stop this, Walpole, on July 8, presented a bill to the House of Commons "to prevent the bringing in of the Infection by the clandestine Running of Goods," which was rapidly pushed through the lower house.[62] On July 20, while it was still in debate, a group of "some of the most eminent Merchants in this City" petitioned against the bill and complained of several clauses which imposed severe hardships on them.[63] Several of these clauses were therefore rejected. The amended bill was passed on July 25 and was then sent to the upper house for concurrence. Here also the merchants petitioned, and again they were favorably received.[64] The bill did not pass, since the concentration of both houses on the problem of restoring the public credit after the South Sea crisis, followed by the early prorogation of Parliament on August 10, prevented it. Besides, the dangers from the plague seemed to abate during the summer. It was left to the fall session to reconsider the whole affair.

[61] *British Gazetteer*, Jan. 28, 1721.

[62] *Journals of the House of Commons*, XIX, 628.

[63] *British Gazetteer*, July 29, 1721; *Journals of the House of Commons*, XIX, 636.

[64] *Journals of the House of Lords*, XXI, 582. Daniel Defoe wrote strongly against these "worthy citizens" who set themselves up against the bill, and urged that effective measures be promptly taken to prevent these "avericious Minds, for private Gain, conveying Goods on Shore at the Hazard of bringing a Contagion upon the Country." "No Mercy," he declared, "is due to a Crime so merciless in its own Nature. Nothing can itself be more cruel. No Thought can be more barbarous, than to venture the Welfare of the whole Kingdom, and the Lives of Men, Women, and Children, for the wretched Gain of a private Man, and perhaps the gain of a Trifle. Such a Man should dye without Mercy, and would dye unpity'd, if ever Man did so" (*Applebee's Original Weekly Journal*, July 29, 1721).

In September the plague had spread with increased severity in France. Methods to prevent its crossing the Channel were at once discussed by the Privy Council, and three of the leading physicians of the kingdom, Sir Hans Sloane, Dr. Richard Meade, and Dr. John Arbuthnot, were called in for consultation.[65] "The plague is at present the topic of most conversations, and the doctors have made a world of simple propositions to the Council, in case it should come," wrote Lady Lechmere to Lord Carlisle.[66]

Various precautionary measures were put into practice. On October 4 the Privy Council made public a proclamation requiring all travelers from France to show certificates of health and issued the proper regulations to make it effective.[67] On October 14 the Justices of the Peace of Middlesex, at a quarter session, issued orders for the better carrying out of the laws for the prevention and removal of all public nuisances and annoyances; for the apprehension of all beggars and vagrants; for the cleaning out of all overcrowded and unsanitary lodginghouses, prisons, gin-shops, and the like; and for the general improvement of conditions in the county.[68] In the City of London, the Grand Jury again repeated its presentments of the previous spring and demanded the more careful carrying out of their duties by the city scavengers;[69] while the Lord Mayor issued orders that the streets be kept clean and threatened prosecution of butchers and others who "poluted" them.[70] Moreover, on October 23, the King signed a proclamation ordering that "a General and Publick Fast be observ'd" throughout the kingdom on December 8 ("on Pain of Suffering Punishment"), to pray for Divine protection from the fatal calamity then threatening them.[71]

The next step was to take parliamentary action; and so, as we have observed above, the King's Speech at the opening of the session called attention to the grave dangers from abroad.

[65] Boyer, *Political State*, XXII, 396, 430.
[66] H. M. C., *Carlisle MSS*, p. 36 (Oct. 17, 1721).
[67] *London Gazette*, Oct. 4 and 8, 1721.
[68] *Daily Courant*, Oct. 16, 1721.   [69] *British Gazetteer*, Oct. 21, 1721.
[70] *Ibid.*, Oct. 28, 1721.   [71] Boyer, *Political State*, XXII, 406.

On November 8, a committee (of which Henry Pelham and Robert Walpole were the chief members) was appointed, and two days later a bill to give his Majesty power "to prohibit Commerce with any Country, as he shall think necessary, in order to prevent the Contagion being brought into this Kingdom" was given its first reading.[72]

On the second reading there was a warm debate, and various amendments were discussed. One of these was to empower the King's officers to fire upon and sink the ships coming from infected places. To this amendment Sir Gilbert Heathcote arose and spoke in opposition. He wished exemption especially for the ships belonging to the merchants who traded with Turkey, alleging that since they were then abroad proper warning could not be given them. He further declared that the measures proposed would practically ruin all the commerce with Turkey, not only depriving the British of imports from that country, but also closing down a very profitable market of the English woolen trade. He was seconded by Sir Nathaniel Gould, another Turkey merchant.[73] Speakers for the government, however, assured them that the measures were chiefly aimed at preventing the plague from being brought in from France and that the King and his ministers would use proper discretion in giving orders for the sinking and destroying of ships coming from infected countries.[74] With this assurance the City merchants had to be content, but they were far from satisfied.

A few days later the bill was passed, and on the twentieth of November it was sent up to the Lords.[75] There, two days later, it was given its first reading, and on the twenty-fourth it was ordered committed for the consideration of the whole house.[76] It was at this point that the opposition lords introduced the subject of the Quarantine Act passed in the previous January and insisted on the repeal of the clauses in that act which gave emergency powers to the government. It should

[72] *Journals of the House of Commons*, XIX, 664-665.
[73] Boyer, *Political State*, XXII, 516-517.
[74] Cobbett, *Parliamentary History*, VII, 928-929.
[75] *Journals of the House of Commons*, XIX, 670.
[76] *Journals of the House of Lords*, XXI, 610-612.

be noted that when this act had passed the Lords in the previous session, it had been agreed to without any amendments and without any recorded opposition. In this session of the parliament, however, the members of the minority group in the upper House, led by Lord Cowper[77] and Bishop Atterbury,[78] were availing themselves of every opportunity to show their dislike for the Walpole administration.[79] They now seized upon the Quarantine Act as a means to stir up trouble.[80] It was therefore ordered that in the Grand Committee, the House should consider both the bill "to prohibit Commerce with infected Countries, etc." and the Quarantine Act, with

[77] William Cowper (d. 1723), first Earl Cowper, had always been considered a Whig. He had served as Lord Chancellor during the first years of George I, and had been created an earl in 1718. With the accession of Walpole to power in 1721, however, he had entered into a decided opposition to the ministry, and because of his influence and ability was considered the leader of the opposition lords. See J. M. Rigg, "William, first Earl Cowper," D. N. B., XII, 389-393.

[78] Francis Atterbury (1662-1732), Bishop of Rochester, had been a Tory High Churchman since the time of William III, and a friend of Queen Anne's last ministers, through whom in 1713 he attained his bishopric. Opposed to the accession of the House of Hanover, he had been active in the interests of the Jacobites in England, and was in correspondence with James and his friends abroad. To Walpole the Bishop was constantly in opposition, speaking against him in the House of Lords, or framing protests against his measures. See J. H. Overton, "Francis Atterbury," D. N. B., II, 233-238: Folkestone Williams, Memoirs and Correspondence of Francis Atterbury, Bishop of Rochester (London, 1869); H. C. Beeching, Francis Atterbury (London, 1909).

[79] Among the others in the opposition group were Philip Wharton (1698-1731), Duke of Wharton, who takes a more leading part a little later in our story, and Lords Trevor (Thomas Trevor, 1658-1729, Baron Trevor of Bromham), Coningsby (Thomas Coningsby, 1656-1729, Earl Coningsby), Bathurst (Allen Bathurst, 1684-1725, first Earl Bathurst), North and Grey (William North, 1678-1734, sixth Lord North, and Baron Grey of Wark), Strafford (Thomas Wentworth, 1672-1739, Baron Raby and third Earl of Strafford), and Orrery (Charles Boyle, 1676-1731, fourth Earl of Orrery, and first Baron Marston). The whole of the opposition of this group during the session has been ably outlined in Realey, Early Opposition to Sir Robert Walpole, pp. 78-88.

[80] "This I very well remember, that a learned prelate [Atterbury] now dead, who had more of a political than of a Christian Zeal, and was one who made the loudest noise about the Quarantine Bill, frankly owned to me in conversation, that though the directions were good, yet he and his friends had resolved to take that opportunity of shewing their disaffection for the ministry." Dr. Richard Meade, in the Preface to his 1744 edition of "A Short Discourse Concerning Pestilential Contagion, and the Methods Used to Prevent It," in The Medical Works of Richard Meade, M.D. (Dublin, 1767), p. 70.

the power to alter, amend, or repeal any part of the latter.[81]

Meanwhile, opposition to the new measures proposed in Parliament and affecting their commerce had been growing among the Londoners. Now the populace was to be further stirred up by the threatened dangers charged by the parliamentary opposition to be existent in the clauses of the old Quarantine Act. The City Fathers, though not so easily alarmed as the common people, were nevertheless concerned; and on December 5, at the first meeting of the Court of Common Council under the new Lord Mayor, Sir William Stewart, they gave their approval to a petition which was to be sent to the House of Lords, praying that they might be heard against the Quarantine Act, since certain clauses of that act affected "not only the Rights, Privileges, and Immunities," but also the "Trade, Safety, and Prosperity of the City of London."[82]

The next day it was presented to the House and read.[83] A warm debate followed. The Government speakers argued for its rejection, and Lord Sunderland insisted that it might establish a bad precedent. The Opposition, of which Lords Cowper and Trevor were the chief speakers, denied this. They urged that the petition be received and declared that both liberty and property were at stake. Finally, after "many and long speeches," the House divided, the motion was negatived, and the City petition rejected by a vote of 63 to 22.[84] The opposition lords then registered their protest, pointing out that the rejection of a petition from so great a body as the City of London was extremely unjust. They also feared that it would act as a check on further presentations of public opinion and would tend to increase the disaffection already prevalent in the kingdom.[85]

---

[81] *Journals of the House of Lords*, XXI, 612.

[82] Journals of the Court of Common Council, 57, f. 92.

[83] *Journals of the House of Lords*, XXI, 622; *Weekly Journal, or Saturday's Post*, Dec. 9, 1721.

[84] Boyer, *Political State*, XXII, 618, 641-644; H. M. C., *Portland MSS*, V, 555 (newsletter, wrongly dated Feb. 19, 1718, actually of Dec. 6, 1721).

[85] *Journals of the House of Lords*, XXI, 622-623. Such protests had a great political significance. Most of them were published and distributed free to the citizens, and were very effective in arousing opposition to the administration, since the debates of Parliament at this time were not published

On the next day, December 7, the House of Lords was put into a Grand Committee to consider the bill to prohibit commerce with infected countries. At once Lord Cowper moved that a clause be added to that bill to repeal as much of the Quarantine Act "as impowers the Government to remove to a Lazaret, or Pest-House, any Persons whatsoever infected with the Plague, or Healthy Persons of an Infected Family, from their Habitations; and also so much of the said Act, as gives Power for the drawing of Lines or Trenches, round any City, Town, or Place infected." These same clauses were mentioned in the City petition. He showed the dangers from isolating such cities as London and Westminster, and charged openly that the powers granted were inconsistent with a free government, were copied from the French military despotism, and were designed to prepare the way for an absolute tyranny in England. He was upheld by Bishop Atterbury, and the Lords Trevor, Coningsby, North and Grey, and Strafford. They in turn were opposed by the Lords Sunderland, Townshend, and Carteret. Nothing, however, was decided that day; and as it grew late, the debates were adjourned to the following Monday (December 11).[86]

Friday, December 8, was the day which had been set aside for the "Public Fast, to implore the Protection of Almighty God, and to avert the Plague." It was observed in the City and the kingdom with all due solemnity, religious services being held in the royal chapel at St. James's, in St. Paul's Cathedral, in Westminster Abbey, and in numerous other places of worship throughout the land.[87]

On Monday the House of Lords again convened, and another spirited debate followed. Lord Cowper showed a second

and the arguments on the ministerial side were therefore not known to the general public. Atterbury composed the greater part of the protests of this session (there were twenty-six of them), and they were revised by Lord Cowper. See Laprade, *Public Opinion and Politics*, p. 255. For the protests of the session see J. E. Thorold Rogers, *A Complete Collection of the Protests of the Lords, with Historical Introductions* (Oxford, 1875), I, 257-308.

[86] *Journals of the House of Lords*, XXI, 624; Boyer, *Political State*, XXII, 618-619.

[87] Boyer, *Political State*, XXII, 619-620.

time the dangers from drawing lines around infected places and attempted to gain exemption for the cities of London and Westminster. Lords Trevor, Coningsby, North and Grey, the Earl of Strafford, and the Bishop of Rochester again supported him; but the weight of the arguments was with the Government speakers, who included Lords Sunderland and Townshend, the Duke of Newcastle, and Lord Carteret. On the division, Lord Cowper's motion was lost by a vote of 45 to 20. Many other points were then brought up, and the bill was fully discussed.[88] On Wednesday, December 13, the bill to prohibit commerce with infected countries was reported complete and was passed by a vote of 47 to 26. It was then sent back to the House of Commons. In the House of Lords Earl Cowper again moved that a bill be brought in to repeal the clauses of the Quarantine Act. Again the same majority divided against it. The minority lords therefore registered their dissent, protesting the powers granted by the Act and expressing alarm at the harmful effects therein latent.[89]

Nor was London less fearful. In fact, the clamor increased amazingly during the latter part of December. The opponents of the administration were responsible for most of this, but the mercantile interests of the City, resentful of the severe restrictions imposed by the quarantine laws with resulting losses in their trade, must share in the blame. There was also a third party, an individual, who deserves in a contributing way to share it likewise, the well-known literary figure of that day, Daniel Defoe.[90]

[88] *Ibid.*, XXII, 621-622; Cobbett, *Parliamentary History*, VII, 931-932.
[89] *Journals of the House of Lords*, XXI, 629-630; Boyer, *Political State*, XXII, 624-627; Cobbett, *Parliamentary History*, VII, 933-935.
[90] Daniel Defoe (or De Foe) (1661?-1731) had begun publishing his pamphlets and essays as early as 1698. He had been very changeable in his political views, having supported the Marlborough-Godolphin administration in 1709, defended the Whig impeachment of Sacheveral in 1710, written in Harley's interest in 1710-1713, been prosecuted by the Whigs in 1713 for treasonable publications, and then in 1716 begun publishing a monthly periodical in the service of the Whig government. In 1717 he began writing for Mist's Jacobite *Weekly Journal*, and in the next few years contributed articles to *Applebee's Journal* and a number of other opposition newspapers, still continuing in the service and pay of the government, but pretending to be a Tory so that he could aid the administration by toning down—"taking

It had been Defoe who, in the previous autumn and again in the spring, had done much to center the attention of the public on the plague in France by his writings, at first in the *Daily Post,* then later on and more fully in *Applebee's Weekly Journal.* Appearing as news articles, but written very graphically, they depicted all the horrors of the plague in Marseilles, Aix, Ailes, and Toulon, and commented on the methods used by the French government to prevent its spread.[91] Defoe was writing on the side of the ministry, and these articles were toned to cause his readers to abhor the plague and look favorably on the administration's attempts to prevent its coming to England. It was quite natural then, in July, 1721, when the bill to prevent "the clandestine Running of Goods" received opposition from the City merchants, that Defoe should write in condemnation of those "worthy Gentlemen!" who showed more concern for their trade than for the lives of their fellow citizens.[92] In this Defoe *did* show himself an administration man, opposing those who would endanger the City and country by preventing the passage of proper precautionary measures.

Yet, throughout his numerous articles, which were renewed in the fall of 1721, it was noticeable that he laid great emphasis on the severity of the plague laws in France and on the despotic methods of the French government, calling attention to the custom of forcing people, whether infected with the plague or not, to remain in infected areas, and of establishing lines, guarded by soldiers, about cities and towns where the plague was raging.[93] Now, the clauses of the English Quarantine Act, which became the subject of so much opposition, gave the English government the power to use almost exactly the same

---

off the edge"—of the attacks on the ministers by those newspapers (Leslie Stephens, "Daniel Defoe," *D. N. B.*, XIV, 280-293; William Lee, *Daniel Defoe, His Life, and Recently Discovered Writings, Extending from 1716 to 1729,* London, 1869 [Vol. I for the "Life"]; Paul Dottin, *The Life and Strange and Surprising Adventures of Daniel De Foe,* translated from the French by Louise Ragan, New York, 1929).

[91] See, for example, his articles in *Applebee's Original Weekly Journal,* Sept. 10, Oct. 1, and Nov. 5, 1720; and May 20 and July 1, 1721.

[92] See p. 37, n. 64 above.

[93] See his articles in *Applebee's Original Weekly Journal,* Nov. 5, 1720, and May 20, Sept. 16, and Nov. 4, 1721.

measures as he had been describing as practiced by the French. There is no doubt then, that in December, 1721, when the parliamentary opposition began its attack, the minds of his readers were receptive for the charges that the King and his ministers were planning to set up a despotism in England on the French system.   Therefore, Defoe must share part of the blame for the ease and rapidity by which the idea took hold on London. The attention of his readers had been called to the evils in France, and while concern for their rights and liberties could genuinely be felt by the general public, it was obviously a situation which the opponents of the administration might capitalize to their advantage; and they made the most of it.

The charges of a military despotism found ready ears in the City, and the large majority vote in favor of the government made many of the citizens "very uneasie."[94]   Rumors spread rapidly, even reports that the proposed pesthouses to be built throughout the kingdom were really to be used for barracks for the quartering of an armed force on the people.[95] Another cause for alarm, to which attention was called by the opposition press, was the extreme punishment for those who disobeyed the rigid quarantine laws—death as a felon without benefit of clergy.[96]   Moreover, the rejection of the City's petition by the House of Lords was taken as a severe snub of the City's government, and broadsides setting forth the contents of the petition, its reception in the upper House, and the protests of the dissenting lords were distributed wholesale, the healths of those lords being drunk "in all Meetings of Citizens."[97]

THE WESTMINSTER BRIDGE BILL

Another matter introduced at this time which contributed to the City's discontent was a proposal to build a bridge for Westminster.   On December 15 two petitions were presented

---

[94] Boyer, *Political State*, XXII, 618.

[95] [Thomas Gordon] *A Complete History of the Centennial Parliament, Wherein All Their Proceedings Are Particularly Enquired into, and Faithfully Related* (London, 1722), p. 62.

[96] *Weekly Journal, or Saturday's Post*, Jan. 6, 1722.

[97] *Ibid.*, Dec. 23, 1721.

to the House of Commons. One was signed by a number of the inhabitants of the City of Westminster, the other by inhabitants of the counties of Kent, Surrey, Sussex, and Southampton. Both petitions set forth the fact that the only convenient and altogether practical means of crossing the River Thames was by a bridge, and that there was none between London and Kingston (eighteen miles up the river). They then pointed out that there had been a great increase in the number of buildings and inhabitants in Westminster and the adjacent parts, and it had become a necessity that better communication be established between Westminster and the counties to the south than was allowed by the uncertain, inconvenient, and hazardous system of ferries then in operation. The petitioners, therefore, suggested that a bridge be erected over the river at Lambeth or Vauxhall, and prayed that leave might be given to bring in a bill for that purpose.[98]

Receiving a favorable hearing, the request was granted, and a large committee was appointed to examine the matter and to report to the House. The committee, of which William Pulteney was chairman, included administration supporters as well as those in opposition, among them the parliamentary representatives from each of the petitioning counties and the districts involved—including the City of London. This committee went immediately to work, a thorough inquiry was made, numerous authorities were consulted, and a full report was prepared to be presented after the Christmas recess.[99]

While it was still in the committee, however, opposition arose in the City. London Bridge had stood in solitary splendor since the twelfth century, and over it passed all the traffic and trade between the counties north and south of the Thames.[100] The enormous advantage thereby given was invaluable to the City, and the citizens were extremely jealous of any attempt to break this monopoly. The proposal to build

[98] *Journals of the House of Commons*, XIX, 694-695.
[99] Ibid., XIX, 694, 708.
[100] "The City has for above 500 Years deriv'd large Advantages from her Communication by the Bridge with Southwark, Kent, Surry, and other neighboring Counties, and has thereby made herself both rich and populous" (Nathaniel Mist, in *Weekly Journal, or Saturday's Post*, Jan. 27, 1722).

a bridge at Westminster, therefore, at once aroused them to take action, and on December 20 a special meeting of the Court of Common Council was ordered by the Lord Mayor, Sir William Stewart. There the members (for the majority of both aldermen and councilmen were dependent on trade solely or in part for their living) almost unanimously opposed the bill. They declared that the building of a new bridge would not only be prejudicial to the interests of the City of London by the diverting of her trade, but would very greatly obstruct the navigation of the River Thames, because the shipping from the upper river would not be able to pass down to the City wharves. They, therefore, moved the sending of a petition to the House of Commons, to inform parliament of their grievances, and to beg that their counsel might be heard against the bill.[101]

In the City agitation made rapid strides. The probable consequences which might arise from the building of a new bridge caused even more apprehension than the possible results that might follow the establishment of a despotism. It affected directly everyone from the lowest apprentice and smallest shopkeeper to the wealthiest of the City merchants.[102] Taken together, the proposed new bridge and the disturbing clauses of the Quarantine Act almost plunged the town into an uproar.

Its first effect was felt on December 21, when the annual elections of Common Councilmen were held in the various wards. The ministry had hoped for the return of a more favorable Common Council this year, but the situation was against them. Moreover, there was a "strange inactivity of the Whigges in the City, especially of ye most substantial among them, who should be examples to their neighbors,"

[101] Journals of the Court of Common Council, 57, f. 93.

[102] "What certain Consequences of Loss and Disadvantage must attend London, in lessening the Number of her Inhabitants, the impairing, if not quite ruining, the Estates and Rents of thousands of Families, whose Fortunes lye in Houses, in Shortening the Supplies of her Markets, and alienating many important Branches of private Commerce . . . by the foundation of a New Bridge," wrote Nathaniel Mist in his opposition *Weekly Journal, or Saturday's Post*, Jan. 27, 1722.

according to a report received by Lord Sunderland.[103] As a remedy the writer suggested that the Minister visit the City and urge the chief of these—naming Aldermen Sir Peter Delmé, Sir Charles Peers, Sir Randolph Knipe, Sir Samuel Stainer, and Sir Thomas Scawen—to more vigorous endeavors.[104] Whether or not Sunderland did this, it failed to bring about the desired results. "Our Friends the Whigs have not had all the good Luck they expected," commented a writer in *Applebee's*,[105] while the *Post-Boy* reported that in the election the several wards had "made Choice of a greater majority than last Year, of Common-Council-Men firm in the Interest of the Church of England, and asserters of the Rights and Privileges of their Fellow-Citizens."[106]

At the end of the month one observer remarked: "The City continues in a high ferment about the quarantine bill, and the new bridge that is to be built betwixt Lambeth and Fox-hall," and he added significantly: "There will be a mighty opposition by the City to that bridge."[107] In January the Quarantine Act was said to be "the greatest Subject of all Conversations," and it was reported that "the fears of the People are rais'd to an extraordinary Pitch."[108] Thus the consideration of both subjects in the House of Commons after the Christmas recess was watched keenly by the citizens of the metropolis.

On January 11 Pulteney reported the findings of the committee appointed to consider the bridge question; namely, that the growth of the City of Westminster and the parts adjacent in recent years warranted the building of a bridge and that it had become not only desirable but a real necessity. The engineers who were consulted had surveyed the condition of the ground on either bank and had recommended that the best place

---

[103] Letter from Edward Calamy on Dec. 11, 1721, printed in John Waddington, *Congregational History, 1700-1800, in Relation to Contemporaneous Events, etc.* (London, 1876), pp. 217-218.

[104] *Ibid.*, p. 218.

[105] *Applebee's Original Weekly Journal*, Dec. 23, 1721.

[106] Dec. 23, 1721.

[107] Dr. Stratford to Lord Harley, Dec. 29, 1721, and Jan. 1, 1722 (H. M. C., *Portland MSS*, VII, 285, 312).

[108] *British Gazetteer*, Jan. 20, 1722.

for it would be from Prince's Wash in Lambeth, to a point just above Peterborough House, in Westminster. Furthermore, they had declared that the bridge could be built so as not to prejudice the navigation of the river. The report had no sooner been read than an effort was made to reject it. This move failed, however, and a bill was ordered to be brought in to build a bridge from Lambeth to Westminster as the committee recommended.[109]

On January 15 the subject of the Quarantine Act was reintroduced. Archibald Hutcheson, a member from Hastings, moved that since certain clauses in that act had "occasioned great Uneasiness," leave be given to bring in a bill to repeal those clauses; namely, those giving the government power to remove persons, whether or not infected with the plague, from out of an infected area to a lazaret or pesthouse, and to draw lines around any infected city, town, or place. He was seconded by Peter Godfrey and Robert Heysham, both City members, who likewise urged that such a bill be brought in. Horace Walpole and other ministerial supporters, we are told, appeared "surpris'd at that unexpected Motion." A two-hour debate followed, during which time we are also told that "Mr. Robert Walpole was silent," and then the motion was approved (115 to 75) and the bill was ordered to be brought in. Hutcheson was made chairman of the committee to prepare it, and his colleagues included three City members, Godfrey, Sir Gilbert Heathcote, and Sir William Thompson.[110]

On January 18 the committee reported, and the bill was given its first reading.[111] In the next two weeks it was freely discussed, and some amendments were made. However, there was little opposition to it, Walpole's silence on the first debate evidently giving the cue to the ministerial spokesmen; and the repeal of the clauses seemed assured. News of this got outdoors, and it was remarked that the report tended "to ease and quiet the Minds of the People."[112]

[109] *Journals of the House of Commons*, XIX, 708; *British Gazetteer*, Jan. 13, 1722.
[110] *Journals of the House of Commons*, XIX, 712; *Historical Register*, VII, 105-106.
[111] *Journals of the House of Commons*, XIX, 716.
[112] *British Gazetteer*, Jan. 20, 1722.

Meanwhile, during the same fortnight, agitation for and against the new bridge at Westminster continued. The bill had been brought in on the sixteenth and its consideration begun by the Commons.[113] Outside, in the City of Westminster, hopes ran high. Various plans for the new bridge were talked of, projects outlined for building up the approaches were presented, and all the advantages to be gained by the inhabitants were everywhere discussed.[114] The Archbishop of Canterbury was even mentioned as one of those who would advance the money to defray the expenses of building (at an interest rate of "5 *l.* per cent").[115] The new bridge had become "the Great Subject of Conversation both in Town and Country," reported the *Saturday Post*, and added: "Tho' this affair be debated very calmly in the Senate, it is with much Warmth and Zeal discours'd in all Places of Publick Resort: Where every one argues, pro or con, as his different Interest leads him, or the Spirit of Opposition inclines him."[116]

Those opposed to the bill resorted to petitions, of which a great number were presented to the House of Commons.[117] The City of London took the lead. On the eighteenth, just after the bill to remove the disturbing clauses of the Quarantine Act had been presented, the Sheriffs of London, Sir George Merttins and Edward Beecher, appeared at the bar of the House and presented the petition approved by the Court of Common Council at its special meeting on December 20.[118] Pointing out that the proposed bridge would "prove inconsistent with and destructive of the Rights, Properties, and Privileges and Franchises of this City"; that it would be "a great prejudice to London Bridge and the Navigation of the River Thames as to render it dangerous if not impracticable"; and that it

---

[113] *Journals of the House of Commons*, XIX, 715.

[114] *Weekly Journal, or Saturday's Post*, Jan. 20, 1722; *British Gazetteer*, Jan. 20, 1722.

[115] *Weekly Journal, or Saturday's Post*, Jan. 20, 1722. One writer (Gordon, *History of the Septennial Parliament*, p. 67) waggishly declared that the bill was brought in because "the Arch . . . p's Horses had rec'd Colds crossing on the Lambeth Ferry."

[116] *Weekly Journal, or Saturday's Post*, Jan. 27, 1722.

[117] *Journals of the House of Commons*, XIX, 717-727.

[118] See p. 47, above.

would "greatly affect the Trade of the City in general, and the properties of many private Persons and Families in particular"—the City Fathers prayed that they might be heard by their counsel before the bill should pass. To this prayer the Commons proved agreeable, and permission was given them to be heard on the second reading of the bill.[119]

Other petitions followed rapidly. The inhabitants of Southwark feared the loss of their trade and the decline of property values in the borough; the owners of houses on London Bridge declared the new bridge would take away their revenues; the managers of the Hospital of St. Thomas in Southwark complained that their property would be endangered by the overflowing of the river, and that their revenues would be endangered; the proprietors of the waterworks at London Bridge said the new bridge would destroy their waterworks, and cut down the water supply of the City; a number of London watermen and lightermen protested that their businesses would be prejudiced and their families ruined; John Pond, tollkeeper for London Bridge, declared that a new bridge would so diminish his income as to ruin him; bargemen and watermen from towns along the upper Thames set forth that the bridge would entirely ruin their business; the governors of St. Bartholomew's Hospital in London declared that their revenues would be seriously depleted; and the owners of markets and wharves in Queenhithe Ward said that they would all be ruined, since the bridge would block the passage of boats from the upper Thames to their wharves. All these were promised a hearing when the bill should be read a second time.[120]

This second reading took place on January 25, and the counsel for each of the petitioners was called in.[121] As it came about, however, only the counsel of the City of London was heard. The case for the City was long, and so many witnesses were called in and examined that at the end of the day the hearing was still unfinished. It was resumed on the following Mon-

[119] Journals of the Court of Common Council, 57, f. 95; Journals of the House of Commons, XIX, 717; British Gazetteer, Jan. 20, 1722.
[120] Journals of the House of Commons, XIX, 718-727.
[121] Ibid., XIX, 728.

day, January 29, "upon which occasion the House and Galleries were filled, nor was the Lobby less crowded."[122] The proponents of the bill made an attempt to block the testimony of the Londoners, but their motion was negatived when put to a vote by the narrow majority of 107 to 89.[123] The counsel for the City then presented their case so ably that at the close of the day the hearing was adjourned until the following week. Reports soon spread about that the bill would be dropped,[124] and time proved them correct. London's influence, her arguments indoors and her clamor outdoors, had been great enough to block the attempt to build the proposed new bridge at Westminster. That subject was not revived again in Parliament for more than a decade.[125]

Consideration of the bill to repeal the objectionable clauses of the Quarantine Act was now completed, and it was passed in the Commons on January 29, the same day that the last hearing of the bridge bill was held.[126] In the House of Lords its consideration was brief, since the support of the opposition lords and the willingness of the administration to concede the issue now made its approval certain. The final vote was taken on February 9.[127] Three days later the bill received the royal assent and became law.[128] The same day the bill passed in December for the prohibition of commerce with infected countries also received the royal approval.[129] Moreover, during the following week the Commons completed the debates and passed (February 20) a bill "to prevent the clandestine Running of Goods," a bill similar to that proposed in the previous

[122] *Applebee's Original Weekly Journal*, Feb. 3, 1722.
[123] *Journals of the House of Commons*, XIX, 731.
[124] *Applebee's Original Weekly Journal*, Feb. 3, 1722.
[125] New plans were made in 1734, sponsored by a small group of the inhabitants of Westminster, including the Archbishop of Canterbury. In February, 1736, a bill was introduced in Parliament; and although protested by the City Corporation, no popular clamor was raised, and it was easily pushed through the quiet session of that year, receiving the royal assent in May. In September, 1738, work was begun; and the bridge, built of stone with fifteen arches, was completed in November, 1749. It was replaced a century later (1854-1862) by the present Westminster Bridge.
[126] *Journals of the House of Commons*, XIX, 731.
[127] *Journals of the House of Lords*, XXI, 667-678.
[128] *Ibid.*, XXI, 683 (8 Geo. I, c. 8).
[129] *Ibid.*, XXI, 683 (8 Geo. I, c. 10). See p. 43, above.

year, which had met the opposition of the City merchants and had been allowed to die at the end of the session.[130]   This bill also had the approval of the House of Lords, and it received the royal assent on March 7.[131]

Thus the proposal to build a bridge at Westminster was defeated, and the offending clauses of the old Quarantine Act were repealed.   The Quarantine Act, when it was passed in January, 1721, and throughout the "noise" of this last session, had been felt by the administration to be necessary, both to prevent the plague from coming into the kingdom and to provide for its control if it should get a foothold.   The clauses of that Act giving the government extraordinary powers in case such a calamity occurred were reasonable, considering the knowledge and experience of the time in matters of contagion. Nevertheless, they could easily be misunderstood or their meaning distorted.   On this ambiguity the opponents of Walpole in Parliament counted.   Not strong enough to overthrow the ministry alone, they sought the support of public opinion and thought to attain their ends by stirring up the London populace.   Neither of the two measures opposed were in themselves enough to provoke such a clamor as was aroused.   The fact that the Quarantine Act was in force for nearly a year without any recorded protest and the fact that an act to build a bridge at Westminster did pass in 1736 without popular dissent seem to prove this.   It was largely because the parliamentary opposition deemed it opportune as an occasion for making political capital that the Londoners were stirred up by newspaper article, pamphlet, and the spoken word.   The rejection of the City petition against the quarantine clauses (which petition was the only one presented on this subject[132]) added fuel to the flames.   All of London was thus aroused, and the popular outcry did not go unheeded by the politically-wise Walpole.   The administration remained in power, but the objectionable measures were repealed.[133]   The whole affair can be classified as an example

---

[130] *Journals of the House of Commons*, XIX, 746-750.

[131] *Journals of the House of Lords*, XXI, 702-716 (8 Geo. I, c. 18).

[132] This point was noted by a writer in the *British Gazetteer*, Jan. 20, 1722.

[133] "Vain and groundless as these fears were, yet the clamours industriously

of the part that public opinion can play in national politics, a public opinion partly aroused by genuine alarm for its liberties and for the safety of its economic interests, but to a greater degree by the machinations of the enemies of the administration in power.

What part did Defoe play in all this? His contribution to the spread of the unrest has already been indicated. Yet he probably did not intentionally aid the opposition. All during the period in which he wrote for the press, he seemed to be genuine in his fear of the possible spread of the plague to England, and on every occasion he attempted to impress his readers with the horrors that would accompany it. His culminating work on this subject was his famous *Journal of the Plague Year*, published on March 17, 1722, in which he realistically pictured the terrible conditions of London in 1665.[134] Written during the height of the clamor, it was intended to be used as an aid to the administration in diverting the minds of the Londoners from a possible establishment of a despotism to the more fearful horrors of the more probable invasion of pestilence and death. Nevertheless, it is not unreasonable to believe that his earlier articles in the newspapers had influenced his readers in an adverse manner, and had put them in a receptive mood for the charges made by the opposition. Defoe was not an active member in the City's government and probably would not normally be included in this story,[135] but the part he played in this particular episode was important, and the history of the opposition to the clauses of the Quarantine Act in this first year of the Walpole administration would not be complete without mention of him.

---

raised from them were so strong, that a great officer in the state [Walpole] thought fit to oblige his enemies by giving way to them; and . . . with his consent the thing was done" (Meade, *Medical Works*, p. 170).

[134] *A Journal of the Plague Year: Being Observations or Memorials of the Most Remarkable Occurences, as well Publick as Private, Which Happened in London during the Last Great Visitation in 1665. Written by a Citizen Who Continued All the While in London* (London, 1722).

[135] Although not an active member, Defoe was connected with the City's life, since he had been admitted (by right of birth, his father being a butcher) as a liveryman of the Butchers' Company in January, 1688. See Dottin, *Daniel De Foe*, p. 50.

THE QUAKERS' AFFIRMATION BILL

Another subject of interest to London during this year meriting attention was the Quakers' Affirmation Bill. Resulting from a petition presented to the Commons by the Society of Friends in London on December 14, it was contemporary with the proposed Westminster Bridge Bill and the repealing of the Quarantine Act clauses, but it did not arouse the same repercussions.

By an act passed during the reign of William III, in 1696, the Quakers had been excused from taking the regular oath used in courts of justice and elsewhere and were given permission to make a solemn affirmation or declaration instead ("I, A. B., do declare in the presence of Almighty God, the witness of the truth of what I say").[136] For a time this oath had been used satisfactorily. Then there grew up among the Quakers themselves an opinion that such an affirmation—using the words "in the presence of Almighty God"—was as sinful as taking an oath. Some attempts had therefore been made, although without success, to make a change. In 1721 the opportunity seemed more favorable, and application was made by members of the London society to various members of the administration. The Earl of Sunderland and the Earl of Carlisle promised support in the Lords, and Lord Morpeth[137] in the Commons.[138] A petition was then sent to the lower house, on December 14, signed by one hundred and thirty-two Friends, and it was presented by Sir John Ward, one of the City members. It set forth the hardships and the inconveniences suffered by the Brethren of the Quakers from their not being able either to take oath or use the form of solemn affirmation allowed them, and prayed that the form of the affirmation might be changed so as not to conflict with their religious scruples.[139] This petition was favorably received, and a bill was ordered to

---

[136] 7 & 8 William III, c. 34.

[137] Henry Howard (1694-1758), Viscount Morpeth, fourth Earl of Carlisle.

[138] John Gough, *A History of the People Called Quakers* (Dublin, 1790), IV, 183-185.

[139] *Journals of the House of Commons*, XXI, 692; Gough, *History of the Quakers*, IV, 181-182.

be brought in, which was called a bill "for granting the People called Quakers, such Form of Affirmation or Declaration as may remove the Difficulties which many of them lie under."[140]

From a desire not so much to curry favor with this particular group of Dissenters as in the interest of peace in general, the administration did give this bill favorable support both in the Commons and in the Lords. Nevertheless, reports were spread about, and came largely to be believed by the London citizens, that its favorable reception was entirely due to the promises made by the Brethren that they would support the ministerial candidates at the next election.[141] From the London viewpoint it is also interesting to note that the bill was sponsored throughout by Sir John Ward and that on the committee appointed to bring in the bill, which included both Robert and Horace Walpole, were three other City men: Robert Heysham, Peter Godfrey, and Sir Gilbert Heathcote.[142]

The Commons passed the bill on January 9, and Sir John was ordered to carry it to the Lords. There it was pounced upon by the opposition minority, but the prelates of the Church of England, led by Bishop Atterbury, took the lead in denouncing the bill, even scornfully characterizing the Quakers as "no Christians." Their motion to prevent the further consideration of the bill, however, was negatived by a vote of 64 to 14 on the division, and on the fifteenth the bill was ordered to be committed.[143]

Two days later the House of Lords formed itself into a grand committee. On that day an unexpected petition was presented by the Archibishop of York from a group of the London clergy, protesting against the endangering of their revenues (inasmuch as the Quakers denied the right of the clergy to

[140] *Journals of the House of Commons*, XIX, 695.

[141] A "Sweetener," James Ralph called it, in his *Of the Use and Abuse of Parliaments: In Two Historical Discourses* (London, 1744), I, 255. See Boyer, *Political State*, XXII, 633; Gordon, *History of the Septennial Parliament*, p. 67; *The Poll of the Liverymen of the City of London at the Election of Members of Parliament, etc.* (London, 1722), p. 2.

[142] *Journals of the House of Commons*, XIX, 699; Cobbett, *Parliamentary History*, VII, 937.

[143] Boyer, *Political State*, XXIII, 108, 112; Cobbett, *Parliamentary History*, VII, 937-938, 941-942.

make them pay tithes to the Church of England) by thus favoring these Dissenters and contending that the extension of such an indulgence would be harmful to the administration and weaken the support of his Majesty's government.[144]   A motion to receive this petition precipitated a hot debate.   The petitioners were supported by the Archbishop of York and Bishop Atterbury and the opposition lords, but as warmly opposed by Lord Townshend, the Earl of Sunderland, Lord Carteret, the Duke of Somerset, and other ministerial supporters.   The irregular method of presenting the petition (the London clergy were not in the Archbishop of York's diocese) was mentioned, and the Earl of Sunderland declared that it was no better than a libel.[145]   On the division the motion to receive the petition was negatived by a vote of 60 to 24, the presence of the leading prelates of England among the minority (including also the Archbishop of Canterbury and the Bishops of Oxford, Litchfield, and Coventry) being duly observed.[146]   The debate on the bill was then resumed and completed on the nineteenth of January, when it passed the House in the affirmative.   The opposition recorded dissent on both occasions, the first being later expunged from the record, but the Quakers' bill became law on February 12.[147]   It repealed all the previous acts involving the Quakers and gave the proper forms to be used by them in declaring their fidelity to George I and their abjuration of the Pretender as well as the proper form of affirmation to be used in courts of justice and other places.[148]   All the Quakers were thereby very highly pleased, and at the end of March the London society presented a loyal address to the

[144] *Historical Register*, VII, 89-91; Boyer, *Political State*, XXIII, 112-115.

[145] The Duke of Somerset later belittled the petition by saying that there were "over five hundred of the clergy in and about London, and we find only fifty-one names to their petition, and these very obscure" (Gough, *History of the Quakers*, IV, 187).

[146] Boyer, *Political State*, XXIII, 115; *Historical Register*, VII, 91.

[147] 8 Geo. I, c. 8.   See the *British Gazetteer*, Jan. 20, 1722; *Journals of the House of Lords*, XXI, 651-656, 683, 713; Boyer, *Political State*, XXIII, 115-116; *Historical Register*, VII, 89-97; Cobbett, *Parliamentary History*, VII, 943-948.

[148] The simple form of affirmation was "I, A. B., do solemnly, sincerely, and truly declare and affirm," and in none of the forms was the name of God mentioned.

King, thanking him for granting the indulgence, and praising him for his goodness and mercy.[149]

But now the first year of the Walpole administration was coming to a close, and it was marked chiefly by the ending of the first Septennial Parliament. There had been talk of this for over a year past, and although according to law it would end in the spring of 1722, yet it was felt by the Jacobites and others that it might be prolonged, since the disturbed condition of the country might prove unfavorable to the administration in a general election.[150] As the spring approached, uncertainty still continued, but it was felt more and more that the end was drawing near.[151] Nevertheless, the dissolution itself, on March 7, did come rather suddenly. "We were agreeably surpris'd," reported the *Saturday Post* in its issue of the following week, "and tho' it came upon us unawares, yet there was a general Joy spread over the whole City and suburbs, more than ever was known upon the like Occasion."[152] To those who looked for better things in the new parliament, the dissolution brought great pleasure. The general mass of the citizens of London and Westminster took it as a time of rejoicing, and in the evening after the Proclamation was made, these "express'd their Joy, by Bonfires, Illuminations, and Ringing of Bells, looking upon it as an extraordinary Deliverance."[153]

Interest in both town and country was now turned on the election of a new parliament.

[149] Boyer, *Political State*, XXIII, 338.

[150] H. M. C., *Clements MSS*, p. 313 (Viscount Molesworth to his son, John Molesworth, May 19, 1721; Flotard to John Molesworth, May 31, 1721); *Portland MSS*, VII, 309 (Dr. Stratford to the Earl of Oxford, Dec. 2, 1721); Coxe, *Sir Robert Walpole*, II, 217 (St. John Brodrick to Lord Midleton, June 10, 1721); Mahon, *History of England, 1703-1763*, II, Appendix, xvii (Earl of Orrery to James, the Pretender, Oct. 28, 1721).

[151] H. M. C., *Portland MSS*, VII, 305-306, 309, 312 (Dr. Stratford to the Earl of Oxford, Nov. 1, Dec. 6, and Dec. 28, 1721); *Clements MSS*, p. 319 (Viscount Molesworth to John Molesworth, Aug. 15, 1721); Fifth Report, Appendix, *The Manuscripts of His Grace the Duke of Sutherland, at Trentham, Co. Stafford* (hereinafter cited as H. M. C., *Sutherland MSS*), p. 189 (Earl Cardogan to Lord Gower, Feb. 20, 1722).

[152] *Weekly Journal, or Saturday's Post*, March 17, 1722.

[153] Boyer, *Political State*, XXIII, 280.

PASSENGER SALES

CHAPTER III

A Parliamentary Election and the Atterbury Plot

THE ELECTION OF 1722

THE PARLIAMENTARY election of 1722 was carried on throughout the country with unusual vigor, and since this was the first return of parliament men in seven years there was great feeling. The opposition leaders hoped to capitalize on the unpopularity of the Government and the ill-feeling among the citizens aroused by the South Sea failure, and still looked for a reaction to the Hanoverian "usurpers." They were at first content to arouse popular excitement by the free use of the press and the inciting of mobs, as in previous elections, but since the voters who controlled the return of the members of parliament were a minority of the population, their methods had to be changed to cope with those of Walpole and the Court; namely, public declarations of their candidates, personal and intensive canvassing of the voters, and the generous use of large sums of money. The "Tories" objected to these methods, but soon adopted them for their own, although not to the same extent or with the same success generally as the administration;[1] for to the great mortification of the opposition at this time, so soon after the South Sea troubles and the unrest that followed, with the country seemingly in deep discontent, the general elections returned a "Whig" parliament of no small majority.[2] A Tory writer in the *Weekly Journal* declared it to be plainly a case of "too much bribery on one side and indolence on the other,"[3] but Dr. Stratford wrote

[1] Cf. Thomas Wright, *Caricature History of the Georges; or Annals of the House of Hanover*, pp. 59-60; Realey, *Early Opposition to Sir Robert Walpole*, pp. 107-111. For the Duke of Newcastle's activities in this election, see Nulle, *Thomas Pelham-Holles, Duke of Newcastle*, pp. 137-146.

[2] Cf. H. M. C., *Carlisle MSS*, p. 37 (Sir J. Vanbrugh to Lord Carlisle, April 24, 1722).

[3] *Weekly Journal, or Saturday's Post*, April 14, 1722.

Lord Harley that the "mighty opportunity" had been lost "for want of concert and understanding amongst [us]."[4]

In London, however, the opponents of the Court had reason to rejoice, for although at the time each faction elected two men, the former actually gained three of the four seats, since one of the men, John Barnard, elected on the "Whig" list, soon turned from supporting the Walpole administration.[5] The London contest was a keen one; the opposition aroused during the past winter months was still apparent in March, when the liverymen prepared to return the City's representatives.[6]

The general feeling was shown in two aldermanic elections held just prior to the parliamentary election. The first became necessary when Sir Thomas Abney, the "Father of the City," died on February 6, in his eighty-third year. He was well beloved, and his death was universally lamented.[7] Sir Samuel Garrard immediately made use of his privilege as new senior alderman and accepted the ward of Bridge Without. To elect his successor in Aldersgate Ward, a Court of Wardmote was held on February 15, at which the freemen "unanimously" agreed upon Richard Levett, a Tobacconist.[8] By these changes the Walpole administration lost a supporter in the Court of Aldermen, since Garrard and Levett were both "Tories," and

[4] H. M. C., *Portland MSS*, VII, 321 (April 15, 1722).

[5] John Barnard (1685-1764), an eminent wine-merchant, served the City as alderman of Dowgate Ward and Bridge Without for thirty years, and was elected as one of her representatives to five successive parliaments. In 1736 he was chosen Lord Mayor. He was elected to Parliament in 1722 as a "Whig," but not agreeing with Walpole's commercial policies, he soon joined the opposition and continued so throughout the administration. His abilities were recognized by all "and by none more than Sir Robert Walpole," according to the latter's biographer Coxe (II, 566 n.). See *Memoirs of the Late Sir John Barnard, Knt. and Alderman of the City of London* (London, 1820); and H. R. Fox Bourne, *Famous London Merchants* (New York, 1869), pp. 199-202.

[6] As early as the first week in January, when the clamor was at its height, rumors that the administration would offer to drop the Quarantine and Westminster Bridge bills if the City would choose members favorable to the Court interest at the coming election had been circulated, but it is doubtful whether such offers were ever made, or accepted if they were made. See H. M. C., *Portland MSS*, VII, 312.

[7] *Daily Post*, Feb. 8, 1722; Boyer, *Political State*, XXIII, 234.

[8] *Daily Post*, Feb. 8, 1722; *Post-Boy*, Feb. 17, 1722; Boyer, *Political State*, XXIII, 234.

the balance in that body was reduced so that the ministry could count on only eighteen of the aldermen, against eight for the opposition.

A far from quiet election followed upon the death of Sir William Lewen, alderman of Castle Baynard Ward, on March 16.[9] The councilmen of that ward, always a strong "Tory" constituency, agreed to support John Barber, the City Printer,[10] and it was thought at first that he also would be elected unanimously.[11] At the wardmote, however, Thomas Ladbroke, a Distiller, was put up by the "Court Interest," and a struggle followed. The show of hands was close, and a poll was demanded and taken. Various artifices were used to sway the voters, and "great Treats were made on both Sides."[12] Finally, Barber was declared elected by a vote of 229 to 191 "to the great Joy of the Ward, and the Interest of the Whole City. The Evening was concluded with Bonfires, Acclamations, &c, more than is usual on those Occasions."[13]

The parliamentary election to choose the City's representatives then followed, the actual election being preceded by much spirited electioneering.[14] This was begun immediately after

[9] *Post-Boy*, March 17, 1722.

[10] John Barber (1675-1741), a confirmed Tory, was a friend of Lord Bolingbroke and Jonathan Swift, and had received many favors from Queen Anne's ministers during the last years of her reign. His employments as Printer of the *Gazette* and Stationer to the Ordnance Department ended with the Queen's death, but he retained the office of Queen's (King's) Printer for several years after the Hanoverian accession. In 1720 he had become very wealthy by fortunate speculation in the South Sea. Shortly after his election as alderman in 1722 he sold out his interest in the printing business and for two years retired to the Continent to regain his health. His contacts with the Pretender and his friends during that time tainted him with the stigma of Jacobitism, and upon his return to England in August, 1724, he was taken into custody, but released soon afterward. He strongly opposed the Walpole administration in the City throughout the remainder of his life. See *The Life and Character of John Barber, Esq.* (London, 1741); *An Impartial History of the Life . . . of Mr. John Barber, etc.* (London, 1741); J. E. Ball, *The Correspondence of Jonathan Swift* (London, 1910-1914), V, 384-385; Boyer, *Political State*, XXVIII, 197.

[11] *Post-Boy*, March 17, 1722.

[12] *Saturday Post*, March 24, 1722.

[13] *Applebee's Original Weekly Journal*, March 24, 1722; *Daily Post*, March 20, 1722.

[14] The King and Lord Townshend both showed their interest in the coming election by personally attempting to cultivate the support of the Dissenters in the City for the administration candidates through their leader,

Parliament was dissolved (March 7). At numerous gatherings of the citizens, in tavern and coffeehouse, or in specially called meetings at one or another of the various Company halls, candidates were suggested and vigorously supported by the opposing factions. On March 13, in Vintners' Hall, in Thames Street, the headquarters of the "Tory" adherents, a meeting of "many Hundreds of Eminent Citizens" was held, where it was agreed to nominate Robert Heysham, alderman of Bishopsgate Ward and member for the City in the late Parliament, Richard Brocas, alderman of Farringdon Ward Within, Francis Child, alderman of Farringdon Ward Without, and Richard Lockwood, a commoner.[15] On the following day these same men were agreed upon at "a numerous meeting of the Worthy and Honest Citizens of London," held at Skinners' Hall, in Dowgate Street.[16] These candidates, according to a writer in the press, were "Gentlemen of known Affection to his Majesty King George, and our happy Constitution both in Church and State; and zealous Assertors of the Rights and Privileges of their Fellow Citizens."[17]

The "Eminent Citizens" who supported the "Whig" cause gathered on March 15 at the Merchant-Taylors' Hall, in Threadneedle Street, and agreed to put in nomination Robert Heysham and Francis Child, and also Peter Godfrey, another of the City's members in the late parliament, and John Barnard, all of whom were likewise specified as being "zealously affected to his Majesty, King George, and the present happy Establishment in Church and State, and in every way qualified for so great a Trust."[18]

There were some changes in these lists before the election finally took place. On March 20 Brocas withdrew from the

---

Edmund Calamy. Walpole later rewarded Calamy by sending him a "present" of fifty pounds "out of his Majesty's royal bounty." See Edmund Calamy, *An Historical Account of My Own Life with Some Reflections on the Times I Have Lived in, 1671-1731* (London, 1829), II, 445-450.

[15] *Daily Post*, March 14, 1722.

[16] *Post-Boy*, March 15, 1722.

[17] *Applebee's Original Weekly Journal*, March 17, 1722.

[18] *Post-Boy*, March 20, 1722. Advertisements for the candidates on both lists appeared almost daily in the *Daily Post* and the *Daily Courant* throughout the latter half of the month.

election completely—"in the interest of the City, and for its Peace and Tranquility," as he said—and his place was taken by Humphrey Parsons, alderman of Portsoken Ward.[19] Heysham and Child had been nominated by both groups, but the latter was dropped from the Whig list early in April,[20] and Heysham soon afterwards refused to allow his name to continue on the Tory list.[21] The best-known personage among the candidates, John Barnard, had been put in nomination by a group of his friends, against his will it was said,[22] and advertisements asking for the votes of his fellow citizens appeared as early as March 14.[23] Such was his popularity, moreover, that a week before the election his name was appearing on both tickets; and Lockwood, whose place he had taken on the Tory list, resenting this, ran a campaign of his own, daily advertising his worth, and denying at the same time the allegations of bribery which were being charged against him.[24]

These charges of bribery and personal aggrandizement, as well as various other abuses, were hurled at all the candidates in the heat of the contest. Strangely enough, no clear-cut issues appeared in this election. The South Sea was occasionally mentioned, and party affiliation was at times brought to the fore, but personal corruption seemed to occupy most attention. Even Barnard, popular enough to be nominated on both of the pre-election lists, was not immune; and in reply to certain attacks on him in regard to his connection with the stockjobbing practices in 1720, he wrote in the *Daily Post* denying all the accusations, and saying that on the contrary he had constantly declared his "utter Abhorrence of all such vile Methods of becoming Rich."[25] The mob also demonstrated for and against the candidates. A "great deal of Riotous

[19] *Post-Boy,* March 22, 1722.
[20] *Post-Boy,* April 7, 1722.
[21] *Saturday Post,* April 14, 1722.
[22] *Memoirs of the Late Sir John Barnard,* p. 8.
[23] In the *Daily Post.*
[24] See *Daily Post, Daily Courant,* and *Post-Boy* from April 3 to April 9, 1722.
[25] *Daily Post,* March 21, 1722.

doings" were reported by one observer,[26] while another wrote that the "rabble" had been very "noisy."[27]

The liverymen of the several City Companies, who were summoned to the Guildhall on April 9 for the election, turned out in great numbers. After the six candidates had appeared on the Hustings, a show of hands was called for, and the sheriffs (Merttins and Beecher) declared that the majority had fallen on Robert Heysham, Humphrey Parsons, Francis Child, and Richard Lockwood; John Barnard and Peter Godfrey were counted out. This did not satisfy the friends of the latter, and they at once demanded a poll for all the candidates, which began the next day.[28]

During the three days that the pollbooks remained open great efforts were made by the friends of all the candidates. Over seven thousand of the liverymen cast their votes, and it was termed "the greatest Poll that was ever known for the City of London."[29] Advertisements appeared daily. One list contained the names of Parsons, Child, and Lockwood. The other included Heysham, Godfrey, and Barnard. The contest was clearly a party one, since the former was backed by the "Tory" interests, and the latter the "Whig."[30] On Saturday, April 14, the numbers of the poll were published as follows:

John Barnard	3,989	Richard Lockwood	4,243
Peter Godfrey	3,852	Francis Child	3,784
Robert Heysham	3,573	Humphrey Parsons	3,594

The sheriffs then declared that Barnard, Godfrey, Lockwood, and Child were duly elected.[31] This action brought a protest from the friends of Heysham and Parsons, who had been named by the sheriffs on the Monday before. They demanded a scrutiny—which was granted, although for some undisclosed

[26] H. M. C., *Clements MSS*, p. 336 (Sir Thomas Hewett to the Hon. John Molesworth, April 5, 1722).
[27] *The Complete Works of John Vanbrugh*, IV, 141 (Vanbrugh to Lord Carlisle, April 6, 1722); H. M. C., *Carlisle MSS*, p. 37.
[28] *Daily Post*, April 10, 1722; *Daily Courant*, April 10, 1722.
[29] *Flying Post, or Post-Master*, April 17, 1722.
[30] *Post-Boy*, April 12, 1722; *Daily Post*, April 10 and 11, 1722; *Daily Courant*, April 10, 11, and 12, 1722.
[31] *Flying Post, or Post-Master*, April 17, 1722.

reason the expenses were ordered to be defrayed by the candidates themselves. Lists of their members were then submitted by the different Companies, and a close check was made of all the votes. On May 8 the scrutiny was finished, and the next day the sheriffs proclaimed on the Hustings that they had gone through it carefully, had found no reason to depart from their April 14 declaration, and announced again that John Barnard, Peter Godfrey, Francis Child, and Richard Lockwood were duly elected members of Parliament as representatives for the City of London. That evening the election was celebrated with the usual "Bonfires and the Ringing of Bells" throughout the town.[32]

The contest had been close, but the friends of the administration in the City had really suffered a signal defeat, since only Peter Godfrey was to be a pro-Walpole representative for London in the new Parliament while the opposition would have the support of three City men. The opposition, moreover, gained another victory a month later at the election of new sheriffs. Although candidates were nominated by the "Whigs" (Sir Thomas Scawen, alderman of Cornhill Ward, and George Cresner, a common councilman), such was the inactivity or disorganization of the "Whig" forces in the City following their defeat in the parliamentary election, that on Midsummer Day, when the liverymen assembled in Common Hall, the two "Tory" candidates, Humphrey Parsons and Francis Child, were chosen by such a great majority upon the show of hands that no poll was demanded.[33]

[32] Ibid.; Applebee's Original Weekly Journal, April 21, 1722; Boyer, Political State, XXIII, 547; The Poll of the Liverymen of the City of London, pp. 198 ff. The necessity of the scrutiny at this election called forth a letter in the British Gazetteer, April 21, 1722, denouncing the scrutiny as showing up the corruption and the rogues on both sides, and declaring that the City elections had become "a Scandal even to the City itself." Something should be done about it, the writer urged, and as a suggestion to prevent such occurrences, proposed that an Act of Parliament be passed providing that "every Livery Man that polls, shall be sworn at the Book, that he is a Livery-Man, that he is the very Person in whose Name he gives his Vote, and that he has not poll'd before." It is interesting to note that in the City Elections Act passed in the spring of 1725 a provision was inserted embodying this very suggestion.

[33] Daily Post, June 2, 16, 25, and 26, 1722; Post-Boy, June 12 and 17, 1722; Boyer, Political State, XXIII, 655.

In the country as a whole, however, the opponents of the administration did not fare so well in the 1722 parliamentary elections, and a large majority was returned in support of the Government.[34] Moreover, the forces of the opposition were further weakened by the failure of the Jacobite, or as it is often called, the Atterbury Plot, which followed immediately upon the heels of the general election. Indeed, the same day that the scrutiny of the poll for London's representatives was finished (May 8), the news broke of the conspiracy to place the Pretender upon the British throne.[35]

THE PLOT

The failure of the Jacobites in 1715 had not made them give up hope of future success. Zealots for the Church and the Stuart line were still numerous in England; and the Pretender, while he lived, would always constitute a threat to the Hanoverian dynasty. The birth of a son and heir to him, on December 31, 1720, gave added encouragement to his supporters. The unrest following upon the South Sea failure seemed to present an ideal situation. Speaker Onslow, who was "at London in the midst of this confusion," later commented on it: "The rage against the Government was such for having as they thought drawn them into this ruin . . . that had some bold men taken advantage of the general disorder mens' minds were in . . . that could the Pretender then have landed at the Tower, he might have rode to St. James's with very few hands held up against him."[36]

Fortunately for George I, this did not happen. Correspondence between the English Jacobites and the Pretender's Court increased markedly, however, and plans for a restoration

[34] A letter to Lord Gower, May 1, 1722 (H. M..C., *Sutherland MSS*, p. 190), reported that two hundred new members would go under "the denomination of the Whigs," and promised only "about one hundred and seventy Tories" in the whole parliament (with a total membership of 588 at the time).

[35] For general accounts of the Plot, see Mahon, *History of England, 1713-1783*, II, 30-50; or Leadam, *History of England, 1702-1760*, pp. 305-309. More detailed accounts of Atterbury's part and his correspondence are found in Williams, *Memoirs and Correspondence of Francis Atterbury*, I, 346-431, and Beeching, *Francis Atterbury*, pp. 275-307.

[36] H. M. C., *Onslow MSS*, p. 504.

were discussed. Of the English Jacobite leaders, Bishop Atterbury was most deeply concerned; but "the five"—the Duke of Ormonde,[37] and Lords North and Grey, Arran,[38] Lansdowne,[39] and Strafford—were all involved. The English agents included John Plunkett, who had figured in the 1715 rebellion; Christopher Layer, a young barrister of the Temple; and George Kelly, a nonjuring clergyman. On the Continent, besides James himself, the chief correspondents were General Dillon, an Irish Jacobite in the French service, and the Duke of Ormonde, who had recently gone to Spain.[40]

The first information disclosing the Plot, which was set for the summer of 1722 when the King should have gone to Hanover, came from the Regent of France; but the above-mentioned correspondence did not go unnoticed by the English ministers, and by opening and copying letters, sending them on to their destination, and noting the answers in the same way, the ministry was able to learn much about the conspiracy.[41] The general public was not informed of these discoveries, but as early as March 7, 1722, Parliament was warned in the King's Speech closing the session, of the enemies who were "reviving, with the greatest Industry, the same wicked Acts of Culumny and Defamation, which have been the constant Preludes to publick Troubles and Disorders."[42]

Just when in 1722 the ministers decided that they had sufficient evidence to proceed against Atterbury is not quite clear. They were probably not at all certain until the first week in May,[43] but even if they had known earlier, it is doubtful that they would have taken action; for such a disclosure during the heat of the parliamentary elections "would have been treated as a ministerial fiction," and might have reacted

---

[37] James Butler (1665-1745), second Duke of Ormonde.
[38] Charles Butler (1671-1758), Earl of Arran, was a younger brother of the Duke of Ormonde.
[39] George Granville, or Grenville (1667-1735), Baron Lansdowne.
[40] Williams, *Memoirs and Correspondence of Francis Atterbury*, pp. 367-368; Mahon, *History of England, 1713-1783*, II, 31-35.
[41] Coxe, *Sir Robert Walpole*, I, 168; II, 220-223.
[42] *Journals of the House of Lords*, XXI, 717.
[43] *Works of Sir John Vanbrugh*, IV, 144 (letter to Lord Carlisle, May 10, 1722); H. M. C., *Carlisle MSS*, p. 39.

unfavorably to the administration. It was therefore "properly delay'd till all electoral contests were entirely ceased."[44]

On the eighth day of May, Lord Townshend, as one of his Majesty's Principal Secretaries of State, sent the following letter to the Lord Mayor of London, Sir William Stewart:

His Majesty, having nothing more at Heart than the Peace and Safety of his good City of London, the Protection of its Inhabitants, and the Support of publick Credit, has commanded me to acquaint your Lordship, that he has received repeated and unquestionable Advices, that several of his Subjects, forgetting the Allegiance they owe to his Majesty, as well as the natural Love they ought to bear to their Country, have entered into a wicked Conspiracy, in Concert with Traitors abroad, for raising a Rebellion in this Kingdom in Favour of a Popish Pretender, with a traiterous Design to overthrow our excellent Constitution both in Church and State, and to subject a Protestant free People to Tyranny and Superstition; but I am persuaded that it will be a great Satisfaction to your Lordship and the City to find, that, at the same Time I am ordered to inform you of this Design, I am likewise commanded by his Majesty to let you know, that he is firmly assured, that the Authors of it neither will be supported, nor even countenanced, by any foreign Power. And as his Majesty has had timely Notice of their wicked Machinations, and has made the proper Dispositions, for defeating them, he has no Reason to doubt but, by the Continuance of the Blessing of Almighty God, and the ready Assistance of his faithful Subjects, this Effort of the Malice of his Enemies will be turned to their own Confusion.

His Majesty makes no doubt but your Lordship, pursuant to the Trust reposed in you, will, in Conjunction with the other Magistrates of his good City of London, exert, with the utmost Care and Vigilance, your Authority at so important a Conjuncture, for the Preservation of the publick Peace, and the Security of the City.[45]

This letter was read to the Court of Aldermen on the following day (May 9), and a formal Address was then drawn up by that body and presented to the King in the evening,

[44] Add. MSS, 9200, f. 70 (Etough Papers).

[45] The letter from Lord Townshend was printed in the *London Gazette*, May 12, 1722, and there are copies of it in the Newcastle Papers (Add. MSS, 34712, f. 24), and in the Repertories of the Court of Aldermen (126, f. 344).

thanking him for his "tender and indulgent Regard" in informing them of the conspiracy, assuring him of their own "steady and unalterable Affection and Zeal" for his Majesty's "Royal Person and Government, and for the Continuance of the Protestant Succession," and congratulating him on the success of the negotiations, which had procured assurances that the conspirators would not be supported by any foreign power. It continued:

When we reflect on the many Blessings which Britons enjoy, under the Protection of a Prince, who makes the Laws of this Land his Rule for the Government of his People; when we consider that neither the civil or religious Rights of your Majesty's Subjects have met with the least Instance of Violation, since your Majesty's happy Accession to the Throne of these Realms; when we recollect your Majesty's Royal Clemency and Benevolence (since the last Rebellion) to Numbers of those who had offended, in the highest Degree, against their King and the Laws of this Country; we cannot but express the utmost Abhorrence of those vile and detestable Persons, who shall again conspire and attempt to bring a free and happy People under the Yoke of Tyranny and Superstition, and involve this Nation in a State of Blood, Misery, and utmost Confusion.

And, as these must be the unavoidable Consequences of attending any Enterprise to alter our present happy Establishment, and to introduce a Popish one, as Englishmen that value our Liberties, as honest Men that have sworn Allegiance to your Majesty, and who have abjured and renounced the Pretender, and as real Friends to our Excellent Constitution in Church and State, (with a Protestant Prince at the head of it) we beg Leave, in the most Solemn Manner, to declare to your Majesty, That, as we are bound in Gratitude, we will exert ourselves, in our several Stations with the utmost Care and Vigilance, for the Preservation of the publick Peace and Tranquility, and for the Restoring of publick Credit; and that we will use our sincere and hearty Endeavours for the firm Support of your Majesty upon the Throne, and for the making your Reign easy and happy.[46]

[46] Repertories of the Court of Aldermen, 126, ff. 344-352. London's example was followed by many other counties and corporations, who all expressed the same zeal and devotion. Some of these addresses may be seen in Boyer, *Political State*, XXIII, 533-543.

His Majesty returned this answer:

Your affectionate and cordial Assurances, upon this important Occasion, of an unshaken Zeal and Fidelity to my Person and Government, give me the greatest Satisfaction.

Your Interest and mine are, and ever must be, inseparable; and I doubt not but that, with the Blessing of God, the Precautions I have taken, and your firm Adherence to our just Cause, will soon convince our Enemies, that their wicked Designs can end in nothing but their own Confusion.

You may depend upon my constant Care and utmost Endeavours to support the publick Credit, to protect the Privileges and Properties of this great and opulent City, and to maintain the Religion, Laws, and Liberties of the Kingdom.[47]

On the same day, May 9, a proclamation was issued that put into execution throughout the country the laws against papists, reputed papists, and nonjurors, requiring them to take the Oath and Declaration, or find bail, depriving them of their horses and arms, and even confining them to their houses.[48] A local order required "all Papists and reputed Papists, to depart from the Cities of London and Westminster, and from within Ten Miles of the same."[49]

Other precautions were taken. The regiments of the Guards were stationed in camp in Hyde Park, and two regiments of horse were quartered on Hounslow Heath. Other regiments were ordered from Ireland and Scotland, all military officers were told to report to their respective commands, and Horace Walpole was sent to Holland to ask for more troops in case they should be needed. Warrants were then issued for the arrest of all the various agents known to be in correspondence with the Pretender's Court or involved in the Plot. These moves proved very effective, and the conspiracy seems to have been nipped in the bud.[50] They also aided in calming the

[47] London Gazette, May 12, 1722.   [48] Ibid.
[49] Repertories of the Court of Aldermen, 126, f. 355. For a copy of the order for the county of Middlesex, see H. M. C., Fifteenth Report, Appendix, Part II, The Manuscripts of J. Eliot Hodgkin, Esq., of Richmond, Surrey (hereinafter cited as H. M. C., Hodgkin MSS) (London, 1897), pp. 348-349.
[50] Boyer, Political State, XXIII, 531-532; H. M. C., Fifteenth Report, Part VII, The Manuscripts of the Marquis of Ailesbury (hereinafter cited as H. M. C., Ailesbury MSS) (London, 1898), p. 226.

general apprehension, and in restoring the public credit, for at the first news of the plot the stocks had fallen, and some of the more "timorous" had begun a run on the Bank.[51]

Throughout the summer the various suspected agents were taken and committed to the custody of the Tower. On May 21 George Kelly was arrested; he was released after examination, only to be retaken later. By August 24 Walpole felt that he had sufficient evidence against his great adversary, and on that date Bishop Atterbury was committed on a charge of "High Treason."[52] In September Christopher Layer was arrested, as were Lord North and Grey, the Duke of Norfolk, and the Earl of Orrery. Intercepted letters during the summer months gave hints of what the conspirators intended to do,[53] but it was not until the trial of Layer, in November, that the whole nature of the Plot was revealed: an advance on London, the capturing of the Tower and Bank, the seizure of the King and the Prince of Wales, and the proclaiming of James in various parts of the kingdom; arms and troops to be furnished by Ormonde and Dillon, and Lord North and Grey to take over command until the Pretender could cross the Channel.[54]

The precautions taken in the early summer, therefore, and the arrests that followed, assured the failure of the Plot. The measures taken by Parliament in the session which opened on October 9, 1722, completed the downfall of the conspirators. A bill to suspend the Habeas Corpus Act for one year was passed, despite the efforts of the Opposition to shorten the term, as was a bill placing a tax on Roman Catholics—a bill which resulted in the raising of a far smaller amount than the £100,000 expected, and gained the administration the enmity of many who were normally its friends.[55] A Declaration of

[51] Boyer, *Political State*, XXIII, 533; H. M. C., Tenth Report, Part IV, *The Manuscripts of Captain Josceline F. Bagot, of Levens Hall* (hereinafter cited as H. M. C., *Bagot MSS*) (London, 1885), p. 345. South Sea stock fell from 90 to 77, Bank from 114 to 109, and East India from 139 to 128. See the *Daily Courant*, May 7-12, 1722.
[52] Add. MSS, 32686, f. 236; H. M. C., *Portland MSS*, VII, 332.
[53] Add. MSS, 32686, f. 237.
[54] See the *Historical Register*, VIII, 59 ff.
[55] See H. M. C., *Onslow MSS*, pp. 463-464; and H. M. C., Seventeenth Report, *The Manuscripts of Lord Polwarth, Preserved in Mertoun House,*

the Pretender, printed copies of which had been distributed in London and other cities, was proclaimed to be a false and traitorous libel and was ordered burnt at the Royal Exchange by the common hangman under the supervision of the sheriffs of London. Moreover, bills of pains and penalties were passed against the arrested conspirators. Bishop Atterbury, despite the pleas of his friends and his own eloquent speech of defense, was banished from the country.[56] Kelly and Plunkett were imprisoned and their estates confiscated. Layer was executed at Tyburn and his head fixed on Temple Bar. Orrery was released on bail after six months in the Tower, and North and Grey was finally admitted to bail and allowed to retire abroad. Others were likewise given their merited punishments.[57]

So the Plot, which would "have seen the whole nation, and particularly the City of London, involved in blood and confusion,"[58] was discovered and foiled. It caused some uneasiness in the City, and the trials of the conspirators excited considerable interest, especially that of Atterbury, but the Plot did not directly affect the Londoners, and, except for those who formed the mob, they refused to get excited.[59] Its great effect was felt by those opposed to the ministry. They lost their great leader, Atterbury, as well as Lord North and Grey, and they

---

Berwickshire (hereinafter cited as H. M. C., *Polwarth MSS*) (London, 1911-1931), III, 283. Reasons for the bill are explained by Lord Carteret in the *Polwarth MSS*, III, 199-200.

[56] Atterbury left England on June 19, 1723, and lived in exile for nine years, most of that time in France, where he was active in the interests of the Pretender and died in 1732. His body was brought back to England and privately buried in Westminster Abbey.

[57] For details of Parliament's action, the report of the Select Committee, and the trials of Atterbury, Kelly, Layer, *et al.*, during the session of 1722-1723, see Cobbett, *Parliamentary History*, VIII, 25-46, 95-364; or the *Historical Register*, VII, 312-331; VIII, 15-378; and IX, 1-99, 296-341.

[58] From the King's Speech, Oct. 9, 1722. See *Journals of the House of Lords*, XXII, 12.

[59] Atterbury had great weight with the parochial clergy, and he was publicly prayed for in most of the churches of London and Westminster, sympathy being stirred up for him by the distribution of prints showing the Bishop looking through the bars of a prison. Nevertheless, he had to be well guarded in going to and from Westminster and the Tower during his trial, for the mob was often very insolent and once "engaged in a pitch'd Battle" over him. See the *British Journal*, May 11 and 18, 1723; the *Daily Journal*, May 13, 1723; and the *British Gazetteer*, May 18, 1723.

had all become tainted with the stigma of Jacobitism. More-over, the Plot reacted favorably for Walpole, Onslow remarking that it "fixed him with the King, and united for a time the whole body of Whigs to him, and gave him the universal credit of an able and vigilant minister."[60] Also, the death of Lord Sunderland in April, 1722, which had removed his great Whig rival from the scene, and the death of Lord Cowper in October, 1723, which removed another of the Opposition's leaders, both contributed to Walpole's advantage; and during the next few years the Walpole administration remained firmly in power, the country continued in peace, and trade and commerce flourished.[61]

Nevertheless, the forces of opposition were by no means destroyed. Newcastle, in a letter to Townshend on July 5, 1723, declared that "the Spirit of Jacobitism is still very strong,"[62] and in April of the following year Townshend, in a letter to the King, repeated the same warning.[63] However, there were many in Parliament who were in opposition not because they were Jacobites, but because they heartily opposed Robert Walpole, and these all rallied to give the administration considerable trouble. Yet, such were the majorities in support of the ministry that the government measures were consistently carried in all the parliamentary sessions, and the general situation of the country was peaceful and prosperous.

[60] H. M C., *Onslow MSS*, p. 513.

[61] On August 3, 1723, Walpole wrote to Townshend, again in Hanover, of the rise of stocks and the flourishing condition of the public credit, saying that he looked for the raising of the whole supply for the next year at a rate of 3 per cent. See British Museum Stowe Manuscripts (hereinafter cited as Stowe MSS), 251, f. 27b.

In reply Townshend wrote that such news gave him "greater satisfaction than I can express"; and he repeatedly urged Walpole "to form a good Scheme for the next Session" which would increasingly contribute to "the Ease of the Nation, and the benefit of Trade and Credit." See Stowe MSS, 251, ff. 6, 30b, and 48b.

[62] Add. MSS, 32686, f. 270.

[63] H. M. C., Tenth Report, Part I, *The Manuscripts of Charles Fleetwood Weston Underwood, Esq., of Somerby Hall, Lincolnshire* (hereinafter cited as H. M. C., *Underwood MSS*) (London, 1895), p. 428.

CHAPTER IV

The City Elections Act

UNLIKE the nation during 1723 and 1724, London was far from peaceful. Economically it prospered, but politically it was torn with conflict. The citizens had not yet become reconciled to the administration of the Norfolk squire, and the factions battled on every occasion. During those years the City was involved constantly in disputed local elections, which were attended by bitter controversy. At one time it was over a new alderman of a ward. Again, it was at the return of a common councilman. Another time it was at the annual election of the London sheriffs. Finally, matters reached such a point that parliamentary interference was necessary to restore quiet, and in the spring of 1725 the City Elections Act was passed, designed to lessen the local election disputes, but at the same time intended to curb the City opposition to the Government. This was not merely an affair of the moment. Disputes had marred the conduct of City elections at intervals for nearly half a century past. Their renewal with greater intensity in 1723 and the close connection of the City aldermen with the Walpole administration combined to bring about the parliamentary legislation.

The causes of the disputes were many. Besides the natural clashes of political factions, there were disagreements over who had a right to vote. At the Common Hall elections, for example, a great many persons, not liverymen of a "Company," always managed to attend and vote illegally. At the wardmote elections, where the voting was supposed to be done only by freemen householders of the ward, paying Scot and Lot, appeared numbers of nonfreemen, who refused to purchase their freedom (on the ground that they would thereby lose the right of complete control over the disposition of their personal estates[1]) and insisted that they had the right to vote because they contributed to the various taxes of their respective wards. This raised the puzzling question of what was meant by "paying Scot and bearing Lot." Another question pertained to the practices of the presiding officers at these elections. Just what powers did they have? Many of them after a scrutiny even kept the results to themselves, and refused to publish which votes had been allowed or disallowed. Especially was this true of some of the Lord Mayors and various members of the Court of Aldermen, and this practice led naturally to the other point of dispute, whether or not the Court of Aldermen was the real executive of the Corporation and had the right of veto over the proceedings of the Common Council, as was claimed.

This last question was the subject of a report of a committee appointed by the Court of Aldermen on February 23, 1724, to examine into the history of the powers of that court. The report, presented on March 10 following, showed that the right to veto the acts of the Common Council had been given to the aldermen by a charter of Edward III, in 1342, and that until 1644 "the Negative Voice of the Lord Mayor and Aldermen, in making of By-Laws in Common Council, was never (that we can find) called in Question, or objected to." Moreover, the committee pointed out, the taking away of that negative voice in 1648 by an Act of Parliament proved that the Court of Aldermen must have been exercising the right of veto then—"else the making of such an Act had been vain and unnecessary." In support of this view the committee also reported the opinions given in 1676 by such distinguished jurists as Sir William Jones, Sir Francis Pemberton, Sir John Maynard, and Sir Francis Winnington, and in 1677 by Sir William Dolben, the Recorder of the City, and Sir George Jeffreys, the Common Sergeant. Furthermore, the report concluded, the Court of Common Council in 1683 had approved the report of a committee appointed to go over the laws then in force, which report

---

[1] By the custom of the City a freeman disposing of his personal estate by will was obliged to leave to his wife one third of that estate, and to his children another third, or, if having only one or the other, one half of his personal estate.

favored the repeal of the Act of 1648, thus showing that the Court of Common Council itself in 1683 had approved of the negative voice of the aldermen.[2]

This report naturally pleased the members of the Court of Aldermen in the spring of 1724, but it was far from pleasing to the members of the Court of Common Council. On March 12, therefore, they voted down a proposal that the Common Council go on record as approving the right claimed by the aldermen.[3] Thus the question became acute and could be settled only by the direct interference of the King, or the King in Parliament.

Before proceeding to the election controversies of 1723 and 1724 which led to the parliamentary action, the picture will be clearer if we stop to consider briefly a few of the disputed elections prior to that time. In the parliamentary election in London in 1710, for example, when "Tories were put in and Whigs were left out," there was much violence and partisanship.[4] The aldermanic elections of the next few years also showed a crying need of electoral reform. At the election of Gerard Conyers as alderman of Broad Street Ward, for instance, in September, 1711, not only did many unqualified persons vote, but the Whig Lord Mayor, Sir Gilbert Heathcote, arbitrarily, and contrary to the results of the poll, declared the scrutiny in favor of the four Whig candidates.[5] An appeal to set the Mayor's decision aside was made to the Court of Queen's

[2] See the published *Report of a Committee of Aldermen, in Affirmance of the Right of the Mayor and Aldermen to Put a Negative to Bills or Acts Depending in the Common Council of London* (London, 1724). There is a copy of the original report in Add. MSS, 33052, f. 47 ff. The opinions of the jurists questioned in 1676 are found in Add. MSS, 35051, f. 206 ff. The opinions of Sir Philip Yorke (Lord Chancellor Hardwicke to-be) in 1724, which are substantially the same, are to be found in Add. MSS, 35875, ff. 18-19.

[3] Journals of the Common Council, 57, f. 110.

[4] Sharpe, *London and the Kingdom*, II, 638.

[5] The practice of nominating four candidates had prevailed since the beginning of the fifteenth century (Act of Common Council, 3 Henry IV, A. D. 1401), but the inconvenience arising from this practice was so manifest during this election of 1711 that even before the election was settled the Court of Common Council passed another act reducing the number of nominations to two, and in 1714 this was repealed, and the "ancient custom" of each ward choosing one of its citizens (not an alderman) to be returned to the Court of Aldermen for approval was restored.

Bench, but the action is not recorded. Conyers, who had been chosen alderman, remained in office.[6]

In July of the next year, a similar dispute arose at the election of Peter Delmé as alderman of the ward of Langbourn. Again the Lord Mayor, this time Sir Robert Beachcroft, declared the votes to be for the candidates he favored, although it was contrary to the results of the poll; and, like his predecessor, Beachcroft refused to explain how he had arrived at that conclusion. Delmé was named to be the alderman, but again the decision was appealed to the Queen's Bench, and, as had been done in the previous year, the Common Council ordered the legal expenses to be paid from the Chamber of London.[7]

Similar disputes, with their resulting appeals to the courts of law, defended at the City's expense, occurred at the election of common councilmen for Cheap Ward in 1713, and for Tower Ward in 1715 and 1717. By the latter case the attention of Parliament was first attracted to the City disputes. Peter Bolton and Edward Bridgen, the two unsuccessful candidates, had appealed to the Court of King's Bench against the ruling of Alderman Sir Charles Peers in favor of Robert Jeffs and Stephen King. For a whole twelve-month the case engaged the attention of the court, the expenses of the plaintiffs again being paid by the City Corporation. By Writs of Error it was then brought to the attention of the House of Lords (January 19, 1719), and the legality of these expenditures by the Common Council out of the City treasury, as well as the practice of the Common Council in assuming the right to judge the contested elections, was questioned.[8]

The lords appointed a committee to examine into the expenditures of the City's Chamber and to ascertain just what was the jurisdiction of the Common Council over the election of its members. A perusal of the records of the Town Clerk

[6] Sharpe, *London and the Kingdom*, II, 640-641. Oldmixon, in his *History of England*, defends Heathcote, saying that his "Behaviour on that Occasion was wise, just and steady" and "according to Law, and the ancient Usage of the City" (p. 728).

[7] Sharpe, *London and the Kingdom*, II, 642-643.

[8] *Ibid.*, III, 13; *Journals of the House of Lords*, XXI, 49.

and the Chamberlain of the City was made, and on April 17 the committee reported to the House that since the eighth day of November, 1711, "the sum of Two Thousand Eight Hundred and Twenty-Seven Pounds, and Ten Shillings" had been "issued out of the City Cash, for carrying on Cause and Suits at Law relating to the Elections of Aldermen and Councilmen."[9] It also reported, concerning the right of the Common Council to judge the elections of its own members, that that court was operating thereby on a procedure of the Common Council of January 9, 1641, in considering the case of disputed elections of that year, but that the procedure had been disclaimed by an Act of Common Council passed in 1683. The committee, therefore, found the Common Council of 1719 at fault.[10] The House of Lords reached the same conclusion, and by a vote of 46 to 19 resolved "That the Common Council of London, having issued great Sums of Money out of the Chamber of London, in maintaining several Suits at Law between Citizen and Citizen, relating to controverted Elections, have abused their Trust, and been guilty of great Partiality, and of gross Mismanagement of the City Treasure, and a Violation of the Freedom of Election in the City."[11]

This action was a direct blow aimed at the Court of Common Council, and a victory for the Court of Aldermen. It was due, doubtless, to the prominuisterial leanings of that latter body. The "Tory" Common Council, however, was not without its supporters, and in the House of Lords the Opposition peers entered a strong dissentient protest against the resolution.[12] Nevertheless, the Court of Aldermen had triumphed.

The disputes continued. At a wardmote held on January

[9] For a detailed account of these expenditures, see the *Journals of the House of Lords*, XXI, 146-147. They were also published by William Cowper, Clerk of Parliament, in a tract entitled *An Account of What Sums of Money Have Been Paid by the City Chamberlain of London, Concerning Any Causes or Suits at Law, Relating to the Election of Aldermen or Common-Council Men, Since the Eighth Day of November, 1711, and by What Warrant* (London, 1719).

[10] *Journals of the House of Lords*, XXI, 71-72; Sharpe, *London and the Kingdom*, III, 12-14.

[11] *Journals of the House of Lords*, XXI, 148-149.

[12] *Ibid.*, XXI, 149.

9, 1719, for the election of an alderman for Bread Street Ward, Robert Baylis (Whig) and Richard Brocas (Tory) were the candidates; and the show of hands being approximately equal, a poll was taken that resulted in 140 votes for Baylis against 170 for Brocas. The scrutiny, held on February 6, reduced the vote to 125 for Baylis and 128 for Brocas. The Lord Mayor, Sir George Thorold, however, declared that he had allowed Brocas as good "pollers" several who had been objected to for not having paid the Orphans' Tax. If he had disallowed them, he said, Baylis would have had the majority. The whole question thus turned on the qualification of some of the voters. Did they or did they not pay Scot? And in what did "paying Scot" consist? The Court of Aldermen was asked to settle the question.[13]

After hearing both sides of the case, and after searching the City charters and records, the Court ruled that paying Scot meant "the paying of all Taxes and Charges in and upon the City, and Inhabitants thereof; the Actual paying of all Taxes, whether assigned upon him or not, demanded of him or not." At the same time, the Court declared in favor of Robert Baylis for alderman of Bread Street Ward.[14] This last decision naturally aroused the Common Council, and litigation was instituted lasting over a year. Nevertheless, the Court of Aldermen would allow no invasion of its rights; and Alderman Baylis continued to hold his seat, the dispute offering fresh causes of dissension between the aldermen and the commoners.[15]

For the next year or two, as the South Sea troubles, the clamor over the Quarantine Bill and the proposed Westminster Bridge, and the Jacobite Plot occupied the public attention, the local elections passed off very quietly, except for the return of parliamentary men. Then in the fall of 1722, with the election of a Lord Mayor to succeed Sir William Stewart, a new phase of the controversy began. For a long time, in choosing

---

[13] Sharpe, *London and the Kingdom*, III, 15.
[14] Repertories of the Court of Aldermen, 123, ff. 210-215.
[15] Sharpe, *London and the Kingdom*, III, 15-16; Repertories of the Court of Aldermen, 123, ff. 223, 242; *A Brief State of the Several Disputes and Grievances at Present Complain'd of in the City of London, etc.* (London, 1724).

a Lord Mayor, the Common Hall had simply returned the two senior aldermen next the chair (who had already served the office of sheriff) to the Court of Aldermen, for the latter to declare in favor of the senior of the two. Rumors of a proposed change in this custom, however, were circulated several days before the election, and on Michaelmas Day (Saturday, September 29) there was an unusually large attendance of liverymen at the Guildhall.[16] On the same day an article in the *British Gazetteer* charged the "Tory" faction with falsehood and the spreading of scandal, and urged the choice of Sir Gerard Conyers for Lord Mayor as "being next the Chair, a Person of undoubted Wealth and Probity, and firmly attached to our happy Constitution in Church and State."[17]

The objections to Conyers, and to Sir Peter Delmé (who was next in line and whose name would be returned with Conyers to the Court of Aldermen), were purely political. The "Tories" wished to follow up their advantage gained in the parliamentary election earlier in the year and, by passing over Conyers and Delmé, elect the next alderman in line, the "Tory" Sir George Merttins. For want of something better, they advanced the argument that Conyers and Delmé had no right to succeed as Lord Mayor because their election as aldermen of their wards had been challenged. This was true,[18] but no such objection had been raised before, and these men had represented their wards for ten years or more. Nevertheless, at the Guildhall, after the sheriffs had declared that a majority of hands were in favor of Conyers and Delmé, the opposition forces demanded a poll in favor of the next two aldermen below the chair—Sir George Merttins, whom they wanted elected, and Sir Francis Forbes, a "Whig" like Conyers and Delmé. But, when he was informed of the matter, Forbes asked that his candidacy be withdrawn and desired his friends not to vote for him, urging "that there should be peace in the City."[19]

The poll began on the Monday following and lasted three days. During that time the City was stirred up, and the voters

[16] *Daily Courant*, Oct. 2, 1722.   [17] *British Gazetteer*, Sept. 29, 1722.
[18] See pp. 76-77, above.
[19] *Post-Boy*, Oct. 2, 1722; *Daily Courant*, Oct. 2, 1722.

were appealed to by advertisements and by articles in the news-papers written for or against the election of Conyers and Delmé.[20] The "Tories" were active, but the "Whigs" seemed suddenly aroused. On Tuesday (October 2) a large number of the latter gathered at the Merchant-Taylors' Hall and led by Alderman Sir John Ward, Sir John Fryer, Sir Edward Beecher, Robert Heysham, Sir Randolph Knipe, and Peter Godfrey, went in a body to Guildhall to vote for Conyers and Delmé. On the next day another group of liverymen met at the same place and were conducted to the poll by a group of Whig aldermen who this time also included Sir Gilbert Heath-cote, Sir Thomas Scawen, and Sir John Eyles.[21] As a result, the vote was strongly in favor of the Whig candidates; and when the returns were made to the Court of Aldermen, Sir Gerard Conyers was chosen and duly declared elected Lord Mayor of London for the ensuing year.[22]

Thus the subject of the contested elections of 1711 and 1712 was revived, although there was a lull before the outburst of May, 1723. The election of William Billers, Haberdasher, on November 1 (1722) as alderman of Cordwainer Ward, on the death of Sir George Thorold;[23] and the election of Joseph (Edward) Bellamy, Fishmonger, on February 28 (1723) as alderman of Billingsgate Ward, in place of Robert Heysham[24] —were attended by no unusual disturbances. Moreover, all four of the aldermen, old and new, in these two elections, were friends of the Walpole administration; the majority in the Court of Aldermen was unchanged. The annual elections of common councilmen on December 21 (1722) were also quiet, and they resulted in the return of the usual majority for the antiadministration forces.[25]

On Monday, April 29, the alderman of Cripplegate Ward,

[20] See *Post-Boy*, *Daily Post*, and *Daily Courant* for Oct. 2 and 3, 1722.
[21] *Flying Post*, Oct. 4, 1722.
[22] *Ibid.*; *Daily Courant*, Oct. 5, 1722. The numbers cast on the poll were: for Conyers, 2,957; for Delmé, 2,912; for Merttins, 1,243; and for Forbes, 1,229.
[23] *Daily Post*, Oct. 31, 1722; *Post-Boy*, Nov. 3, 1722; *British Gazetteer*, Nov. 3, 1722.
[24] *Post-Boy*, March 2, 1723; *British Gazetteer*, March 2, 1723.
[25] *Post-Boy*, Dec. 22, 1722.

Sir William Stewart, died, in his eightieth year. He had been Lord Mayor in 1721-1722, and although in politics he was known as a confirmed "Tory," yet it was said of him that he had "executed that high office to the general Satisfaction of all the differing Parties in this great City."[26]   To elect his successor, a Court of Wardmote was held on May 1 before the Lord Mayor, Sir Gerard Conyers, at the parish church of St. Giles's Cripplegate.[27]   The political animosity then engendered was to be carried over into the election of sheriffs on June 24. So bitter did the controversy become, indeed, that the Cripplegate Wardmote was not adjourned until June 20, and its election not decided until July 23; while the election of sheriffs was not finally declared until September 28.

THE DISPUTED ELECTIONS OF 1723

There were three candidates for the aldermanship of Cripplegate Ward. The contest, however, lay between two of them: Sir John Williams, a Mercer and a "Tory," and Felix Feast, a Brewer and a "Whig." The latter, who had been Deputy of the ward since 1718, on the show of hands was declared by the Lord Mayor to have the majority. This did not at all please the friends of Williams, and they immediately demanded a poll, which began that afternoon.[28]

A keen interest in this contest was at once displayed by the voters, and the excitement spread throughout the ward. Advertisements were inserted in the newspapers for the two candidates, and one for Sir John Williams mentioned Aldermen Brocas, Levett, and Parsons (one of the sheriffs), and Richard Lockwood (one of the City's representatives in Parliament) as his supporters.[29]   For Feast, Alderman Robert Baylis was said to have exerted himself "prodigiously."[30]   The voting was fairly equal, but at the end of the poll Feast was reported to have 623 votes and Williams 597. Again Feast was declared elected, but again the friends of his opponent were un-

[26] *British Journal*, May 4, 1723.   [27] *Daily Post*, May 2, 1723.
[28] *Ibid.*; J. J. Baddeley, *The Aldermen of Cripplegate Ward, from 1276 to 1900* (London, 1900), pp. 87-89.
[29] *Daily Post*, May 2, 1723.
[30] Add. MSS, 32686, f. 176 (Newcastle to Townshend, June 28, 1723).

satisfied. A scrutiny was therefore granted, and after naming the scrutineers the wardmote was adjourned until May 22.[31]

At that date the scrutiny had not been finished, however, and another fortnight went by before the Lord Mayor was ready to report. Then there was a further postponement until he could consult the Recorder about the qualifications of some of the voters. Finally, on June 20, his Lordship reported that the scrutiny was completed and that in his opinion Sir John Williams had received the majority of "voices."[32] Nevertheless, because of certain unusual irregularities, he did not declare Williams elected. The Lord Mayor disclosed that certain evidence had been presented showing that Sir John and Sheriff Parsons had taken it upon themselves "to menace and threaten" the scrutineers of Felix Feast, and had so "Intimidated, Terrified, and Discouraged" them that they had not been able to examine properly the votes. His Lordship therefore ordered the Court of Wardmote dismissed, declaring that he would lay the whole matter before the Court of Aldermen for that court to decide the election.[33]

On three successive weekly meetings following, the Court of Aldermen considered the case, read the affidavits presented, examined witnesses on both sides, and debated the evidence. On July 23 the Court gave its decision. The aldermen agreed that "unjustifyable Menaces were used by Sir John Williams upon the Scrutiny of the said Election," but they had come to the conclusion that "the said Scrutiny was not affected by the said Menaces, so as to turn the said Election in favour of Mr. Feast," and therefore Williams should be declared to be the duly elected alderman for Cripplegate Ward.[34] Sir John, who was then called in, was immediately sworn into office.[35] There was great rejoicing in the ward when the news was made public.

[31] *Daily Post*, May 3, 1723; *British Journal*, May 4, 1723; Baddeley, *Aldermen of Cripplegate Ward*, pp. 89-90.
[32] *British Journal*, June 22, 1723.
[33] Baddeley, *Aldermen of Cripplegate Ward*, pp. 90-91; *British Journal*, June 22, 1723; *Saturday Post*, June 22, 1723.
[34] Repertories of the Court of Aldermen, 127, ff. 394, 402, and 416.
[35] *London Journal*, July 27, 1723; Repertories of the Court of Aldermen, 127, f. 416.

That night (July 23) the mob ran riot. The streets were filled, friends of the candidates were insulted, their windows smashed, and a number of houses broken into. The proclamation against rioting had to be read twice, and several ringleaders apprehended, before quiet could be restored.[36]

But neither the conduct of the mob, nor the irregularity of the methods used by Sir John to gain the election, were perhaps as unusual as that a Court of Aldermen, proadministration in the majority, should decide the election against Feast, a proadministration man, with such an opportunity as Williams' "Menaces" offered. Perhaps the explanation lies in the contested election of sheriffs, begun on June 24 but still in progress, in which both Williams and Feast were involved, and through which the local contest in the ward of Cripplegate spread through the whole City.

The 1723 sheriffs' election showed plainly the need of reform in the election laws of the City in that it indicated the arbitrary powers of sheriffs in their conduct of the Common Hall elections, and how a partisan sheriff could thereby exert almost a complete control over those elections, unless sufficient opposition could be aroused to overcome his decisions. It showed also the need of defining more clearly the qualifications of voters.

Advertisements for the candidates appeared in the press as early as June 12. The "Court Party" adherents, who met at the Merchant-Taylors' Hall, put Felix Feast in nomination, and with him Sir Richard Hopkins, an East India merchant. They were termed as "being Persons Zealously affected to his Majesty King George, and the present happy Establishment in Church and State, and every way qualified for so great a Trust."[37] The "Tories," meeting at Vintners' Hall at the same time, nominated Sir John Williams, and with him Richard Lockwood, one of the four members of Parliament for the City, proposing them also as "being Gentlemen well-affected to his

[36] Add. MSS, 32686, f. 285b (Walpole to Newcastle, July 24, 1723); London Journal, July 27, 1723; Boyer, Political State, XXVI, 114.

[37] Daily Courant, June 12, 13, and 24, 1723; Daily Post, June 12 and 15, 1723.

Majesty King George, and our present Constitution in Church and State, and every way qualified for the great Trust."[38] Both parties considered the election of great importance. The friends of the administration, in the City as well as at Court, were anxious to regain the ground lost in the City by the parliamentary election and the sheriffs' election of 1722. Their opponents were eager to repeat their victories in those contests. As Walpole wrote to his brother-in-law, Lord Townshend, on June 20: "The Tories have set up Sr. Jn. Williams and Lockwood for Sheriffs. There never was a point more laboured on both sides; and both sides full of Hopes."[39]

On Monday, June 24, being Midsummer Day, the liverymen gathered at the Guildhall, and the Court of Common Hall was called to order by the sheriffs then in office, Humphrey Parsons and Sir Francis Child, Sheriff Parsons presiding. Expectation of a close contest was forecast by a note of admonition by the City Recorder, Sir William Thompson, in his speech before the election took place:

You are here assembled to elect Sheriffs for this City, and the County of Middlesex, for the Year ensuing.

Your Privileges having been hitherto used in so prudent a Manner, as to answer the Ends for which they were obtain'd, viz, the Preservation of your Liberties and the Public Welfare, there is no doubt but you will be govern'd by the same Temper and Discretion in the Affair under your present Consideration.

You must be sensible, that your Sheriffs will have . . . important Trusts repos'd in them, therefore you will think it necessary to have Regard to Persons of Abilities and Capacities proper for such a Station.

I shall not presume to descend to particular Qualifications; but you are so good Judges, as to know it is of the highest Moment that they should be Gentlemen of Character for their Honour and Integrity, eminent for their Zeal to our present happy Establishment in Church and State, and remarkable for their unfeigned Affection to our most gracious Sovereign King George: A Prince, who makes

[38] *Daily Courant*, June 13, 15, and 24, 1723.
[39] Stowe MSS, 251, f. 3.

the Laws of the Land the Rule of his Actions, and whose chief Delight is the Happiness of his People.[40]

Sheriff Parsons then called for a show of hands for the candidates, and "notwithstanding the great Appearance for Sir Richard Hopkins and Mr. Feast," the sheriffs declared the majority to be for Sir John Williams and Richard Lockwood.[41] Immediately the friends of Hopkins and Feast protested. They claimed "that the Livery chose one, and the Sh ... ff's the other."[42]   There was "a very great bustle" about the Hustings, and a "Cry of No White Roses, &c." A poll was demanded, and granted to begin the next morning.[43]

For three days the poll went on—"with great Party Zeal." "The Poll for our Sheriffs goes on with great fury on both Sides & reflections run very high," Viscount Perceval read in a newsletter.[44]   On one side charges were made that orders had been given "to some in publick Posts, requiring y^m to Exert y^r Interest for Sir Richard Hopkins and Mr. Feast." It was even said that threats had been sent to various "Tenants & Tradesmen, if they would not vote for Hopkins and Feast," and that special constables had been brought in "to abuse & knock down & commit friends of Williams and Lockwood." Both sides were charged with "forming a Mobb to obstruct ye Liverymen as they were coming to Poll."   There was also much talk about the Duke of Wharton's "Influence" in promoting "ye Election of Sir Jn. Williams & Mr. Lockwood."[45]

The Duke of Wharton, as leader of the Jacobite faction after Atterbury's deportation, had found ample opportunity to show his opposition to Walpole and the administration in the upper house of Parliament.   "Those in Parliament have great Opportunities to distinguish their Zeal for the Good of

[40] Boyer, *Political State*, XXV, 673-674.
[41] *Daily Courant*, June 25, 1723; *British Gazetteer*, June 29, 1723.
[42] *British Gazetteer*, June 29, 1723.
[43] Add. MSS, 27980, f. 80 (newsletter addressed to Viscount Perceval, June 25, 1723); *Daily Post*, June 25, 1723.
[44] Add. MSS, 27980, f. 81b.
[45] Add. MSS, 27980, ff. 81b, 85b (newsletter, July 2, 1723).   See also the *True Briton* (London, 1723), I, 78-79 (No. 9, July 1, 1723).   The biweekly *True Briton*, an opposition newspaper, was started on June 3, 1723, by the Duke of Wharton, and continued until February 17, 1724.

their Country," he himself wrote in the *True Briton*, and added that "those who are Without-Doors should do their Duty by supporting such Patriots, and acting in Concert with Them."[46] Acting on this principle therefore, he "did not confine his Spirit of Opposition to the House of Lords; but exerted it both in the City and Country, promoting in all kinds of Elections, Persons who were suppos'd to be no Favorites of the Court."[47] In London he was very active. In the spring of 1723 "he push'd himself into the Metropolis, invested himself with all the Rights and Privileges of a Citizen, and was received a Member of the Wax Chandlers' Company, in virtue of which he appear'd at all Meetings, charm'd all Societies, and voted in his own Right upon all Occasions."[48]

On Midsummer Day, he "appeared in the Gallery over the Hustings in Guildhall at the Election for Sheriffs,"[49] and when the majority of hands were declared to be for Williams and Lockwood, "it was observed y^t ye Duke of Wharton who was in ye Balcony over ye Hustings waved his Hat with ye Livery Men."[50] The next day he "headed a Party for Sir John Williams and Mr. Lockwood" to vote at the poll.[51]

The voting on the poll was heavy. By Tuesday night (June 26) the numbers were: for Hopkins, 2,519 votes; for Feast, 2,518 votes; for Williams, 2,317 votes; and for Lockwood, 2,320 votes.[52] That evening the balloting continued, as did the electioneering for the candidates. To promote the interests of Hopkins and Feast, there was a large gathering at the Merchant-Taylors' Hall, while the friends of Williams and Lockwood met at Vintners' Hall—"at Each of wch places Such Treats are made as ye like were Never known."[53] The Duke

---

[46] *True Briton*, I, 43 (No. 5, June 17, 1723).

[47] *Memoirs of the Life of his Grace Philip, late Duke of Wharton, by an Impartial Hand* (London, 1731), I, 13.

[48] *Ibid.* The Duke was made free of the City and of the Wax Chandlers' Company on February 7, according to the *Saturday Post*, Feb. 8, 1723. The account in the *British Journal* of the same date adds that he went home with Sheriff Parsons.

[49] *London Journal*, June 29, 1723.

[50] Add. MSS, 27980, f. 80 (newsletter, June 25, 1723).

[51] *British Journal*, June 29, 1723.

[52] *Daily Courant*, June 29, 1723.

[53] Add. MSS, 27980, f. 82 (newsletter, June 27, 1723).

of Wharton also was active in all this, and continued "to busy himself in favour of y[e] 2 last Named Candidates with Such a Zeal as is very Surprising."[54] On July 1 he devoted the whole of his letter in the *True Briton* to the election which was "at present the Subject of all Conversation." His intention, he said, was "only to justify the Reputation of several Gentlemen, and the Character of all the Livery-Men, who appeared for Sir John Williams and Mr. Lockwood." The Duke spoke very highly of the characters of both Williams and Lockwood; but Feast, who he admitted had always shown a "remarkable Zeal . . . for the Support of the present Government," he charged with using bribery in his efforts to obtain the office of sheriff.[55]

On Thursday, June 27, the books for the poll were closed, but the declaration of which candidates had the majority was deferred until the following Tuesday, July 2.[56] Both sides claimed victory:

> . . . the Court Party gave out that it [the Poll] stood thus, viz.

Sir Richard Hopkins	3244
Felix Feast, Esq;	3241
Sir John Williams	3187
Rich. Lockwood, Esq;	3193

But the Tories gave out that upon the most exact Computation, the Poll stood thus.

Sir John Williams	3188
Rich. Lockwood, Esq;	3190
Sir Rich. Hopkins	3163
Felix Feast, Esq.	3155

Upon which the Sheriffs deferr'd the Declaration till Tuesday the 2d. of July.[57]

On Friday, June 28, the Duke of Newcastle wrote to Lord Townshend about it. "Last Night," he said, "our Poll for

---

[54] Add. MSS, 27980, f. 82.

[55] *True Briton*, I, 71-75 (No. 9, July 1, 1723).

[56] *British Gazetteer*, June 29, 1723.

[57] Boyer, *Political State*, XXV, 674. The *British Journal*, June 29, 1723, carried the figures showing Hopkins and Feast in the lead, and the *Saturday Post* of the same date printed those showing Williams and Lockwood in the lead.

Sheriffs ended, where We had a Majority of about Four score, (as I hear), but Mr. W.[alpole] will give a full account of it. The Torries have demanded a Scrutiny, which is judged by the Old Sheriffs, so we cannot yet Say what will be done, but undoubtedly We have a fair Majority. The Spirit of Jacobitism . . . has Show'd itself again upon this occasion and if it had not been for great pains & Industry, We should not have carried our point."[58]

The issue was not settled at once, because the old sheriffs refused to co-operate with those who were appointed to carry out the scrutiny. The *Daily Courant* of July 5 carried the following account:

Mr. Falkingham, appointed by Sir Richard Hopkins and Mr. Feast, attended Mr. Sheriff Parsons, and Mr. Langley Hill, the other Person appointed by Sir John Williams and Mr. Lockwood, on Saturday, the 29th of June at Guildhall, to cast up the Poll Books, and after having cast up the several Pages of the Books, Mr. Falkingham desired the Sums of the Pages might be added together, but Mr. Sheriff Parsons chose to adjourn the Matter to Monday, the 1st of July.

Mr. Falkingham attended patiently from Nine till One a-clock on Monday, and then sent to acquaint Mr. Hill therewith, who return'd for Answer, that he would come presently, but did not so, tho' Mr. Falkingham staid 'till three a-clock, in all which time Mr. Sheriff was not pleased, either to come or send.

After this several Livery Men went twice the same Evening to Mr. Sheriff Parsons' House, to complain of this Usage, but he could not be found 'till Tuesday Morning, at Guild-Hall Coffee-House, where he was again requested to add the Sums of the Pages, but he still declin'd it.[59]

On Tuesday afternoon, the adjourned Court of Common Hall met to hear the Declaration, and there was "such an Expectation among ye Partys to hear ye Issue thereof y^t ye Guildhall was as much Crowded as on Midsummer Day."[60] The sheriffs then mounted the Hustings and reported that "upon

[58] Add. MSS, 32686, f. 176.
[59] *Daily Courant*, July 5, 1723. See also Boyer, *Political State*, XXVI, 108-109.
[60] Add. MSS, 27980, f. 86 (newsletter, July 2, 1723).

Examination of the Poll Books & Computation of the Numbers" they saw no reason to depart from their former Declaration, and again declared that Williams and Lockwood were the duly elected sheriffs of London and Middlesex.[61]

Again a demand for the numbers of the Poll was made, but these the sheriffs refused to disclose. Complaint was then made to the Lord Mayor, Sir Gerard Conyers, and the Court of Aldermen, which met at once and questioned Mr. Falkingham and others upon their oaths. Suspecting that Hopkins and Feast had a larger majority than they were given credit, the Court ordered the sheriffs to report at once the numbers of the Poll. This being refused, the sheriffs were then ordered to bring in the books so that they might be looked over. This order was also refused. The Court of Aldermen then resolved that the declaration of the sheriffs in favor of Williams and Lockwood was "Irregular and Unwarrantible," and declared that they (the aldermen) "would take Care that Justice should be done to their Fellow Citizens in this Affair." All of this being reported by the City Recorder, Sir William Thompson, to the Common Hall, it was then adjourned until the following Friday.[62]

On that day, at noon, the two sheriffs appeared on the Hustings, and Parsons made a speech complaining of the lack of co-operation of the Court of Aldermen. He reported that he and his brother sheriff, nevertheless, had made a careful scrutiny themselves of the poll—"with indefatigable Pains"—and had found Williams and Lockwood elected by a majority of legal votes.[63]

About three o'clock of the same day, however, the Recorder (by order of the Court of Aldermen) gave the real story of what had occurred. He told the liverymen that the Court of Aldermen had examined under oath Mr. Falkingham and several other persons concerned in taking the Poll, and was agreed

[61] Daily Courant, July 3, 1723; London Journal, July 6, 1723; Add. MSS, 27980, f. 86.

[62] Daily Courant, July 5, 1723; London Journal, July 6, 1723; Boyer, Political State, XXVI, 109-110; Add. MSS, 27980, f. 86.

[63] London Journal, July 6, 1723; Post-Boy, July 6, 1723; Evening Post, July 6, 1723; Add. MSS, 27980, f. 89.

that the proper numbers stood thus: for Hopkins, 3,248 votes; for Feast, 3,244 votes; for Williams, 3,188 votes; and for Lockwood, 3,191 votes. He further declared that since not one person from the party of Williams and Lockwood had appeared to deny the truth of these figures, and that since the two sheriffs had refused to declare the numbers of the Poll or show their books to the Court, or appear before the Court when summoned, and had conducted themselves in an arbitrary and partial manner, the Court of Aldermen had concluded that the majority upon the Poll was in favor of Sir Richard Hopkins and Felix Feast, and therefore declared them to be duly elected Sheriffs of the City of London and the County of Middlesex for the ensuing year. The Court of Common Hall was then declared dismissed.[64]

The liverymen were slow in dispersing, and at five o'clock a great many of the friends of Williams and Lockwood still lingered in the Guildhall. Sheriff Parsons, who entered about that time, was urged to do something about the decision. "But by this Time Mr. Parsons thought it adviseable to submit to the Authority of the Court of Aldermen," and excusing himself, he sent an officer to announce that since the Lord Mayor had ordered the Common Hall dismissed, he desired "that they would all depart in Peace."[65]

So ended the bitterly contested sheriffs' election of 1723. The national administration was well pleased at the outcome and the part played by the Court of Aldermen. On July 5 the Duke of Newcastle wrote to Lord Townshend at Hanover that that Court had shown "a pure Spirit."[66] A week later in another letter he noted that the aldermen had "exerted themselves with an unusual Zeal and Vigour in the affair of the Sheriffs," and added: "Everybody is very well Satisfied with their proceedings upon this occasion, and I believe the behavior of the opposite Party has turn'd very much to the advantage of the friends to the Government."[67]

[64] *Daily Courant*, July 6, 1723; *Flying Post, or Post-Master*, July 6, 1723; *Evening Post*, July 6, 1723; Add. MSS, 27980, ff. 88-89.
[65] *British Journal*, July 13, 1723.
[66] Add. MSS, 32686, f. 270.
[67] Add. MSS, 32686, f. 276 (July 12, 1723).

Moreover, the attitude of the old sheriffs came in for much condemnation. On July 20 Lord Townshend wrote in reply to the Duke's letters: "I hope, as we have justice on our side in the Election of the Sheriffs, all the Methods that the Law allows of, will be made use of to chastise the Insolence of the present Sheriffs, if they should persist in declaring Williams and Lockwood duly elected in defiance of all Equity & reason."[68] Nevertheless, no action seems to have been taken, although it was seriously considered. Walpole, on August 2, wrote to the Duke of Newcastle, then at his country home: "On Wednesday, several of ye Court of Aldermen with Mr. Recorder and Mr. Woodford, mett the Attorney & Solicitour Gen[rl] at my house for dinner, to consider what method to take in proceeding against the present sheriffs of London, & altho' they did not finally agree, what measures to pursue, and were of opinion that something might & ought to be done, I believe it will end in filing information."[69]

The outcome of the election, with the naming of new sheriffs friendly to the Government, also received the approval of his Majesty, and Lord Townshend wrote to Walpole on August 6: "The King is wonderfully pleased with the vigour shewn by the Court of Aldermen." He then added for Walpole's benefit: "I am persuded that some popular Bills next Session in favour of Trade and Credit will effectually confirm the City in their present good disposition." Referring again to the sheriffs' election, he expressed the hope that "our Lawyers will take care that no Chicanery of the present Sheriffs shall hinder the New Ones from entering quietly on the Execution of their office."[70]

He need not have worried. The old sheriffs had evidently decided to let well enough alone. At a meeting of the Court of Common Council on September 4, if we may believe a con-

[68] Add. MSS, 32686, f. 273.

[69] Add. MSS, 32686, f. 289. This incident certainly illustrates the close relationship between Walpole and the aldermen of the City. The attorney general at this time was Sir Robert Raymond (1673-1733), first Baron Raymond; the solicitor general was Sir Phillip Yorke (1690-1764), first Earl of Hardwicke.

[70] Stowe MSS, 251, f. 21b.

temporary chronicle,[71] the legality of the election was questioned; but Sir William Thompson, the City Recorder, at once stood up and fully explained the laws dealing with the election of sheriffs. At the same time he "set the Proceedings of the present Sheriffs in so true a Light, as likewise those of the Lord Mayor and the Court of Aldermen, in relation to the Declaration of Sir Richard Hopkins and Mr. Feast, that there was no reply made, notwithstanding some seem'd prepared to favour Sir John Williams and Mr. Lockwood. On September 28, Hopkins and Feast were, without opposition, duly declared elected, and on the same day were sworn in by the Lord Mayor at the Guildhall."[72]

That same day also (September 28) there "came on" the annual election of a Lord Mayor. It was a quiet procedure in contrast to the election just finished, and no opposition was manifested. Sir Peter Delmé and Sir George Merttins, the aldermen next the chair, were returned by the Common Hall, and the Court of Aldermen duly declared the former to be the Lord Mayor of London for the year ensuing.[73] At the December elections of common councilmen, when the antiadministration forces again returned their usual majority, there were some complaints of "Irregular practises,"[74] but no real contest developed and the year closed with the City comparatively quiet.

THE 1724 ELECTIONS

The year 1724 was not many days old before dissension again broke out. This time it was first seen at the election of an alderman for Lime Street Ward, to succeed Sir Lancelot Skinner, who died on January 28, 1724.[75] At the wardmote, held in the Church of St. Mary-Axe on January 31, the candidates were Sir Richard Hopkins, one of the recently elected sheriffs, and Edward Bridgen, a Cutler. On the show of hands, Sir Richard was declared to have the majority, but Bridgen's

[71] Boyer, *Political State* (Sept., 1723).
[72] Boyer, *Political State*, XXVI, 319-320.
[73] *Present State of Europe, or, The Historical and Political Monthly Mercury*, XXXV, 296.
[74] *Daily Courant*, Dec. 23, 1723.
[75] *British Journal*, Feb. 1, 1724.

friends demanded a poll. A poll being taken, Hopkins was again declared elected by a vote of 88 to 72.[76] Still not satisfied, Bridgen's friends demanded a scrutiny. This was dragged on through the month of February, but it brought no change in the result. A number of the votes were disqualified, and the numbers reduced to 66 for Hopkins and 48 for Bridgen. On March 4 Sir Richard Hopkins was finally declared alderman of the ward.[77]

A controversial election which affected the whole City, and which inspired demands for parliamentary intervention in London elections, was precipitated by the death of one of the recently sworn sheriffs, Felix Feast. Feast's health had been the cause of alarm to the friends of the Government for some time. On November 5 (1723) the Duke of Newcastle had written to Lord Townshend, still in Hanover: "We were in a great fright y[e] other day, for one of our New Sheriffs Mr. Feast, who was very dangerously ill. Our friend Capt. Bell was with me on Sunday, & told me the Tories had determined to set up Alderman Brocas, upon w[ch] we agreed that Alderman Bellamy must be set up on our side, & I wrote accordingly to my Lord Mayor, S[r] G. Heathcote, S[r] J. Ward & Alderman Bellamy."[78] The Duke sent the same message to Robert Walpole, then at Houghton, but added that he had just heard that Feast was much better, and he hoped "quite out of danger."[79] Three months later, however, on February 22, 1724, Sheriff Feast was seized with the "Dead Palsey," and died the next day.[80]

Immediately, the parties showed the same spirit manifested the previous June. Meetings were held to name the candidates, and advertisements were run daily in the newspapers.[81] A meeting of the "Court Party" was held at Merchant-Taylors' Hall, and it was agreed to support Edward Bellamy, alderman of Billingsgate Ward, as had been suggested by the Duke of Newcastle. The friends of the opposition met at Vintners' Hall

[76] Ibid.; British Gazetteer, Feb. 8, 1724.
[77] British Gazetteer, Feb. 8 and March 7, 1724; Saturday Post, Feb. 22, 1724.
[78] Add. MSS, 32686, f. 391b.   [79] Add. MSS, 32686, f. 393.
[80] Boyer, Political State, XXVII, 216.
[81] See the Daily Courant, Feb. 28-March 5, 1724.

and put in nomination their candidate who had been beaten in the previous sheriffs' election, Sir John Williams, alderman of Cripplegate Ward.[82] The Duke of Wharton also came into the picture again to give his hearty backing to Alderman Williams. Nevertheless, it was said that "some of y[e] Party begin to Distrust his Sin——ty."[83]

On Thursday, March 5, the election was held at the Guildhall. Upon the show of hands Bellamy was declared to have the majority, but a poll was granted and began that afternoon. That evening the numbers were 604 for Williams and 449 for Bellamy.[84] The next day, Friday, the voting was very heavy; in the evening the count showed that Sir John had received 2,516 votes, with Bellamy still behind but in the running with 2,209 votes.[85] According to a report sent to Viscount Perceval, "the Party Struggles in ye Election of a Sheriff in room of Sir Felix Feast Deceased are remarkably great. The Duke of Wharton headed a great Body from ye Bell Tavern in ye Strand to Poll, & when his Grace came himself to give his Vote as a Liveryman of ye Wax Chandlers Company, he desired y[m] to take notice that he Polled for Sir John Williams, & yt they would make no mistake. 'Tis endless to relate all ye particulars yt occur at this Election, wch is carried on by both Partys with such Zeal & Assiduity as ye like has not been known."[86]

On Saturday, March 7, the books were closed and sealed up until the Monday. On that day they were opened and the votes counted, and reported as showing 3,102 for Alderman Bellamy, but 3,557 for Sir John Williams.[87] On Tuesday, therefore, Sheriff Hopkins declared the election for Sir John. But the friends of Bellamy demanded a scrutiny, and it was ordered to begin on March 18.[88] In the intervening days the livery companies brought in true lists of their members, at the order of the Lord Mayor, and advertisements were inserted in

[82] British Gazetteer, Feb. 29, 1724; Saturday Post, Feb. 29, 1724.
[83] Add. MSS, 27980, f. 292 (newsletter, Feb. 29, 1724).
[84] British Gazetteer, March 7, 1724.
[85] British Journal, March 7, 1724.
[86] Add. MSS, 27980, ff. 296-297 (March 5, 1724).
[87] Daily Courant, March 10, 1724.
[88] British Gazetteer, March 14, 1724.

the newspapers urging the citizens to "declare themselves" to prove the scrutiny.[89] A great many bad votes were thus found. At the end of the first day, out of 1,002 votes scrutinized, 144 of those for Williams were declared to be illegal, and 44 of those for Bellamy. It was then computed, according to one writer, that since the lists presented by the livery companies showed that the total number of the liverymen was 8,399, and since the number of liverymen who had not polled was 1,586, there remained 5,811 legal votes yet to be scrutinized. But since a total of 6,659 votes appeared on the pollbooks, it was plain to be seen that 848 of them must be illegal votes.[90]

Immediately there was much talk of the need of reform. Advertisements continued to be run urging the citizens to detect the bad pollers. Many votes were challenged for failure to pay taxes, and on both sides charges were made that "names had been used of Persons who are dead, who were absent, or who never lived."[91] "All ye Discourse of ye City is upon ye affair of ye Elections of a Sheriff," said a newsletter report sent to Viscount Perceval on March 24. "They talk of great Frauds & Abuses in ye Poll, but it can't be Supposed they are all on one Side. They talk likewize of Something to be laid before ye Parliament in Relation to ye Election of ye City officers, but whatever it be 'tis not doubted such Impartial Methods will be taken as are Most agreeable to ye Laws and Usages of ye City."[92]

On March 20, after the lists of thirty-three companies had been scrutinized, 410 bad votes had been found for Williams and only 132 for Bellamy.[93] At the end of the next day, after fifty-five companies had been examined, there were 595 bad pollers for Williams and 193 for Bellamy, and the report in the press prophesied: "It is not doubted but the continued Zeal of the Citizens to detect bad Pollers, will determine the Election in favour of Edward Bellamy, Esq."[94]

[89] *British Journal*, March 14, 1724. See *Daily Courant*, March 11, 13, 14, 17, and 18, 1724.
[90] Boyer, *Political State*, XXVII, 317.
[91] *Daily Courant*, March 25, 1724.   [92] Add. MSS, 27980, f. 300.
[93] *Daily Courant*, March 21, 1724.   [94] *Ibid.*, March 23, 1724.

On Thursday, March 26, the scrutiny was completed, and the number of bad votes for Williams had increased to 715, while Bellamy was credited with but 232. Again the writer in the *Daily Courant* mentioned his belief that now without doubt Bellamy would be declared elected "to the Mortification of those who have invaded the valuable Rights of the worthy Citizens, by introducing the vile Practise of bad Polling, and to the great Joy of those who have a due regard to the Honour of this Great City."[95]

And Bellamy was elected, for the next day Sheriff Hopkins declared upon the Hustings that the scrutiny of the Poll having been completed, the number of legal voters for Edward Bellamy was 2,868 and for Sir John Williams 2,850. He therefore named Alderman Bellamy as the duly elected Sheriff of London and Middlesex in place of Sir Felix Feast for the remaining part of the year, an announcement "which was received with universal Acclamations" and "the Night concluded with the ringing of Bells, &c."[96] "The Detection of the corrupt Practises of false Polling upon the Scrutiny, gives a generous Satisfaction to all sorts of honest Citizens, and Occasions an impatient desire among them to have this Threatening Evil redressed," was the parting comment of the writer in the *Daily Courant*.[97]

The citizens were indeed getting tired of the continual wrangling.[98] Moreover, friends of the Government in the City began to bestir themselves. In the regular election of sheriffs which followed soon after, on June 24, they became unusually active. Their candidates were Robert Baylis, alderman of Bread Street Ward, and Joseph Eyles, a Turkey Merchant, chosen at a meeting held at Merchant-Taylors' Hall on June 4.[99] The opposition forces met on June 16 at Vintners' Hall

[95] *Ibid.*, March 28, 1724.
[96] *British Gazetteer*, March 30, 1724; Boyer, *Political State*, XXVII, 318.
[97] *Daily Courant*, March 30, 1724.
[98] The *British Gazetteer*, on March 21, 1724, reported that it had received a number of letters, complaining of "the late Increase of the scandalous Practise of False Polling," and mentioned one remedy that had been suggested— a scheme of voting separately by Companies, to do away with the "Mobbing" so prevalent in Common Hall, and to prevent the trouble and expense of a scrutiny. It then added that this, and other schemes for regulating the growing election evils, would be speedily submitted to Parliament for consideration.
[99] *Daily Courant*, June 5, 1724.

and proposed Richard Brocas, alderman of Farringdon Ward Within, and Richard Levett, alderman of Aldersgate Ward.[100] Again the Duke of Wharton was active, and an advertisement in the press in support of Brocas and Levett asked the liverymen "to meet his Grace at the Five Bells Tavern near the New Church in the Strand" before going to the Guildhall for the election.[101]

But his influence and "hospitality" were both unavailing, and at the meeting of the Common Hall on Midsummer Day, Baylis and Eyles were elected by "the greatest Majority that was ever known on any such Occasion."[102] The Guildhall was completely filled with liverymen, it was reported, and they "came with great Resolution and Zeal, to prevent the Evils for the future which have been so much practis'd, and to assist in the Redress thereof; and therefore did almost unanimously elect Mr. Alderman Baylis and Joseph Eyles, Esq; the Majority in the Hall for those worthy Candidates being so great, no Poll was demanded. The Satisfaction of the Citizens shew'd on this happy Occasion, was express'd in an extraordinary Manner, by Ringing of Bells, Bonfires, and other Demonstrations of Joy."[103]

Quiet prevailed in the City through the summer. An election in Aldgate Ward for the successor of Sir Samuel Stainer, who died on August 28, was very peaceful; and Francis Porten, Mercer, nephew to Sir Samuel and Deputy of the ward, was "unanimously" elected in his uncle's room "without any Opposition."[104] On September 29, when the election of Lord Mayor came on, Sir George Merttins, who had figured as the "Tory" candidate in the controverted election of 1722,[105] but who was next the chair now, was declared elected also "without Opposition."[106]

Then came the election of a successor to Peter Godfrey, one of the members of Parliament from the City, who died on November 10.[107] With it came more irregularities of polling.

[100] *Ibid.*, June 18, 1724.   [101] *Ibid.*, June 24, 1724.
[102] *Ibid.*, June 25, 1724.   [103] *British Gazetteer*, June 27, 1724
[104] *Saturday Post*, Sept. 5, 1724; *British Journal*, Sept. 5, 1724.
[105] See p. 80, above.   [106] *Daily Courant*, Sept. 30, 1724.
[107] *Ibid.*, Nov. 11, 1724.

The candidates were Sir Richard Hopkins, recently a sheriff of London, and Charles Goodfellow, a Russia merchant and formerly a Consul in Muscovy. At the election on Monday, November 23, the show of hands favored Hopkins, but leave was given to take a poll.[108] There was a warm contest, and charges such as the "hiring of several Watermen and others to appear at Guildhall with Clubs to intimidate" the voters, flew fast.[109] There were also many votes challenged, most of them credited to Goodfellow; and many of those who had voted on the first day, for trying to repeat their move the next day— "in a very bare-faced Manner"—were committed to prison.[110] There was even "one Fellow, famous for such Things, who took on him to personate one Mr. Wood who had been in his Grave a Month." He, too, was detected and committed.[111]

Hopkins, whose friends claimed that eighteen of the Court of Aldermen were on his side (the eighteen favorable to the administration),[112] led the poll throughout, and had 3,332 votes when the books were closed on Saturday, November 28; while Goodfellow, whose friends claimed only five aldermen supporters (Garrard, Parsons, Child, Levett, and Williams),[113] received 2,911 votes.[114] Goodfellow not being satisfied, a scrutiny was demanded and granted, but on Wednesday, December 9, he conceded the election to Hopkins, who by that day had increased his majority to 560, and who was declared by Sheriff Baylis to be duly elected.[115]

It was at this time that Parliament began to take the steps that led to the City Elections Act of 1725.

THE CITY ELECTIONS ACT OF 1725

A governmental move to regulate the local City elections had been suggested as early as April 21, 1722, and had been talked of considerably during the contested election of a sheriff in March, 1724.[116] The direct action was foretold by Lord Townshend in a letter to the King in April, 1724, urging him

---

[108] *London Journal*, Nov. 28, 1724. [109] *Daily Courant*, Nov. 23, 1724.
[110] *Ibid.*, Nov. 26, 1724. [111] *Ibid.*, Nov. 28, 1724.
[112] *Ibid.*, Nov. 23, 1724. [113] *Ibid.*, Nov. 25, 1724.
[114] *London Journal*, Dec. 5, 1724. [115] *British Gazetteer*, Dec. 12, 1724.
[116] See p. 65, n. 32, and p. 97, above.

not to make his customary trip to Hanover that summer. Commenting on the improved situation in England, and the "flourishing Condition of Trade & publick Credit," and referring to the recent victories of their friends in the City elections, he reported that "a very great change has been wrought, in favour of your Ma^{ty}, in the City of London," despite "the utmost Efforts & most Indirect Practises of the United Party of Jacobites"; and he promised that with the support of the King's presence in England that year, their friends in the City would not only carry all the other elections during the summer, but with the help and assistance of the ministry would "be prepared to lay before the Parl^t Such Bills as may for the future secure the Government of y^t important Place entirely in ye hands of those who are Zealous in your Ma^{tys} Interest."[117]

And Townshend's promise proved true, for not only were the sheriffs' and Lord Mayor's elections favorable to the ministry, as was also the return of Hopkins to be a member of Parliament for the City in place of Godfrey (already described), but in December came the move for the reform and control of City politics.

It was arranged that this first move should appear to come from the City. Accordingly, on December 16, a petition was presented to the House of Commons, signed by "many Citizens of the City of London, in behalf of themselves, and their Fellow Citizens," setting forth that "the Animosities and Divisions between Citizen and Citizen, and also between the Magistrates and the Commons, of the City of London," had grown "to such a Height and Flame," that they were obliged to seek "Releif" from Parliament.

At the Elections by the Liverymen, Numbers of People, that have no Right to Vote, break in, with Noise and Violence, upon the legal Electors; and poll, in their own or borrowed Names; and personate absent Electors, as often as they think they may, without being detected; and at the late Election of a Sheriff, in the room of Sir Felix Feast, deceased, many Hundreds appear to have polled, without any Colour of Right; and, at the preceding Election, Even the Sheriff of London, without Example, concealed the Number of

[117] H. M. C., *Underwood MSS*, pp. 428-429.

the Poll for each Candidate, though the Liverymen, several Times, demanded the same.

Moreover, the petition continued: ". . . for want of a Law, Non-jurors, and Persons receiving Charity have demanded, and been admitted to vote." The frequent contests at the ward elections were pointed out, and the claims of the nonfreemen that since they contributed to the charges of their respective wards, they were thereby entitled to vote in the election of ward officers. The meaning of "paying Scot" was still unsettled, according to the petition; and the disputes between the Court of Alder-men and the Court of Common Council continued to divide the City administration. Altogether the situation was deplor-able, and the petitioners were now come to the House of Commons to urge that something be done "for preserving the Liberties and Peace, and quieting the Minds of the Citizens: and for punishing all Intruders upon their Rights and Privi-leges; and settling their Elections upon a just and lasting Foundation."[118]

The House acted at once by giving leave to bring in a bill "for regulating Elections within the City of London; and for preserving the Peace, good Order, and Government, of the said City"; and a committee consisting of Richard West, Sir Gilbert Heathcote, Sir William Thompson, and Sir John Eyles[119] was appointed to prepare it.[120] This being done, West, as chairman, presented the bill for its first reading on Wednesday, January 27, 1725.[121]

Two days afterward a meeting of the Common Council was held at the Guildhall, and the members were informed of the bill that had just been introduced. Thereupon, a proposal was made that the Common Council petition against it. This being agreeable to the majority, a committee was ordered to prepare such a petition. The committee included four aldermen (Gar-

[118] *Journals of the House of Commons*, XX, 363.
[119] The three latter were prominent City men, but were representatives of other constituencies. Heathcote sat for St. Germains, Thompson for Ipswich, and Eyles for Chippenham. West sat for Bodmin. All were pro-Walpole men.
[120] *Journals of the House of Commons*, XX, 364.
[121] *Ibid.*, XX, 377.

rard, Levett, Barber, and Williams) and eight commoners, all being antiadministration men; and when read to the Court, their draft was approved, signed by the Lord Mayor, Sir George Merttins, and ordered to be presented to the House of Commons. The presentation at first threatened to be held up, since the sheriffs (Baylis and Eyles), being politically contrary-minded to those who were sponsoring the petition, refused to carry it to Westminster. The Council finally decided that it should be presented by any two of the aldermen and four of the commoners on the committee which had prepared it.[122]

On Monday, February 1, the petition "of the Lord Mayor, Aldermen and Commons of the City of London, in Common Council assembled" was presented at the Bar of the House of Commons and read. The petitioners stated that if the proposed bill should pass into law, it would "be destructive to many of their Rights and Privileges, which by ancient Charters, they, and their Fellow Citizens are entitled to." They therefore prayed that they might be heard, by their counsel, against the impending bill. This was so ordered.[123]

Two days later a petition was presented to the House in favor of the bill, entitled as from "the major Part of the Aldermen of the City of London." It had been drawn up and presented to the Court of Aldermen on Friday, February 2, by a committee of which Sir Gilbert Heathcote was chairman. On a motion that it be approved, however, the Lord Mayor declined to put the question, on the ground that he had already signed the petition against the bill which had been presented to Parliament in the name of the Lord Mayor, Aldermen, and Commons in Common Council. Nevertheless, over his protest, the petition was approved and signed by the majority of the aldermen of the Court and presented accordingly on February 3.[124]

In this petition the aldermen gave their approval to the proposed bill, which they believed was the only remedy that could do away with the disputes so prevalent in recent years in

[122] Journals of the Common Council, 57, ff. 119b-120.
[123] Journals of the House of Commons, XX, 387.
[124] Repertories of the Court of Aldermen, 129, f. 123.

the City and restore peace and tranquillity therein. They also drew attention to the clause in the bill touching on the passing of acts or bylaws by the Common Council. The right of the Court of Aldermen to veto measures had never been questioned until the time of the Civil War, they said, nor since then, until recently. Moreover, attempts by the aldermen to enlist the co-operation of the common councilmen in submitting their differences to the courts of law at Westminster or to Parliament for settlement, had previously resulted in failure. The petitioners, therefore, prayed that they too might be allowed a hearing, by their counsel, in regard to the proposed bill. This hearing also was so ordered when the second reading should be held.[125]

The second reading came on Monday, February 8, and counsel for and against the bill were called in to present their cases. The hearings continued throughout the month; the Journals of the Common Council, the Repertories of the Court of Aldermen, the Returns of the clerks of the livery companies, and various other records and papers were introduced and read and witnesses examined. Also, petitions from a number of the livery companies were received and read, and their counsel was given a hearing. Next, the various clauses of the bill were discussed and amendments suggested.[126] Finally, on Friday, March 19, the question was put, and the bill passed the Commons by a vote of 139 to 83.[127]

In the House of Lords the procedure was similar. Petitions were again presented by the Common Council against the bill,[128] and by the "major Part of the Aldermen" for it, as well as another petition from a group of freemen who objected to certain parts of it. Counsel were heard, the whole matter was debated, amendments were made, and at the third reading on April 13, the bill was passed by a vote of 79 to 27. On April

[125] Journals of the House of Commons, XX, 389; Repertories of the Court of Aldermen, 129, ff. 123-124.

[126] Records of the speakers or speeches during these debates are not available.

[127] Journals of the House of Commons, XX, 403-462.

[128] The majority of the common councilmen again favored this petition, but only five aldermen (Merttins, Levett, Barber, Williams, and Brocas) voted for it.

19 the Commons agreed to the Lords' amendments, and on the following day the royal assent was given and the bill became law.[129]

This Act of April 20, 1725,[130] was entitled "for regulating Elections within the City of London, and for preserving the Peace, good Order, and Government of the said City," and in its preamble explained that it had come about because of the "great controversies and dissensions" that had arisen in the City at the elections of citizens to serve in Parliament, and of mayors, aldermen, sheriffs, and other officers; because of the large number of persons who had voted illegally at these elections and had been the cause of much disturbance; because of the large number of wealthy persons who had refused to become free of the City, yet insisted on enjoying the full rights of freemen; and because of the great dissensions which had arisen between the Court of Aldermen and the Court of Common Council.[131]

The Act proposed to bring about peace at elections (1) by making it necessary for all voters at elections to take an oath that they were freemen of London and entitled to vote, as well as an oath of loyalty to his Majesty King George I, and by imposing penalties for falsely taking such oaths; (2) by giving instructions concerning the proper methods of taking the polls and fair and legal scrutinies to all, and imposing a penalty (of £200) on offending presiding officers; and (3) by stating what persons could or could not vote for the various officers, especially declaring that the right of election of aldermen and common councilmen for the several wards should belong only to freemen of the City, being householders of the ward, and paying scot and bearing lot as required[132]—provided that such

---

[129] *London Gazette*, April 20, 1725; *Journals of the House of Lords*, XXII, 459-499; *Journals of the House of Commons*, XX, 496; Journals of the Common Council, 57, ff. 121-121b; Repertories of the Court of Aldermen, 129 f. 218. The Duke of Wharton, who was again active in arousing the opposition in the City, claimed that the royal assent was obtained so quickly in order to prevent the Common Council from appealing directly to the King for aid, as the Duke and his friends had planned. See Mahon, *History of England, 1713-1783*, II, Appendix, xxii (Stuart Papers).

[130] 11 Geo. 1, c. 18.

[131] For full text of the Act, see the *Statutes at Large, of the Reign of George I*, XV, 221-230.

[132] "Paying scot and bearing lot" was defined as contributing to all the

householders were sole occupiers of houses of at least £10 a year value, and dwellers in the same for a space of twelve calendar months previous to the election.[133] The liverymen who voted at the Common Hall elections of mayor, sheriffs, representatives to Parliament, and so forth, were required to be in good standing upon the livery for the twelve months previous to an election, and to have paid their rates. By these provisions it was hoped that disorders at City elections would be eliminated. To end the disputes between the aldermen and commoners touching upon the passing of acts, orders, and ordinances in Common Council, it was definitely provided that no such act, order, or ordinance should be passed by the Common Council without the assent of the Lord Mayor and aldermen there present, the aldermen thereby being confirmed in their claim to a veto over acts of Common Council. To end the objections of the nonfreemen in regard to control of their personal estates, and to encourage the more wealthy to take their freedom, the Act provided that, with a few exceptions, all persons free of the City should have the right of disposing of their personal property by will as they thought fit.

These were the main provisions. The clauses dealing with the regulation of the elections were in large part good, and long needed. Nevertheless, the Act was not received with unanimous approval. The "aldermanic veto," so called, the provision that Common Council acts could not be passed without the consent of the mayor and aldermen, aroused the greatest furor. Clearly it was a move to make certain the supremacy of the Court of Aldermen over the Court of Common Council—and thus was a victory for the adherents of the national government over the opposition factions in the City.

Support of the Act naturally came from the aldermen friendly to the Walpole administration, and to the number of eighteen they had signed the petitions to Parliament favoring

rates imposed by the Corporation (the church, the poor, the scavenger, the orphans, the watch, etc.), or paying a minimum of thirty shillings to some or all of them.

[133] This clause had the effect of disenfranchising some three thousand freemen householders who occupied houses under £10 per annum value. See Boyer, *Political State*, XXIX, 155-156.

its passage. The aldermen wished to aid the national administration, but were perhaps even more interested in solidifying
their own power in the City government. In this they were
successful, for during the next few years the power of the
Common Council was drastically curtailed, and for a time the
Lord Mayor summoned a session only when he thought fit—
as long as thirteen months on one occasion being allowed to
elapse without a single meeting.[134] Nevertheless, although the
Act pleased the aldermen, the majority of the Londoners did
not like it. They were said to have been very "uneasy" about
the affair even in February, when the bill had been first introduced.[135] Its passage through Parliament "occasion'd a great
Ferment among the Citizens,"[136] and it was not passed in April
without a "violent outcry."[137] On May 1 the Duke of Wharton wrote to James (the Pretender) that "the rage which in-
flames both parties in the City . . . increases every day, and will
blaze more and more as they feel the great distinctions which
must attend the execution of it."[138]

During the progress of the bill through Parliament, as was
customary, public opinion had been appealed to, and pamphlets
written to state the case of both sides.[139] Efforts also had been

[134] From May 24, 1728, to June 5, 1729. Soon after, however, a slight
move was made to remedy the situation, and an ordinance was passed compelling the Lord Mayor to summon a meeting of the Common Council at
least once a quarter. See the Journals of the Common Council, 57, f. 198.
[135] H. M. C., *Clements MSS*, p. 384 (John Lekeux to John Molesworth,
Feb. 15, 1725).
[136] Boyer, *Political State*, XXIX, 260.
[137] Mahon, *History of England, 1713-1783*, II, 76.
[138] *Ibid.*, II, Appendix, xxii (Stuart Papers). The Duke did not remain
much longer on the English scene. In July of that year (1725) he went to
Vienna, and openly attached himself to the Pretender's court. In 1726 he
went to Madrid as James's ambassador, there turned Catholic, and married an
Irish maid of honor of the Queen of Spain. He had various adventures in
the Pretender's service, was outlawed by Parliament, squandered and lost his
money, and finally, destitute and broken in health, he died in a Spanish mon-
astery. There, at the age of thirty-two, "amongst strangers, and without one
friend to close his eyes, this last heir to a most aspiring family and most
princely fortune, ended his career of baleful wit, miserable frolic, and splen-
did infamy" (*ibid.*, II, 141). See J. R. Robinson, *Philip, Duke of Wharton,
1698-1731* (London, 1896), pp. 149-260.
[139] For example, the *Daily Journal* of March 31, 1725, urged the citizens
to sign petitions against the bill, on the ground that it would take away their
freedom. In reply the next day, the *Daily Courant* denounced the scandalous

made to arouse the mob to a demonstration. One such attempt, for instance, occurred on Wednesday, March 24, with the distribution of a printed summons inviting the citizens to assemble at Guildhall. Upon receiving notice of this, the Lord Mayor and Court of Aldermen, resenting such an action undertaken without their approval, ordered the Guildhall gates to be closed, circulated a printed notice to the effect that the suddenly scheduled meeting was only calculated to precipitate the citizens to some disorders in opposition to the bill then pending in Parliament, and urged a reasonable support for the said bill which aimed to provide a remedy for the unsettled state of affairs in the City. They also acquainted the ministers with the affair, who ordered the guards doubled at St. James's Palace, Leicester House, and Somerset House. By these precautions, the scheduled meeting was prevented, no disorders occurred, and the aldermen scored a moral victory.[140]

Nor was it all clamor. Various organized groups in the City respectfully opposed the bill. The Common Council, several livery companies, and a number of freemen, as has been noted above, petitioned against it. Moreover, three of the four representatives of the City (Richard Lockwood, Sir Francis Child, and John Barnard) actively worked against it during its progress through the lower House, and though their efforts were in vain, the Common Council, on March 22, in recognition of "their great Pains and Application, and for their brave, strenuous, and very Hon'ble behaviour" in defending "the ancient Rights, Franchises, and Libertys" of the Corporation, tendered the three men a formal vote of thanks.[141]

proceedings of the opposition paper, charging gross misrepresentations. The *British Journal*, of April 3, urged the citizens to favor the bill and, supposing that the clamor against it was for want of a knowledge of what the bill really was, published an abstract of its provisions. Typical pamphlets preserved in the Guildhall Library in London are *The Report of a Committee of Aldermen, in Affirmance of the Right of the Mayor and Aldermen to Put a Negative to Acts . . . in the Common Council* (1724); *A Brief State of the Several Disputes and Grievances . . . in the City of London, with Some Observations upon the Bill Now Depending in Parliament* (1724); *The Art of Managing Popular Elections, etc.* (1724); and *A Letter from a Citizen to a Member of Parliament, against the Bill Now Depending, etc.* (1725).

[140] *Weekly Journal: or British Gazetteer*, March 27, 1725; Boyer, *Political State*, XXIX, 261-262; Oldmixon, *History of England*, p. 760.
[141] Journals of the Common Council, 57, f. 121b.

In the House of Lords there was much dissent by the opposition peers. It was first voiced on April 13 and was led by Wharton, Gower,[142] Strafford, and Lechmere.[143] While the bill was still pending, upon a motion to ask the opinion of the King's Counsel whether it would affect the ancient customs and liberties of the City restored in 1690 by William and Mary, which motion received a negative vote (83 to 24), these lords protested that the provisions giving the aldermen the veto power over the Common Council would endanger the long-established legal rights of the City.[144] These same lords then signed a protest when the bill was passed (by a vote of 79 to 27) on April 19. At the same time they declared that the penalty against presiding officers at wardmote elections was too small, deplored the loss of the franchise by so many householders who occupied houses of less than £10 per annum value, and objected to the clause abolishing the custom relating to the distribution of the personal estates of freemen. They declared that the bill was really giving a new constitution to the City, and they feared for its ancient rights and titles. They were especially opposed to the clauses which prohibited the passing of an act in Common Council without the assent of the major part of the aldermen present, charging that it gave them too great an addition to the power they already possessed, that it was a dangerous innovation upon the City, and that it would be the source of even greater "disputes, divisions, and distractions" in the future.[145]

In all this the dissenting lords had grounds for their contention, but the substantial issue was political, their opposition to the administration, which by this Act was to gain more power in the City. There was really more emphasis on the aldermanic veto than was called for. Actually the veto power was not dangerous as such, and did not prove to be so in the following years.[146] Anciently it had been one of the prerogatives of the

[142] John Leveson-Gower (1694?-1754), first Earl Gower.
[143] Nicholas Lechmere (1675-1727), Lord Lechmere.
[144] *Journals of the House of Lords*, XXII, 499.
[145] *Ibid.*, XXII, 500.
[146] Although the right of the aldermen to negative the Council proceedings was seldom called on during the years that followed, it continued to be

Court of Aldermen, and so used, not being questioned or objected to until the time of Charles I. During the troubled years of the Commonwealth that followed, it had been a bone of contention. Then there was a period of peace. Only in the later years, when differences between the political groups in the City had become so bitter, did this privilege assume importance in the eyes of the councilmen. It thus served in 1724 as a screen for the real issue, when the matter was put up to Parliament to make the privilege a permanent law in the City's constitution. On one side stood the councilmen, a majority of whom were opposed to the Walpole ministry and the Court, and who were supported by the parliamentary Opposition. On the other side stood the majority of the aldermen, supporters and adherents of King George I's ministers, and heartily in favor of the measure.

The real issue was understood at the time, and Walpole came in for much censure from the Opposition. John Barnard, representative of London in Parliament and himself an alderman, but a great opponent of Walpole's policies, even charged that minister, in a speech in Parliament in 1746, with downright corruption in forcing through the Act of 1725. He declared that in giving the power to the Court of Aldermen Walpole knew he would be able to control the City government, as by posts or promises he could secure a majority of the aldermen to his interest.[147] In the same debate, Alderman George Heathcote, another representative of London at that time, declared that Walpole's design was "to get the government of the City into his hands, or at least to prevent her opposing any of his future schemes," and to that end "he contrived to throw as much power into the hands of the aldermen

highly unpopular. The Common Council was very active about it, agitation was carried on, pamphlets were written, and later on the candidates for aldermanic vacancies were persuaded to pledge themselves to the repeal of the hated "negative." Gradually, as the political views of the Court of Aldermen and the Court of Common Council came to a closer agreement, and with the end of the Walpole administration in 1742, and the defeat of the Young Pretender in 1745, political opinion was won over finally to the side of repeal, and the unpopular clause of the Act was repealed in March, 1746 (19 Geo. II, c. 18).

[147] Cobbett, *Parliamentary History*, XIII, 1146 ff.

as possible, because, by working on their averice or their vanity, he thought he might prevail with a majority of them, to make use of their power upon all occasions for his service."[148]

The purpose of the ministry was noted even in December, 1724, just after the bill was first proposed. Dr. Stratford, writing to his former pupil, Edward Harley, declared (December 17) that it was "to give the mayor and aldermen a negative upon the Common Council, and to abolish some other privileges which are not used as the ministry would have them." This move to regulate City affairs, he added, was "the highest attempt of its nature that was ever made, and much beyond the taking away of charters in King Charles and King James days."[149] Dr. Stratford was certain that the Government was determined to push it through Parliament, despite any objection from the citizens, for a week later he wrote that "the bill against the city will be carried with a high hand."[150]

Another contemporary also mentions the real purposes of the City Bill. John Lekeux, a friend of Walpole, writing to John Molesworth, British envoy to Turin, on February 15, 1725, declared that "the aim is . . . to strengthen the Court party, for if they reduce the government of the City to only the Lord Mayor and aldermen's power, the Court can at any time gain their worthships."[151] On April 12 he wrote again: "The City Bill will pass. I hope it will prove for the good of the nation. For it was a great shame that the cits should oppose the designs of the Government at all elections with so much mutiny, and carry themselves with so much ignorant pride, followed by a brutish behavior, as they have for several years practised, This will bring them to reason."[152]

The City Elections Act then was a movement for reform of London election conditions, but at the same time it was designed to be a means whereby the national administration could exert greater control over the metropolis. Popular objection to the measures of the ministry was not thereby completely suppressed,

---

[148] *Ibid.*, XIII, 1162.
[149] H. M. C., *Portland MSS*, VII, 394.
[150] *Ibid.*, VII, 395.
[151] H. M. C., *Clements MSS*, p. 384.
[152] *Ibid.*, p. 391.

nor was the opposition by any means destroyed, but the chief
stronghold of the Opposition in the City, the Common Council, was made less effective.   The Duke of Newcastle, writing
to Lord Townshend, who was again with the King in Hanover,
reported on November 5, 1725, that London had quieted down
considerably, and the opposition of the Common Council had become of little consequence—"now the power is taken from them
by our late Bill."   He asserted that the ministers were "very
well Satisfied with the Situation."[153]   They might well be at
that, for during the next few years London proved to be more
amenable to the men in power.[154]

This was shown in the elections that were held during the
following year.   In June "came on" the election of sheriffs.
Francis Porten, alderman of Aldgate Ward and a Mercer, and
Jeremiah Murden, a Merchant-Taylor, were the candidates of
the friends of the administration.[155]   They had little opposition,
although at one time the ministry was not too sure of the situation; and Lord Townshend commented in a letter to the Duke
of Newcastle, on June 18, that "if it should happen that we
cannot be able to carry but one sheriff in the City, I question
whether the Administration in that point would make the figure
I desire it should, notwithstanding all the pains you promise
to take on it."[156]   The Duke's "pains," however, proved to be
sufficient, and on June 25 he was able to write in reply to
Townshend: "I have . . . at present the pleasure to acquaint
you that yesterday in a very large full meeting at Guildhall,
computed to have consisted of above 3,000 persons, the Gentlemen proposed by our Friends, viz. Alderman Porten and Mr.
Murden, were without any opposition elected Sheriffs of London and Middlesex for the year ensuing."[157]

In September, when the Lord Mayor was chosen, custom
again prevailed, and Sir Francis Forbes, who was next the chair,

[153] Add. MSS, 32687, f. 183.
[154] Cf. Laprade, *Public Opinion and Politics*, p. 283; Realey, *Early Opposition to Sir Robert Walpole*, p. 145.
[155] *Daily Courant*, June 24, 1725.
[156] Add. MSS, 32687, f. 87.
[157] Add. MSS, 32687, f. 95.   The *Daily Courant* for June 25, 1725, reported that these men were elected "unanimously."

was elected without opposition.[158]   In December, when the elections of common councilmen were held in the several wards, the friends of the administration were far more successful than they had been in several years; and although no figures were given, it was stated that "the Whigs gain'd considerable Advantage."[159]

No aldermanic elections were held during the remainder of the year following the passage of the City Elections Act, but on Saturday, March 12, 1726, Sir John Ward, alderman of Candlewick Ward, died, and on Tuesday, John Thompson, "a Gentleman of known Loyalty, Worth, and Probity," was elected his successor "without any opposition."[160]   This same John Thompson was put up for sheriff a few weeks later in the place of Sir James Murden, who caught the "goal-distemper" trying to stop a riot in Newgate Prison and died on March 27.[161]   There was a slight contest by Alderman Richard Brocas, who asked for a poll after the show of hands had been declared for Thompson.   Soon after it had been started, Brocas, however, "thought fit to decline the Poll"; and Alderman Thompson was again declared, and sworn in for the remainder of Murden's term.[162]

The regular sheriffs' election that year had no contest at all, and Sir John Lock, a Turkey Merchant, and William Ogbourn, a Carpenter, were "unanimously" chosen to the shrievalty.[163]   The same quiet was observed at the Lord Mayor's election in September, when Sir John Eyles, the alderman next the chair, who was very popular in the City, was chosen "and not one Hand lift against him."[164]

In that month (on September 11) Sir John Fryer, the alderman of Queenhithe Ward, died.[165]   To succeed him, Robert Alsop, Haberdasher, who had served the ward for many years

[158] Boyer, *Political State*, XXX, 310.
[159] *Brice's Weekly Journal*, Dec. 24, 1725.
[160] *British Gazetteer*, March 19, 1726.
[161] *Ibid.*, March 19 and April 2, 1726.
[162] *Daily Courant*, April 2, 4, and 8, 1726; *British Gazetteer*, April 2, 1726.
[163] *Daily Courant*, June 25, 1726.
[164] *Daily Post*, Sept. 30, 1726; *British Journal*, Oct. 1, 1726.
[165] *Daily Courant*, Sept. 13, 1726.

as Deputy, was "unanimously" chosen alderman.[166] According to one reporter, although he was fully qualified for the office, Alsop at first declined the honor; but was finally prevailed upon by the inhabitants of the ward to accept the office on the ground that his unanimous selection would be "an Example worthy of Imitation, and, if followed, will much contribute to the Quiet of the City."[167] The Common Council elections that December were also carried on quietly enough in the several wards, and it was reported that the men chosen were "generally the same as before."[168]

Thus the City Elections Act of 1725, as shown in the conduct of the various elections which followed its passing, seems to have fulfilled its purpose of preserving the peace and good order of the City of London.

THE FOREIGN SITUATION AND THE DEATH OF GEORGE I

London was now quiet, but it was not so everywhere. Outside the country things were happening which, though they did not touch the capital directly, nevertheless affected the citizens to a large degree. The peace of Europe, which had been maintained since 1720,[169] was apparently threatened with disaster. Friction between the members of the Quadruple Alliance had existed for some time, but the Emperor and the King of Spain had gradually drawn together in opposition to England, France, and the Netherlands. On April 30 and May 1, 1725, Charles VI and Philip V signed the Treaty of Vienna.[170]

During that summer rumors of war with Spain were spread about, and the stocks fell alarmingly. England was confronted

---

[166] *British Journal*, Sept. 17, 1726.
[167] *Daily Journal*, Sept. 15, 1726.
[168] *Daily Post*, Dec. 22, 1726; *British Gazetteer*, Dec. 24, 1726.
[169] See p. 7, above.
[170] By this treaty Spain guaranteed the Pragmatic Sanction (providing for the succession of Maria Theresa to the throne of Austria), agreed to give the Emperor's commercial subjects preference over those of Britain and Holland, and sanctioned the trade of the Ostend Company with the East Indies and the ports of Old and New Spain. The Emperor, on his part, confirmed the concessions that the Quadruple Alliance had made earlier to Spain, and undertook to support Spain in her efforts to obtain the return of Gibraltar and Port Mahon. See Leadam, *Political History of England, 1702-1760*, p. 323; and Basil Williams, "The Foreign Policy of England Under Walpole," *English Historical Review*, XV, 492-493.

with serious possibilities. The loss of Gibraltar and Port Mahon was threatened,[171] the trade of the merchants to the Indies was put in jeopardy, and there were also tales of renewed attempts to put the Pretender on the English throne, with Spanish support. Of all this the Londoners were highly sensible, and there was much talk in the City of "the monstrous Ingratitude of the Emperor, and the insufferable Insolence of the King of Spain."[172]

To offset the Austro-Spanish agreement, the Treaty of Hanover was negotiated, and approved by Parliament in February, 1726, drawing Great Britain, France, and Prussia together in a closer alliance.[173] The following year was a period of international negotiation and diplomatic intrigue. Threats were made, and even some actual fighting was carried on, although no formal declaration of war was made.[174] All this left the nations in a high state of uncertainty. In London the stocks fell "lower and lower," and rumors of war continued.[175]

At the end of January, 1727, the Lord Mayor, Aldermen, and Common Council together presented a loyal Address to the King, expressing resentment at the action of the King of Spain in demanding Gibraltar and Port Mahon, in supporting the Pretender, and putting trade in jeopardy; and assuring his Majesty that they would be loyal to him, even to the sacrifice of their "Lives and Fortunes."[176] For this the King expressed his thanks, and assured them that the utmost endeavors would

[171] Gibraltar had been captured from Spain in 1704, and Port Mahon (on the island of Minorca) was taken in 1708.

[172] *British Gazetteer*, Jan. 26, 1726.

[173] There were several provisions, but the chief one was that in case of any attack on one of the contracting powers, the others should furnish a certain quota in troops, or their value in ships or money. See Mahon, *History of England, 1713-1783*, II, 81-82; Williams, "Foreign Policy of England Under Walpole," *English Historical Review*, XV, 676.

[174] See Leadam, *History of England*, pp. 324 ff.; Williams, "Foreign Policy Under Walpole," *English Historical Review*, XV, 677 ff.; XVI, 67 ff. For a complete study of this period, see James F. Chance, *The Alliance of Hanover: A Study of British Foreign Policy in the Last Years of George I* (London, 1923).

[175] H. M. C., *Portland MSS*, V, 10; VII, 413-417; H. M. C., Fifteenth Report, Vol. VIII, *The Manuscripts of the Hon. Frederick Lindley Wood, Preserved at Temple Newsam, Leeds* (hereinafter cited as H. M. C., *Wood MSS*), p. 102.

[176] Journals of the Common Council, 57, f. 149.

be made for the continuance of peace, the settlement of affairs with Spain, and the preservation of trade. He then bestowed knighthood on Aldermen William Billers, Edward Bellamy, and John Thompson, and on Sheriff William Ogbourn, afterwards entertaining them all most sumptuously at dinner in St. James's Palace.[177]

The King's promise to continue negotiations was kept; these were successful, the Emperor being finally brought over from Spain's influence; and on May 31, 1727, at Paris, the preliminaries of a peace with Britain, France, and Holland were signed by the Austrian ambassador.[178] Before the news could be announced in London, however, Britain had lost her king. On June 3 George I left for Hanover. On June 11 he was dead. A new reign was to begin, with George II upon the throne.

[177] *London Gazette*, Jan. 31, 1727; *Daily Post*, Feb. 1, 1727; *British Journal*, Feb. 4, 1727. The whole City government must have turned out on this occasion, for there were "above a hundred Gentlemen's Coaches" in line. At the dinner they were served with "near a Thousand Dishes of Meat, the most exquisite and most in Season, besides a fine Desert of Sweatmeats and Fruit. Everything was done in the handsomest Manner without the least Disorder, to the Satisfaction of every Person there. The Lord Mayor and Aldermen were honoured with all the Prime Ministers of State at their Table, and each Table had at the Head of it a great Officer of the Household. There was a vast Plenty of all sorts of the finest Wines, and the greatest Cheerfulness appear'd throughout the whole Company." See the *British Journal*, Feb. 4, 1727.

[178] See Chance, *The Alliance of Hanover*, pp. 729 ff.

CHAPTER V

A New Reign and a New Opposition

GEORGE II BECOMES KING

THE NEWS of the death of George I reached Sir Robert Walpole,[1] then at Chelsea, on the afternoon of Wednesday, June 14 (1727); he immediately carried it to the Prince and Princess of Wales at Richmond, who came at once to Westminster. The next morning his Majesty, King George II, was proclaimed with the usual ceremonies at Leicester House, in Leicester Square at Charing Cross, within Temple Bar (after the gates of which, upon admission to the City being requested, had been "order'd open'd by the Right Honourable the Lord Mayor, accompany'd by the Aldermen and Sheriffs in their Robes"), in Cheapside, and at the Royal Exchange.[2]

Losing no time in paying their respects to the new sovereign, the Lord Mayor and Court of Aldermen waited on the King the next day with an Address; and the Recorder, Sir William Thompson, presented their congratulations and compliments at his Majesty's succession to the British Crown and their condolences on the death of his father, the late King. The City Fathers also assured him of their allegiance and their loyal support. To this the new King gave them thanks for their "early Marks of Zeal and Affection." Their compliments were also paid to her Majesty, Queen Caroline. The aldermen were cordially received by the royal couple, and to show his pleasure the King conferred the honor of knighthood on Alderman Robert Baylis.[3]

[1] Walpole had been made a knight of the Order of the Bath on May 27, 1725, and a year later he received the Garter, the first commoner to be so honored since 1660.

[2] *Daily Post*, June 16, 1727; *London Journal*, June 17, 1727.

[3] *London Gazette*, June 17, 1727; Repertories of the Court of Aldermen, 131, 285-291; *Applebee's Original Weekly Journal*, June 17, 1727; *Craftsman*, June 17, 1727.

The Common Council also wished to congratulate his Majesty upon the occasion of his accession; at a meeting on June 22 the same was so ordered, and a committee appointed to prepare an Address. When it was submitted to the Council for approval, however, trouble developed because the committee had tried to make use of the occasion to criticize and cast aspersions on his Majesty's ministers.[4] There were six clauses, or paragraphs, in the proposed Address,[5] and objections being

[4] The committee was chosen by the common councilmen present, the aldermen not participating; it consisted of eight commoners and four aldermen. The latter were Richard Brocas, John Barber, Richard Levett, and Sir John Williams, all antiadministration men.

[5] The Address was as follows:

To the King's Most Excellent Majesty.

The Humble Address of the Lord Mayor, Aldermen, and Commons of the City of London, in Common Council Assembled.

May it please your Majesty,

1. We your Majesty's most Dutiful and Loyal Subjects, the Lord Mayor, Aldermen, and Commons of the City of London in Common Council assembled, presume to approach your Throne upon this Solemn occasion; and whilst we congratulate your Majesty's happy Accession, we beg leave to express the deep Sense we have of the Loss which this Kingdom sustains by the Death of your Royal Father, our late most gracious Sovereign: So great and so unexpected a Loss, in so critical a Conjuncture, would fill our Minds with the justest Apprehensions, if we did not find, in the Love and Affection which your Majesty bears to this Country, to the Church of England as by Law established, to our Laws, and to our Liberties; and in those great Qualities which enable you to assert their Honour, and support the Interest of the Nation, so many Reasons for assuaging our Grief, for preventing our Fears, and even for raising our Hopes.

2. We promise ourselves from the Wisdom of your Majesty's Councils, that those beneficial Branches of Trade, which are at present cut off, and in Danger of our being totally lost, shall be restored to us; that our undoubted Right to those Possessions and Privileges, which were yielded to the Nation by former Treaties, and especially to those important Possessions of Gibraltar and Port Mahon, (so necessary for the Preservation of the Commerce of these Kingdoms) shall be no longer called in question by our Enemies, nor left at the Mercy even of our Friends; that They shall not be provided for by dark and doubtful Expressions, but acknowledged and confirmed in the strongest, plainest, and most authentick Manner.

3. As your Majesty's known Resolution and Courage gives us just Reason to depend on your Care and Interest abroad; so, when we reflect on your great Wisdom, and Mildness of your Government during the Time of your Regency; we make no doubt of enjoying at Home all those Blessings which a just, prudent, and a frugal Administration can procure to any People.

4. The Weight of the National Debt is severely felt, tho' cheerfully borne; and however vain the Hopes which have been hitherto given of sinking it, gradually, have proved, we have assured ourselves that this Glory is reserved for your Majesty's Reign; that Measures effectual to this great End will now be taken; that our Trade and Manufactures, the only Source of our Wealth and Riches, will be restored to the most prosperous and flourishing Condition; and that real Credit will grow up, and be established on true and natural Principles.

5. Thus will this Nation increase in Riches and Power, under your Majesty's auspicious Government; and whilst you cultivate Alliances for restoring the Tranquility, and preserving the Balance of Europe, your Majesty will be sufficient to your self,

at once raised, they were ordered to be read one by one. The first, which was simply a statement of congratulations and condolence, was passed favorably. The following clauses, chiefly the second, fourth, and fifth, which touched upon various phases of national policy, such as the question of Gibraltar and Port Mahon, the state of the National Debt, and of Public Credit—aroused opposition, especially from the majority of the aldermen present, who upon this occasion exercised their right of veto, so that when put to a vote all these clauses were rejected "as insinuating Reflection on the Conduct of his late Majesty's Government, and containing Matters not fit to be offer'd to his present Majesty, especially by that Court, and upon that Occasion."[6] The Lord Mayor, Sir John Eyles, then proposed that the offending clauses be changed or left out, or that the Address might consist of the first, third, and sixth clauses, which were not offensive, or even of the first clause only. All these suggestions, however, were refused by the committeemen and their supporters. "All or None" was their cry. The Lord Mayor, therefore, put an end to any further discussion and declared the Council meeting ended.[7]

A week later the Lord Mayor received a petition signed by twelve of the councilmen, asking him to call another Council meeting to consider again an Address to the King. This request he refused, after consultation with and upon the advice of the Court of Aldermen. He told the petitioners that in the first place they had no right to make such a request, and that in the second they had given no satisfaction that the conduct of a new Council meeting would be any different from the last. Moreover, he pointed out, there was really no need of another meeting now since an Address, highly complimentary to his

---

will promote the Interest of other Princes and States, without standing in Need of their Assistance for the Security of your own.

6. Be pleased, Sir, graciously to receive the Assurances, which we, your most dutiful and loyal Subjects, humbly presume to give your Majesty, That we will, to the utmost of our Power, and at the Expense of our Lives and Fortunes, support your Majesty, and the present happy Establishment in Church and State, against all your Enemies whatsoever.

[6] Boyer, *Political State*, XXXIV, 29.
[7] Journals of the Common Council, 57, ff. 154-155b; *British Journal*, June 24, 1727; Boyer, *Political State*, XXXIII, 569-571; XXXIV, 28-33.

Majesty, had already been drawn up and was then "lying" at various coffeehouses in London to be signed by the citizens.[8]

This Address, signed by "the Lord Mayor, the Aldermen, Recorder, Sheriffs, about a Hundred of the Common-Council, and by many Thousands of the most wealthy Merchants and other substantial Citizens," was presented to the King on Saturday, July 8.[9] The Lord Mayor, members of the Corporation, and other citizens of London turned out in great numbers to carry it to St. James's, "nearly 400 Gentlemen's Coaches, the greatest Part with 4 in a Coach," being in the procession from the Guildhall.[10] The King and Queen received them graciously, and allowed everyone to kiss their hands; the King then bestowed the honor of knighthood on the two sheriffs-elect,

[8] Repertories of the Court of Aldermen, 131, ff. 345-348; *Daily Post*, June 29, 1727; *London Journal*, July 1, 1727; *Daily Journal*, July 3, 1727.

[9] *British Gazetteer*, July 15, 1727. The text of the Address was as follows:

We your Majesty's most faithful and Dutiful Subjects, humbly beg Leave to approach your Royal Presence, being sensible of the Loss we have sustained by the Death of your Royal Father, our late most gracious Sovereign, and at the same Time to express the highest Satisfaction that Providence has secured to your Majesty a peaceable and happy Accession to the Throne.

Our Knowledge and Experience of your Majesty's eminent Bravery, your prudent Conduct, your Mildness and Clemency, give us Reason to hope for all the Blessings which can be expected under the best of Governments.

Your Majesty's most gracious Declaration of your paternal Love and Affection to this Country; of your indulgent Care for the Honour, Interest and Security of your People, confirms our Reliance on your Majesty, that you will preserve our Excellent Constitution in Church and State; that you will protect and effectually secure our Trade and Commerce, the Source of Wealth and Prosperity to this Nation.

Permit us, Sir, to assure your Majesty as becomes truly loyal Subjects, of our unfeigned Affection and most hearty Attachment to your Royal Person; and that we will exert ourselves upon all Occasions, for the Support of your Majesty's Government, and the happy Establishment in your Royal Family; and as we are too sensible of our Felicity in the Enjoyment of the Protestant Religion, our Laws and Liberties, to have the least Inclination to exchange them for Popery, Arbitrary Power and Misery; we shall always return an utter Abhorrence of any Measures which may favour the Hopes of the Pretender to your Majesty's Crown.

And we presume to add our most sincere Wishes for Health and long Life to your Majesty, your Royal Consort, and to all your Royal Offspring, not doubting but they will follow the Example and inherit the Princely Virtues of their Illustrious Parents: Thus your Majesty will have the Glory of yielding Happiness to your People in your own Time, and to be the Means of transmitting numberless Blessings to the latest Posterity.

[10] A writer in the Opposition's paper, the *Craftsman*, of July 15, insisted that there were only 176 coaches, but even this was an imposing number. The *Craftsman* had favored the previous Address which had been vetoed, saying at the time (issue of July 1) that "however improper some Expressions in the Address may be justly esteemed, the Substance of it cannot be supposed to be altogether repugnant to the good Sense of the City."

Richard Grosvenor and Thomas Lombe. "Thus was his Majesty pleased to favour the Zeal of the loyal Citizens; and thus impolitikly have those Gentlemen acted, who with the duty of an Address of Condolence and Congratulations would have mixed indecent Reflections," as Boyer commented in the following month's compilation of political news.[11]

The new King was well received in London. When he went to open Parliament on Tuesday, June 27, he was "follow'd with the Huzzas and Acclamations of a prodigious Number of People."[12] On Saturday, July 15, the King and Queen went "in an open Shallop with 12 Oars" for a boat ride on the Thames. As they passed by, flags waved from the embankment, ships hoisted their colors, and guns were fired. After landing, they proceeded to St. James's "amidst the Acclamations of Infinite Numbers of their delighted People."[13] This popular reception in London had its larger effects, also, for it was said that "the universal joy, satisfaction and congratulation which the People of this City expressed on his Majesty's accession, were soon communicated thro' the whole Kingdom and exerted the same general Demonstrations of Loyalty and Affection."[14]

The coronation of George II, in Westminster Abbey, was one of great splendor and magnificence, and took place on October 11, the day being concluded "with Bonfires, Illuminations, Ringing of Bells, and other publick Demonstrations of a general Joy and Satisfaction."[15] The King's first official visit to the City was made on the Lord Mayor's Day, when he was invited to the annual banquet at Guildhall, it being the custom for the monarch to attend the first one after his accession.[16] On that day, October 30 (October 29 falling on a Sunday in 1727), "their Majesties, the Princess Royal, and her Royal Highness

[11] *Political State*, XXXIV, 34. See the *London Gazette*, July 11, 1727, and the *British Gazetteer*, July 15, 1727.

[12] *Daily Post*, June 28, 1727.

[13] *London Journal*, July 22, 1727.

[14] *Craftsman*, Oct. 17, 1727.

[15] Boyer, *Political State*, XXXIV, 329-344.

[16] The Lord Mayor-elect was Sir Thomas Beecher, alderman of Bishopsgate Ward and next the chair, who was chosen on September 29, "without opposition." See Boyer, *Political State*, XXXIV, 298.

the Princess Carolina, came into Cheapside, about Three in the Afternoon, attended by the great Officers of the Court, and a numerous Train of the Nobility and Gentry, in their Coaches, the Streets being lined from Temple Bar by the Militia of London, and the Balconies adorned with Tapestry." At the Guildhall a magnificent dinner and entertainment were provided, speeches were made and toasts drunk to the royal guests and to the City of London, the King ordered a thousand pounds to be paid for the relief of the poor, and the evening was concluded with a Grand Ball. Then their Majesties returned to St. James's "with the same State they came. The Streets were again lined by the Trained Bands, the Houses all the way were Illuminated, and the People made loud Acclamations of Joy."[17]

THE "NEW OPPOSITION"

The new king might be popularly enthroned in the hearts of the citizens, but a new and rising opposition was developing against his Majesty's ministers. The rise of this "new opposition" has been described adequately by Charles B. Realey in his *Early Opposition to Sir Robert Walpole*.[18] Nevertheless, for the completeness of this story, it is necessary to mention here briefly its leaders, so that the reader may understand who was behind the formidable attacks on Walpole and his administration which developed during the reign of George II.

Previously, in the first years after Walpole had come into power, there had been noticeable weaknesses in the parliamentary opposition, chiefly through a lack of co-operation. The Jacobites, the Tories, the Whigs, and others were each working

[17] *Ibid.*, XXXIV, 358-388; Journals of the Common Council, 57, f. 162; Maitland, *History of London*, I, 541-543. Maitland also gives some details of the banquet, the whole cost of which was £4889 4 *s.* A total of 1,075 dishes was served the guests. The menu is not given, but 315 dozen bottles of wines (varying from "Champaigne" and Burgundy to Port and Old Hock) were ordered for the occasion.
[18] Pp. 155 ff. See also Walter Sichel, *Bolingbroke and His Times* (London, 1901-1902), II, 235 ff.; John, Lord Hervey, *Some Materials Towards Memoirs of the Reign of George II*, ed. Romney Sedgwick (hereinafter cited as Hervey, *Memoirs*) (London, 1931), I, 6 ff.; James Ralph, *A Critical History of the Administration of Sir Robert Walpole* (London, 1743), pp. 504 ff.; Taylor, *Robert Walpole: And His Age*, pp. 238 ff.; and H. M. C., *Onslow MSS*, pp. 465-472.

for themselves. There was "no centralized organization, no unified leadership, and no common principle" to make their opposition effective.[19] In the later years, however, although there was no party organization in the modern sense of the term, the opposition did have leadership and an increasingly effective organization, and its leaders became definitely united in their common hatred of the chief minister. Moreover, the scene of attack was shifted from the House of Lords to the House of Commons; and, by means of the press, an endeavor was made to arouse and enlist the support of the general public to the cause.

The rise of this "new opposition," as Realey terms it, may be dated in the spring of 1725. At the beginning of that year Walpole had no formidable rival. Of his earlier opponents, Bishop Atterbury had gone into exile (June, 1723) and Lord Cowper had died (October 10, 1723). Lord Sunderland, the chief of his Whig rivals, had also passed away (April 19, 1723); and Lord Oxford,[20] the leader of the old Tory group, had followed a year later (May 21, 1724). Lord Carteret, who had great aspirations, had been temporarily shelved by being sent to Ireland as Lord Lieutenant; he had been succeeded as Secretary of State by the less imaginative, but more dependable, Duke of Newcastle (April 3, 1724). So, during the years immediately following the suppression of the Jacobite plot, although there was opposition to the administration in Parliament, it was not of any consequence; and the country being at peace and trade flourishing, the national political scene remained relatively quiet.

It was in April, 1725, that William Pulteney first spoke in the House of Commons against Walpole and the administration, attacking the increased debts of the Civil List; and he continued to be in opposition until Walpole's fall in 1742, the year that really marked his own political retirement when he accepted a peerage and moved to the upper House as the Earl of Bath. Pulteney had been in close alliance with Walpole and his faction for many years, following him into opposition

[19] Realey, *Early Opposition*, p. 156.
[20] Robert Harley (1661-1724), first Earl of Oxford.

to Stanhope and Sunderland in 1717, and returning with him as a member of the administration in 1721. He had been rewarded with some offices and places, although not high ones; for although he had real abilities, he also had many weaknesses, and he did not command the confidence of Walpole. Therefore, he was passed over in 1724, when choice was made of a Secretary of State in place of Carteret. It was after this that Pulteney openly turned against Walpole, and from 1725 on he was a leading spirit of the opposition.[21]

Among his colleagues were Sir William Wyndham,[22] the leader of the so-called Hanoverian Tories, and William Shippen,[23] the admitted leader of the Jacobites in the House of Commons. Lord Hervey, in his *Memoirs,* speaks of Pulteney and Wyndham as the "Consuls" of the "Patriots (for so they were pleased to christen their faction)." He further notes the rivalry and jealousy between them.[24] Other important figures were Daniel Pulteney (a cousin of William), Sir Samuel Sandys, Sir John Rushout, and that able City merchant, John Barnard, in the lower House; and Lords Strafford, Lechmere, and Bathurst in the upper. In 1730 the latter were joined by Lord Carteret, following his dismissal from the Lord Lieutenancy; and in 1733 Lord Chesterfield,[25] dropped from favor

[21] Realey's excellent characterization of Pulteney (*Early Opposition,* pp. 160-166) leans slightly in his favor. See Taylor, *Robert Walpole,* pp. 238-241, for the opposite view.

[22] Sir William Wyndham (1687-1740), third baronet, had been a Tory member of Parliament since 1710. He was secretary at war in 1712-1713, and served as Chancellor of the Exchequer during the last year of Anne's reign. He was arrested for complicity in the rebellion of 1715, but was liberated on bail and never brought to trial. With Oxford and Bolingbroke out of the picture, Wyndham became the acknowledged leader of the Tory opposition to the new government. Not a great leader himself, however, he was generally considered little more than Bolingbroke's mouthpiece (J. R. MacDonald, *D. N. B.,* LXIII, 252-254).

[23] William Shippen (1673-1743) had been a Tory member since 1707. After the accession of George I he became the leader of the Jacobite members of the Commons, and was constantly in opposition to the ministers, on one occasion (in 1718) being sent to the Tower for a time because of his outspoken criticism of the King. He was known for "his courage, his incorruptibilty, his good humor, and his frankness of purpose" (Thomas Seccombe, *D. N. B.,* LII, 117-119).

[24] Hervey, *Memoirs,* I, 21.

[25] Philip Dormer Stanhope (1694-1773), first Earl of Chesterfield. Never friendly with Walpole, he had become temporarily reconciled in 1730 and was serving as Lord Steward of the Household (Sidney Lee, *D. N. B.,* LIV, 24-37).

because of his opposition to Walpole's Excise Bill, became one of their number.

Probably the most notable figure among the Opposition, however, was Henry St. John, Viscount Bolingbroke,[26] who sat in neither House, but contributed much to the strategy and the plan of attack, and the keeping together of the rivals Pulteney and Wyndham. He had been relieved of his attainder by Parliament in May, 1725, but Walpole's opposition had prevented the recovery of his seat among the Peers. He therefore, in the following year, began to vent all his personal antagonism on the Minister, and joined with the Pulteneys, Wyndham, and the others in their campaign to overthrow him. Many of their plans were made at Bolingbroke's farm at Dawley; there, too, they were joined by a number of the literary figures of the day, Alexander Pope, John Arbuthnot, John Gay, and Jonathan Swift, all united in opposition to Sir Robert Walpole.

Their chief weapon in stirring up public opinion against the ministry was the *Craftsman.* First published on December 5, 1726, as a single sheet, it appeared twice a week until May 13, 1727, when it was enlarged to four pages and continued as a weekly newspaper entitled *The Country Journal: or The Craftsman.*[27] Containing the usual news items, personal notes, and advertisements (of varied and sundry nature), the *Craftsman* put its chief interest in the letter or essay touching on some particular topic, which usually graced the front pages. Although contending that they presented the true situation to the general public, these essays were more often direct attacks on the Government. While they may now claim some place in English literature, truth and fair dealing were not the ideals of the writers, and they often descended to mere scurrility and in-

[26] Henry Saint-John (1678-1751), first Viscount Bolingbroke, had entered Parliament in 1701, the same year as Robert Walpole, and they continued bitter rivals throughout their careers. Leader with Harley of Anne's last ministry, Bolingbroke had fled to France in 1715 to escape impeachment. He served the Pretender a short time, and then spent the years following in philosophical studies, and in attempts to obtain a pardon from George I. See Leslie Stephen, "Henry Saint-John," *D. N. B.*, L, 129-144; Sichel, *Bolingbroke and His Times;* or Arthur Hassal, *Life of Viscount Bolingbroke* (Oxford, 1915).

[27] Implying by its name that it was the spokesman for the "Country" interests as opposed to the "Court."

vective, for which the printer and publisher were several times arrested and fined. The *Craftsman* was conducted by Nicholas Amhurst, who usually wrote under the pseudonym of "Caleb D'Anvers," while Lord Bolingbroke, William Pulteney, and his cousin Daniel were among the constant contributors. It soon became the official organ of the Opposition, and played a large part in appealing to the general public and in arousing resentment and hostility to the ministry. It was aided by Mist's *Weekly Journal* (renamed *Fog's* in 1728) and the *London Evening Post*, begun in 1727. Pamphlets and broadsides were also used effectively, and particular letters in the newspapers were often published in pamphlet form for a wider distribution.

Of course the ministry was not without its weapons and a host of "scribblers." Each morning the *Daily Courant* (succeeded in 1735 by the *Daily Gazetteer*) and the *Daily Journal* were distributed among the coffeehouses and to private homes, and weekly the administration's policies were likewise defended and the Opposition attacked in the *British Journal*, the *London Journal*, the *British Gazetteer*, and the *Free Briton*. Walpole himself was not averse to taking up his pen on occasion, and he was ably supported by men like Bishop Benjamin Hoadley, Lord Hervey, Thomas Gordon ("Cato"), William Arnall (who first wrote as "Roger Manley," later as "Francis Walsingham"), and James Pitt. "Francis Osborne" was the pseudonym of a number of ministerial writers contributing to the *London Journal*.

The writings of all these men, on both sides, while effective as political weapons, were naturally not great pieces of literature. Too often the writers let their passion run away with their reason, and the amount of "adjectival vapour" was large in proportion to the solid argument. Facts were blithely misrepresented in order to make out a good case, and personal attacks on opponents became the common thing. Nevertheless, they were sharp weapons, and they fulfilled their purpose of arousing public opinion. This was not accomplished in a moment, of course, but through the years, by constant attack and counterattack.[28]

During the last period of the reign of George I this new Opposition made little headway. With the accession of George II in the summer of 1727, however, hopes for a change in the ministry ran high. The new King, while Prince of Wales, had not been too friendly with Walpole; and at first it seemed that George II would lay him aside in favor of Spencer Compton, the speaker of the House of Commons. Walpole, however, was able to prove his ability to get things done. His control of a majority in Parliament assured the passing of an increased Civil List and the doubling of the Queen's jointure. Moreover, he had the active support of Queen Caroline. Therefore, he was soon in the good graces of the sovereign. With the new elections of parliamentary men in the fall, Walpole and his administration were made more secure than before.[29]

Parliament, which had reconvened on June 27, at the order of the King, was on August 5 ordered dissolved. Five days later a proclamation was made for the return of a new Parliament. The elections were hotly contested in all parts of the country. From some places came reports of riots and disorders, while charges of "barefaced Bribery" and "Corruption" were very common.[30] Neither side was free from this, but the administration's supporters, who were returned in a greater majority than before, naturally were given a full share. Consequently, the Opposition's spokesmen, finding solace only in abuse, according to one writer, "were reduced to vent their mortification in strictures against bribery, corruption, undue influence, and those secret intrigues in which they themselves were such adepts."[31]

[28] See Bourne, *English Newspapers: Chapters in the History of Journalism*, I, 96 ff.; Stevens, *Party Politics and English Journalism, 1702-1742*, pp. 118 ff.; and Stanley Morison, *The English Newspaper, 1622-1932* (Cambridge, 1932), pp. 81 ff. Valuable material is to be found in Laprade, *Public Opinion and Politics in Eighteenth Century England* (refer to newspaper articles and writers in the Index). See also *A Census of British Newspapers and Periodicals, 1620-1800*, by R. S. Crane and F. B. Kaye (Chapel Hill, 1927).
[29] Coxe, *Sir Robert Walpole*, I, 282 ff.; Hervey, *Memoirs*, I, 22 ff.
[30] Boyer, *Political State*, XXXIV, 152, 155.
[31] Joseph Grego, *A History of Parliamentary Elections and Electioneering in the Old Days . . . from the Stuarts to Queen Victoria* (London, 1886), p. 84. See Realey, *Early Opposition to Sir Robert Walpole*, pp. 228-229; and

The Parliamentary Election in the City

As had become the custom, the parliamentary election in the City was held after the majority of the country boroughs and towns had made returns of their representatives. In 1727, whereas these latter elections had been held beginning August 15, the London election did not take place until October 10. Nevertheless, it had been anticipated even before the old Parliament had been dissolved, and candidates were considered and named early in July. Thus there was time for a long and hard campaign which, though advantageous to the politicians, contributed, according to one writer, to "keeping up a continual Ferment, occasioning Disorders," and "giving Interruption to Business."[32]

The first newspaper advertisements appeared on July 12 and continued during the following days. Some of these asked support for a group which included Sir John Eyles (then Lord Mayor), Sir Gilbert Heathcote, Sir Richard Hopkins (member for the City in the late Parliament), and Sir John Thompson—all aldermen and loyal supporters of the national administration. Others contained the single name of Humphrey Parsons, alderman and opponent of the Walpole ministry. On July 15 there began a few days' run of notices nominating Micajah Perry, a tobacco merchant; on July 17 first notice was given of the nomination of four anti-Walpolians: Sir Francis Child, Richard Lockwood, and John Barnard (all elected at the last City parliamentary election), and Sir John Williams. The next day there began also advertisements for John Barnard alone.[33]

On July 19, at a meeting of the antiadministration forces in the City, held at Skinners' Hall, in Dowgate Street, Sir Francis Child was dropped from the previously proposed list, Humphrey Parsons was added, and Parsons, Williams, Lockwood, and Barnard were agreed upon as the list of candidates to be supported.[34] Advertisements for these men appeared, there-

S. H. Nulle, "The Duke of Newcastle and the Election of 1727," *Journal of Modern History*, IX, 1-22.

[32] "Caleb D'Anvers" in the *Craftsman*, Oct. 7, 1727.

[33] See issues of the *Daily Courant, Daily Journal, and Daily Post* beginning with those of July 12, 1727.

[34] *Daily Post*, July 20, 1727; *Daily Courant*, July 21, 1727.

fore, and continued to be run in the newspapers until the election on October 10, and afterwards while the poll was being taken, as were also those for the list agreed upon by the friends of the administration in the City at a meeting at the Crown Tavern, behind the Royal Exchange, on July 22. Sir Gilbert Heathcote, declining to run because of advancing age, was replaced by Micajah Perry; and the citizens there assembled agreed that their support would be given to Perry, Hopkins, Thompson, and Eyles.[35]

During August and September the campaign "was carried on, on both sides, with more than ordinary Industry, Application, and Animosity."[36] On October 7, "Caleb D'Anvers," writing in the *Craftsman*, gave the liverymen their final charge. He reminded them that London was the "Metropolis of this powerful Kingdom," that it was "the richest, if not the greatest City and Emporium in the Universe," and that it was "the Center of all the Wealth and Trade of the whole Kingdom, and consequently the fundamental Basis and Support of all our Manufactures, Navigation, and Maritime Power." He warned them that because of this importance "the Eyes of the whole Nation are constantly fixed on the Conduct and Proceedings of this City," and thus that London had "almost at any Time, in its Power to give a Turn to the Affairs of the whole Kingdom." He desired them, therefore, to be prudent and wise, to lay aside party distraction and "the foolish names of Whig and Tory," and to make good use of their opportunity to return to Parliament gentlemen who had previously been "the most strenuous Assertors" of their rights and privileges, and who are loyal supporters of the King—rather than "blind and servile" adherents of the ministry. "Let Party, Faction and meer Names have no weight in the Business of that day," he concluded, "but let an unbyassed Zeal for the Publick go hand in hand with Loyalty to your Prince; let your only Contention be, who are the most Worthy of your Choice; and let no Cries be heard against you, on that Occasion, but what are accom-

[35] *Daily Journal*, July 25, 1727; *Daily Post*, July 25, 1727.
[36] Boyer, *Political State*, XXXIV, 358.

panied with Liberty, King George, a Flourishing Trade, and the Present Happy Establishment."[37]

On Tuesday, October 10, the liverymen assembled at the Guildhall for the election, and a show of hands for the candidates was asked. The voting was fairly close, but, without putting up the candidates a second time, the sheriffs (Sir John Lock and Sir William Ogbourn, both administration supporters) declared that in their opinions the majority had fallen upon Sir John Eyles, Sir Richard Hopkins, Sir John Thompson, and Micajah Perry. A vigorous dissent was at once raised by the supporters of the other list; and the poll demanded, being granted, was begun the next morning. Since it was the day of the King's coronation, the poll was stopped after half an hour and was resumed Thursday morning, October 12.[38]

Then followed "a great Struggle between the two Parties."[39] Again a vigorous campaign was waged. Advertisements appeared in the newspapers, letters were published, and citizens, both for and against each list of candidates, gathered daily at various taverns and halls. The result of the poll was published each day to keep everyone informed, and the liverymen who had not voted were urged to cast their ballots. Charges of various sorts were freely made, and several arrests were made for false polling (including three Irishmen who were said to have each voted several times for John Barnard's list).[40] Of the reported bribes, one was of a certain Mr. Cowper of Southampton Street, who was said to have received five Guineas for a vote for Sir John Eyles and his list.[41]

On Wednesday, October 18, the poll closed, and the result was given as follows:[42]

Proadministration		Antiadministration	
Sir John Eyles	3,633	John Barnard	3,630
Micajah Perry	3,495	Humphrey Parsons	3,364
Sir John Thompson	3,339	Richard Lockwood	3,087
Sir Richard Hopkins	3,010	Sir John Williams	3,017

[37] *Craftsman*, Oct. 7, 1727.
[38] *Daily Journal*, Oct. 11, 1727; Boyer, *Political State*, XXXIV, 358.
[39] *Craftsman*, Oct. 21, 1727.   [40] *London Journal*, Oct. 21, 1727.
[41] *Craftsman*, Nov. 25, 1727.   [42] *Daily Courant*, Oct. 19, 1727.

According to this report, Eyles and Perry, Barnard and Parsons had the highest number of votes, and this was so declared by the sheriffs at a Court of Hustings held on the following Saturday (October 21). But the other candidates were not satisfied, and a scrutiny was demanded and granted, to begin on November 6.[43]

This scrutiny was the first demanded since the passage of the City Elections Act, and resulted because of the keen interest in the contest and the unwillingness of either side to admit victory or defeat. The election, however, was not marked by the disorders which had characterized those held previous to 1725. The scrutiny was conducted very carefully. The livery companies submitted their lists of members, and many of them were printed in the *Daily Journal,* the voters being urged to check them and report any frauds. By this means a number of false voters were readily discovered, yet the result of the poll as previously announced, was not affected since the number of these was about the same on both sides.[44] When, on Friday, November 24, the result of the scrutiny was announced, there was "a prodigious Number of People at Guildhall to hear the Declaration," and Sir John Eyles, Micajah Perry, John Barnard, and Humphrey Parsons were declared by the sheriffs to be duly elected representatives of the City in the forthcoming Parliament.[45]

Thus it turned out that two of the men chosen (Eyles and Perry) were of those friendly to the administration, while two (Barnard and Parsons) were definitely in opposition. By the friends of the latter two, this was considered a victory, especially so, since, as a writer in the *Craftsman* pointed out—or charged—just after the poll had been completed, there were so many citizens of London who were under the influence of the Government, they being "in some Degree or other, em-

---

[43] *Daily Journal,* Oct. 23, 1727.

[44] The number of votes was reduced for Eyles to 3,539, for Perry to 3,396, for Thompson to 3,244, and for Hopkins to 2,921—an average of 97 bad voters for each proadministration man. The number of votes for Barnard was reduced to 3,514, for Parsons to 3,255, for Lockwood to 2,977, and for Williams to 2,914—an average of 109 bad voters for each man on the antiadministration list. See the *Daily Post,* Nov. 25, 1727.

[45] *Daily Post,* Nov. 25, 1727.

ployed by, or under Obligations to, and Dependance upon the
Bank of England, the South Sea Company, the East India
Company, the Customs House, the Ordinance, the Excise Of-
fice, the Post Office, the Victualling Office, the Navy Office, and
the Salt Office, as well as several other powerful Companies,
Offices and Men in Authority."[46]

Dr. Stratford had taken cognizance of this point in a letter
to Lord Harley, a few weeks before, when he remarked that
"should the Tories carry it [the City Election] against the
Whigs, Court, Ministry, and the three great Companies, it
would be such a proof of their strength as never any party
gave before."[47] Although the Tories were not so fortunate,
nevertheless, after the election, Dr. Stratford was jubilant.
"The carrying of two in the City, under the present circumstances, is a great victory. Had all that were influenced by
Bank, South Sea and East India, by custom house, excise, post
office, &c., and all that did not vote at all, been left to themselves, it must have been carried by at least 4 to 1."[48]

But the ministers were also happy. Although they could
claim only two of the City representatives as being friendly,
this was one more than they had been able to count on in the
previous Parliament. Moreover, from the country as a whole
the returns had been so favorable that their majority in Parliament was now stronger than ever; and despite the rise of
the new leadership among the Opposition, the administration
in 1727 was firmly entrenched and confident of remaining in
power for some years to come.[49]

Nevertheless, despite this seeming security, the ministry did
not always have its own way, and its members were constantly
under fire from Pulteney and Bolingbroke and their supporters.
During the next five years opposition, in Parliament and in the
press, was manifested on every possible occasion, attacks were

[46] *Craftsman*, Oct. 28, 1727.

[47] H. M. C., *Portland MSS*, VII, 451 (Oct. 12, 1727).

[48] *Ibid.*, VII, 453 (Nov. 28, 1727).

[49] On November 7, 1727, the Duke of Newcastle wrote to the Earl of
Carlisle: "Things at home go extremely well; the King is in mighty good
humour, very gracious to us all, and I hope and believe, perfectly satisfied
with the management of his affairs" (H. M. C., *Carlisle MSS*, p. 52).

made on the chief minister, and repeated efforts were made to overthrow the administration. Not until 1733, however, did they have some success. Because of this fact and because the City of London was not drawn into the national picture (except as its representatives in the Commons took part in the debates there—of which our knowledge is very limited), these five years of the national situation can well be passed over as adding little to the London story. It was not until 1733, the year of the Excise Bill, that the Opposition at last attained sufficient strength to inflict a serious defeat on the chief minister. It was not until that year also that the City was again involved in the national picture. The local situation, meanwhile, during these first five years of the reign of George II, merits a thoughtful glance.

The London Political Scene, 1727-1732

On the whole, politics in London during this period were peaceful in character. There were no unusual contests at the local elections; no controversial subject was important enough to bring about a clash in the City between the friends and the foes of the administration. Yet it is to be noticed that in the elections of various Corporation officials during these five years unmistakable gains were made by those in the City who were opposed to the Walpole ministry. From Lord Mayor to members of the Common Council, the returns showed more and more the growing influence of the Opposition in City politics.

The election of Lord Mayors, of course, was still according to custom, the senior alderman below the chair being regularly elected to that highest office. Nevertheless, the circumstances were such that even here the friends of the opposition to the national administration fared very favorably; and following the mayorality of Sir Robert Baylis (a Walpole man), aldermen of the opposite political group were elected four years in a row. Sir Richard Brocas was chosen in September, 1729, Humphrey Parsons in 1730, and Sir Francis Child in 1731.[50] In 1732

[50] *Craftsman*, Sept. 30, 1729, and Oct. 1, 1731; *British Gazetteer*, Oct. 2, 1730; *Monthly Chronicle*, II (1729), 196; III (1730), 172; IV (1731), 170.

the choice fell on John Barber, the old Tory friend of Bolingbroke and Swift and a consistent opponent in the City of Sir
Robert Walpole, who held office until the autumn of the Excise
year of 1733.[51] These magistrates had great influence in the
Corporation and did much during their periods of office to turn
the City against the national administration.

Moreover, the elections of sheriffs during these years
showed also the return of a majority of antiadministration men.
The midsummer election of 1728 returned Aldermen Richard
Brocas and Richard Levett by a great majority.[52] It was very
gratifying to the opposition faction, and the writer in that
week's issue of the *Craftsman* congratulated the citizens on their
show of independence and their refusal to be influenced "by the
Artifices of any Tools of Powers within their own Walls, or
by Threats or Promises, Messages or Letters, from Persons at
the other End of the Town."[53] The next year John Barber
and Sir John Williams, two more aldermen of the same political creed, were elected, and the "Unanimity of the Liverymen" on this occasion was also very pleasing to the opposition
supporters.[54]

Then followed two years in which the pendulum swung
back and the elected sheriffs had the approval of the national
administration. Two commoners, Sir Isaac Shard, a Glover,
and John Fuller, a Distiller, were elected in June, 1730;[55]
and in June, 1731, Samuel Russell, a Cook, and Thomas Pinder,
a Salter, also both commoners, received the majority of hands.[56]
In the latter election a poll was demanded for Robert Westley,
a close friend of Alderman Barber; but the voting was light,
and no change appeared in the result.[57]

In 1732 the "Country" interests again gained control of the
shrievalty when Alderman Robert Alsop and Henry Hankey

[51] *Daily Courant*, Sept. 30, 1732; *Craftsman*, Oct. 4, 1732.
[52] *Brice's Weekly Journal*, June 28, 1728; *Mist's Weekly Journal*, June
29, 1728; Boyer, *Political State*, XXXV, 601.
[53] *Craftsman*, June 29, 1728.
[54] *Fog's Weekly Journal*, June 28, 1729; *British Gazetteer*, June 28, 1729.
[55] *Daily Courant*, June 25, 1730; Add. MSS, 27981, f. 155b (newsletter,
June 25, 1730).
[56] *Daily Post*, June 25, 1731.
[57] *Daily Courant*, June 30, 1731; *Monthly Chronicle*, IV (1731), 113.

were chosen. The majority of hands for them was so great that the taking of a poll was not even considered, and such was the quietness of City politics that year, a writer in the *Daily Courant* reported, that "the Friends of the abovesaid Gentlemen heard the Declaration with all the Temper and Quiet imaginable, without the use of the least Insult to their losing Opponents."[58] It was the quiet just before the storm which the Excise Bill blew up.

During all of these five years friction continued between the Court of Aldermen and the Court of Common Council. Nevertheless, the powers given to the Court of Aldermen by the City Elections Act kept the Common Council in a subservient position, and its infrequent meetings were in large part devoted merely to routine local matters. In their attitudes toward the national administration the two groups also continued to differ. The Common Council remained strongly antiadministration, and although the annual elections of councilmen saw struggles in some wards, the newspapers regularly reported that there was "very little Variation," or "no considerable Alteration," or that "a great Majority of the same Gentlemen who served before, were re-chosen" to that Court.[59] The Court of Aldermen, on the other hand, remained favorable to Walpole and the ministry. Nevertheless, here too, the opposition interests gained considerable ground during these first years of the reign of George II. At the beginning of the reign eighteen of the aldermen could be counted on as friends of the national administration, while eight voted regularly in opposition on questions involving national issues. In January, 1733, however, only fifteen of the former could, by their activities up to that time, be classed as Walpole men, while eleven aldermen cast their votes in opposition.

The first change came in September, 1727, upon the death of a pro-Walpole man, Sir Francis Forbes, alderman of Dowgate Ward. In his place was elected John Crowley, a wealthy

---

[58] *Daily Courant*, June 26, 1732. See also the *Daily Journal*, June 26, 1732, and the *London Magazine*, I (1732), 154.

[59] *Daily Post*, Dec. 25, 1728, Dec. 23, 1729, Dec. 24, 1730, and Dec. 22, 1732; *Craftsman*, Dec. 25, 1731; *Daily Journal*, Dec. 23, 1729, and Dec. 22, 1732; and *Gentleman's Magazine*, I (1731), 529, and II (1732), 1124.

Ironmonger,[60] who had been an Opposition member in the late Parliament for the town of Okehampton in Devonshire.[61] Then followed three aldermanic elections in which no change resulted. The first saw Thomas Preston, Vintner, in November, elected alderman of Bridge Ward Within to succeed Sir George Merttins. His proadministration opponent, Sir John Grosvenor, then one of the sheriffs of London, had demanded a poll after the show of hands, but Preston won by a majority of forty votes (150 to 110).[62] The second election came in January. Then antiadministration supporters were successful in retaining their gain of September in Dowgate Ward, when, upon the sudden death of Alderman Crowley, John Barnard was chosen his successor. Barnard, who had been persuaded to stand after repeated urgings by the inhabitants of the ward, was elected "without any opposition."[63] The third election saw Aldgate Ward stay in the pro-Walpole ranks; in February of the same year (1728) Micajah Perry was "unanimously" elected to succeed Alderman Sir Francis Porten.[64]

Following these came two important elections which deprived the majority aldermen of two of their number, and returned to the Court instead men critical of the national administration. The first was held on June 5. Two days earlier, Sir Randolph Knipe, alderman of Bassishaw Ward, had been found in one of the fishponds on his Epsom estate, accidentally drowned. At the Wardmote at Cowpers' Hall to elect his successor there was a close vote, but Sir Thomas Lombe,[65] one of the sheriffs then in office, was declared to have the majority,

[60] Crowley was "reckon'd the greatest Ironmonger in the King's Dominions, if not in all Europe," employing "above 20,000 Persons" in his works. His grandfather was the first to bring "the Art of making Steel" into England (from Germany), according to the *Daily Post*, Jan. 3, 1728. See also *British Gazetteer*, Jan. 6, 1728.

[61] Boyer, *Political State*, XXXIV, 298, 309.

[62] *Daily Post*, Nov. 7, 1727; Boyer, *Political State*, XXXIV, 510, 515.

[63] *Daily Post*, Jan. 5, 1728; *Daily Journal*, Jan. 3, 1728; *Craftsman*, Jan. 6, 1728.

[64] *Daily Journal*, Feb. 26, 1728; *Monthly Chronicle*, I (1728), 37, 38.

[65] Sir Thomas, a wealthy silk merchant, was responsible for developing in England the manufacture of the fine twisted silk called Italian *organzine*. See Cobbett, *Parliamentary History*, VIII, 924-929; *London Evening Post*, June 4, 1739.

an election which seems to have been largely influenced by Aldermen Humphrey Parsons and John Barnard.[66] Then, on September 4, Sir Peter Delmé, alderman of Langbourn Ward, died "in his Compting-House, of a fit of Apoplexy."[67] His successor was chosen only after a struggle. The candidates at first proposed were Henry Hankey, Haberdasher, and George Champion, Cooper. At the Wardmote at Pewters' Hall, however, Champion declined to run; and Edward Bridgen, a Turkey Merchant, was put up as the candidate of the friends of the ministry. The show of hands was close, but on the poll which followed, Hankey received the majority of votes (146 to 90) and was declared elected.[68] By these two elections, therefore, the majority group in the Court of Aldermen was reduced for the time being to fifteen members.

A little over a year later they succeeded in getting back one of the votes they had lost, when George Champion was elected alderman of Bridge Ward Within to succeed Thomas Preston, who died suddenly on Christmas Day, 1729.[69] And they retained this advantage in the following September, when John Salter, Merchant-Taylor, was "unanimously" chosen to succeed Sir Thomas Scawen as alderman of Cornhill Ward.[70] Nevertheless, they lost it again a year later, when Robert Godschall, Ironmonger, and brother-in-law of John Barnard, was elected by the antiadministration supporters to succeed the pro-Walpole Sir Edward Beecher, as alderman of Bishopsgate Ward.[71]

The last aldermanic election before the affair of the Excise came in January, 1733. On the twenty-fifth Sir Gilbert Heathcote, that staunch old Whig and friend of Walpole, and "Father of the City," died in his eighty-third year.[72] He was succeeded as alderman of Bridge Ward Without by the next senior alderman, Sir William Humphreys, alderman of Cheap Ward and likewise a Walpole supporter. To succeed Humphreys, the

---

[66] *Craftsman,* June 8, 1728; *British Gazetteer,* June 8, 1728.
[67] *Daily Journal,* Sept. 5, 1728; *Monthly Chronicle,* I (1728), 201.
[68] *Daily Journal,* Sept. 6 and 7, 1728; *Monthly Chronicle,* I (1728), 202.
[69] *Craftsman,* Dec. 27, 1729; *London Journal,* Dec. 27, 1729.
[70] *Daily Post-Boy,* Sept. 23, 1730; *British Gazetteer,* Sept. 26, 1730.
[71] *London Magazine,* I (1732), 313.
[72] *London Evening Post,* Jan. 27, 1733. Heathcote was perhaps the richest commoner in Great Britain, being worth £700,000 at his death.

"Court" interests put up Robert Kendall, a Fishmonger; and the "Country" party, Robert Westley, a Merchant-Taylor. On the show of hands at the Wardmote (January 27) the Lord Mayor, John Barber, declared in favor of Westley, but the supporters of Kendall immediately demanded a poll. When it was finished on January 30, Kendall was in front by a vote of 135 to 105. At this the followers of Westley demanded a scrutiny, but two days later they decided to give it up, and on February 3 Robert Kendall was declared duly elected alderman.[73]

In 1733, therefore, Walpole still had a majority of the Court of Aldermen favorable to him, although not as decisive a majority as it had been in the previous years. On questions affecting their own interests, however, the year would prove that even this declining majority could not be held in full allegiance. In the year 1733 came the Excise Bill.

[73] *London Evening Post*, Jan. 30, 1733; *British Gazetteer*, Feb. 3, 1733; *London Magazine*, II (1733), 44.

CHAPTER VI

The Excise Scheme

The Arousing of the Opposition

The story of Sir Robert Walpole's proposed bill to levy an excise tax on the import trade of tobacco and of its reception has often been told, and from various angles.[1] The part played by the City of London in this story has often been pointed out, but never described completely. It is doubtful if it ever will be possible to ascertain all of the facts concerning the trickery and wirepulling which stirred up the citizens against the scheme. Chiefly, of course, it was the mercantile interests of the City who were most concerned, and who were first aroused to take action. Yet, as in the case of the clamor raised in 1721 over the Quarantine Act,[2] the matter became in time of concern to all the citizens and to their government, and the defeat of the Excise Bill may be largely attributed to an "aroused" public opinion.

The controversy arose because Walpole, interested in developing the commerce and trade of the nation, was at the same time concerned with retaining the support of the landed gentry. For many years they had borne, by the Land Tax, the main strain of the national expense,[3] and Walpole was determined

[1] Lord Hervey's account in his *Memoirs of the Reign of George II*, I, 135-184, is the contemporary story, but it was not published (first edition in 1848) until after Archdeacon Coxe had written his *Memoirs . . . of Sir Robert Walpole* (1798). Coxe's version (I, 372-407), therefore, remained the authority for a long time. Of more recent studies the economic viewpoint is uppermost in Briscoe's *Economic Policy of Robert Walpole* (1907), pp. 94-126. Paul Vaucher, in his *La crise du ministere Walpole en 1733-1734* (1924), gives a general view based on previous works with some attention to the newspapers and pamphlets of the period. E. R. Turner's "The Excise Scheme of 1733," *English Historical Review*, XLII (1927), 34-57, is based on a more intensive review of the newspaper and pamphlet war carried on by the Opposition and the ministry.

[2] See pp. 33 ff., above.

[3] Since the Revolution they were said to have paid in over sixty-four million pounds. See Sir Thomas Robinson's speech of March 16, 1733, in Boyer, *Political State*, XLVI, 504.

that the merchants and men of trade should share the burden. "I have, Sir, with the deepest Concern observed, how heavy and unequal a Burthen has been long borne by the Landed Gentlemen of this Kingdom: I have long had it in my View to procure them some Ease."[4] As a first step the inland duties (or excise) on salt were revived, and in the session of 1732 the land tax was cut to one shilling in the pound.[5] Walpole declared a tax on salt was the most equal and the most general, therefore the most just.[6] Nevertheless, the salt duties and their collection had always been the cause of much complaint—which is why they had been abolished in 1730—and their revival was eagerly taken up by the Opposition. For this opportunity Pulteney and Wyndham and their followers had long been waiting. They immediately attacked the ministry, charging that the renewal of the excise on salt was but the prelude to further and more burdensome taxes. "This tax upon Salt . . . is one Step towards a General Excise," declared Sir William Wyndham in the Commons,[7] and his words were soon echoed in the public press.[8]

In October of that year (1732) the cry was repeated and taken up in earnest. The horrors of a "General Excise" were vividly depicted. Trade would be decreased, and the liberties of the people would be endangered. The number of excise men (revenue officers) would be increased to an army, and all rights taken away, homes subjected to search, elections brought under the control of the Crown, and other dark doings introduced. The *Craftsman* and *Fog's* led the attack; and pamphlet

[4] From Walpole's speech moving the revival of the salt duties on Feb. 9, 1732. See Richard Chandler, *The History and Proceedings of the House of Commons from the Restoration to the Present Time* (hereinafter cited as Chandler, *Commons' Debates*) (London, 1741-1744), VII, 160.

[5] 5 Geo. II, c. 5 and 6. The land tax in 1721, when the Walpole administration began, was three shillings in the pound. Walpole reduced this to two shillings in 1722, where it remained until 1727, when it was raised to four shillings because of the threatened war with Spain. It was reduced to three shillings in 1728 and to two shillings in 1730.

[6] Chandler, *Commons' Debates*, VII, 160.

[7] *Ibid.*, VII, 171.

[8] *Craftsman*, March 27, 1732. See the pamphlet attributed to William Pulteney, *The Case of the Revival of the Salt Duty, Fully Stated and Considered; with Some Remarks on the Present State of Affairs* (London, 1732).

and broadside, ballad and caricature, exaggerated the story.[9] The public was aroused almost to a state of frenzy.[10]   Nor was this hard to bring about, for a general excise had long been held in detestation and odium by the English people.[11]   In vain the *Courant,* the *Free Briton,* and the other organs of the administration denied that such a tax was being considered.   In vain, likewise, did they try to show that excise laws had great advantages in decreasing smuggling and in increasing revenues. Such explanations only added to the general apprehension and increased the belief that obnoxious measures were intended in the next session of Parliament.   Meetings, therefore, were held in protest, and letters were sent to members of Parliament from all over the kingdom.   "No slavery!   No excise!   No wooden shoes!" was the universal cry.[12]

London was the center of this excitement.   Her citizens were at all times exposed to the wordy barrage laid down by both the Court and the Opposition for and against the intended scheme, for it was in London that most of the newspapers and

[9] The study of the newspaper and pamphlet war has by no means been exhausted, and the material is voluminous.   This is most complete in the British Museum and the Guildhall Library, but the pages of the *Gentleman's Magazine* (II, 1732, 1021-1106, and III, 1733, 19-225) and of the *London Magazine* (I, 358-472, and II, 14-241) are a valuable aid to an understanding of the subject for those unable to go to London.

[10] "So universally were these terrors scattered through the nation, and so artfully were they instilled into the minds of the people . . . that there was hardly a town in England, great or small, where nine parts in ten of the inhabitants did not believe that this project was to establish a general excise, and that everything they eat or wore was to be taxed; that a colony of excise officers was to be settled in every village of the kingdom, and that they were to have a power to enter all houses at all hours; that every place and every person was to be liable to their search; and that such immense sums of money were to be raised by this project that the Commons would no longer be under the necessity of calling Parliaments for annual grants to support the Government, but be able to provide for itself, for the most part; and whenever it wanted any extraordinary supplies, that the excise officers, by their power, would be able at any time to choose just such a Parliament as the Crown should nominate and direct.

". . . Every alarm sounded from the faction in London came reverberated by a thousand echoes from every part of the country.   The whole nation was in a flame, and fresh fuel was constantly supplied by those who first kindled it, to keep it blazing" (Hervey, *Memoirs,* I, 145-146).

[11] Boyer, *Political State,* XLVI, 400; E. R. Turner, "Early Opinion About English Excise," *American Historical Review,* XXI (1915), 314-318.

[12] Hervey, *Memoirs,* I, 147.

pamphlets were published and first distributed. The people were, therefore, very readily aroused. Moreover, St. Stephen's Chapel was not far away, and the citizens of both high and low degree could be moved to fill its lobbies and crowd around its doors—demonstrations that made no small impression on the Parliament members. Nevertheless, in this Excise business, it was the merchants who took the lead, for, influenced by the leaders of the parliamentary opposition, and led to believe "that their own private Interests might suffer, they took all imaginable pains to make it the Concern of the Public."[13]

By December, 1732, the press campaign had effectively stirred up the bugbear of the Excise, and apprehension of further taxes and restrictions on trade was widespread. Tobacco, wines, and sugar were to be the first taxed; other goods would be included shortly thereafter.[14] The London merchants trading in these commodities naturally became alarmed. On December 22 a considerable number of them met at the Swan Tavern, in Cornhill, and unanimously resolved: "That the Merchants, Traders, and Citizens, here present, will act with the utmost Unanimity, and by all dutiful and lawful Methods, strenuously oppose any new Excise, or any Extension of the Excise Laws, under whatever Name or Pretence it may be attempted." They appointed a committee of twenty-five (which included such men as Aldermen Godschall and Champion, Sir William Chapman, John Bosworth,[15] Robert Willimot, Sir John Grosvenor, Richard Lockwood, and Daniel Lambert) to wait on the four members of Parliament for the City (Sir John Eyles, Sir John Barnard,[16] Humphrey Parsons, and Micajah Perry) with the resolution, and to urge them "to oppose with

[13] *An Impartial History of the Life . . . of John Barber*, p. 30.

[14] *London Evening Post*, Jan. 2, 1733.

[15] Bosworth, who was to be elected Chamberlain of London in 1734, was said to be the leader of the London tobacconists in their fight against the Excise; he "spared no Expense, Industry, or Interest, to disconcert that Scheme, and to oppose the Intentions of the Ministry" (*An Impartial History of the Life . . . of John Barber*, p. 30).

[16] Barnard had been knighted on September 27, 1732, upon the occasion of the City's presenting an Address to the King congratulating him upon his safe return from Hanover.

the utmost Vigour and Resolution any Motion of that kind in the House of Commons."[17]

During the next month there were frequent meetings of these and other merchants and traders "to consider Methods, & to oppose, in a dutiful Manner, a general Excise, if such a Thing should be offer'd."[18] On January 5 a general meeting of the Tobacconists of London was held,[19] and a week later the Grocers met together.[20] The Vintners, the Merchant-Taylors, and the Brewers also held meetings, and the spirit of opposition was taken up by groups all over the City.[21] "As for news, there is nothing here talked of but the new scheme of excise," wrote John Arbuthnot to Dean Swift on January 13.[22] A great many committees were appointed. One waited on Speaker Onslow and asked him to intercede for them.[23] Others engaged in sending letters to all parts of England, urging other cities and corporations to instruct their representatives in the Commons to work against the proposed measures.[24] "The affair of the Excise makes a great noise," wrote Lady Irwin to Lord Carlisle on January 9. "Bristol and Leicester have already sent instructions to their Members to oppose it, and 'tis said all the great towns in England will do the same. The merchants of London having informed their correspondents in the country, the apprehension is become general, especially amongst the traders in wine and tobacco, those being the first branches that will be attempted, as 'tis said."[25]

In February the subject was considered by the London Common Council, a special meeting being called by the Lord Mayor, John Barber.[26] Barber had long been opposed to Wal-

[17] Daily Journal, Dec. 23, 1732; Craftsman, Dec. 30, 1732.

[18] London Evening Post, Jan. 2, 1733. See also the London Journal, Jan. 13, 1733; London Evening Post, Jan. 17, 1733; and London Magazine, II (1733), 38.

[19] London Evening Post, Jan. 6, 1733.   [20] Craftsman, Jan. 13, 1733.

[21] London Evening Post, Jan. 11, 1733; British Gazetteer, Jan. 13, 1733.

[22] Ball, Correspondence of Jonathan Swift, IV, 379.

[23] London Evening Post, Jan. 13, 1733.

[24] Ibid., Jan. 13, 1733; London Magazine, II (1733), 38, 41; Gentleman's Magazine, III (1733), 43-44.

[25] H. M. C., Carlisle MSS, p. 95.

[26] Meetings of the Common Council were still limited to four a year, except when specially called by the Lord Mayor.

pole, but his opposition had been further strengthened by the activities of Walpole's enemies—Pulteney, Wyndham, and Lord Litchfield[27] being among those who had come into the City and so "Visited, Caressed, and abundantly Flattered" him, that he had become "more firmly Attached to them than ever."[28] The Council met on the fifteenth and unanimously voted "to Represent to their Members [in Parliament] the Inconveniences that will attend any new Excise or Extension of the Laws of Excise, and earnestly to Request them to Oppose the Same whenever any Attempt of that Kind shall be made in Parliament."[29] It then appointed a committee to draw up the Council's "Representation," or instructions.

The chosen members included many of the same men who had formed the committee appointed at the meeting of merchants and traders on the previous December 22, including Aldermen Brocas and Godschall (antiadministration), Aldermen Champion and Salter (proadministration), and a number of common councilmen who also held differing political views. At this time political affiliation was not binding. Aldermen and common councilmen joined together in one opposition. They had all been convinced that an attack was intended on their trade, and that the proposed measures (they had not yet been presented in Parliament) would be harmful to them. "The whole conversation of the Town is on the scheme we expect from Sir R——, which will extend the Excise Laws to wine and tobacco," wrote Sir Thomas Robinson to Lord Carlisle.[30] The press campaign had indeed done its work well, and the influence of the writings of Pulteney and Bolingbroke and the others may readily be discerned in the wording of the Representation "unanimously" agreed upon to be sent to the City members, which was as follows:

The Lord Mayor, Aldermen, and Commons of the City of London, in Common Council assembled, doth Represent;

That this Court doth apprehend from the Experience of the

[27] George Henry Lee (d. 1743), second Earl of Litchfield.
[28] *An Impartial History of the Life of . . . John Barber,* p. 30.
[29] Journals of the Common Council, 57, f. 274.
[30] H. M. C., *Carlisle MSS,* p. 101.

Laws of Excise now in being, that extending those Laws to any Commodities not yet Excis'd must necessarily be very prejudicial to Trade, both as it will probably diminish the Consumption of the Commodity to be Excis'd, and subject the Fair Trader to the frequent and Arbitrary Visitation of Officers and the Judicial Determination of Commissioners removeable at pleasure, from whom there is no Appeal.

That the Extension of such Laws must necessarily increase the Number and Power of Officers, which will be inconsistent with those principles of Liberty on which our happy Constitution is founded, and will further deprive the Subjects of England of some of those valuable Privileges which have hitherto distinguished them from the Neighboring Nations.

Wherefore this Court doth earnestly recommend it to You their Representatives, to use Your utmost Diligence in Opposing a Scheme of this Nature, should any such be offered in Parliament in any Shape or however limited in its first appearance; being fully convinced that an Inland Duty on Goods now rated at the Customs House, cannot be effectually collected even with an Extension of the Powers or the severest Exercise of all the Rigours of the present Laws of Excise.[31]

The long-awaited presentation of Walpole's "Scheme" was speeded up by the fact that the returns from the Salt Duty did not prove to be as great as had been expected. On February 23, 1733, Walpole asked that £500,000 might be taken from the Sinking Fund to supply the current expenses of the year. At once Pulteney objected, and in his speech he openly charged Walpole with planning a General Excise. "There is," he declared, "a very terrible Thing impending! A monstrous Project! Yea, more monstrous than has ever yet been represented! It is such a Project, as has struck Terror into the Minds of most Gentlemen within this House, and into the Minds of all Men without Doors, who have any regard to the Happiness of the Constitution of their Country. I mean, Sir, that Monster, the Excise!"[32] Walpole denied the monster, but admitted that he had a scheme in mind for the increase of

[31] Journals of the Common Council, 57, ff. 274-274b. See the *Weekly Miscellany*, Feb. 17, 1733.
[32] Boyer, *Political State*, XLVI, 118.

the revenues, and promised that he would soon disclose it. And he was not long in fulfilling his promise. On March 7 the Commissioners of the Customs were ordered to prepare an account of the frauds in the tobacco and wine trades since 1723, and at the same time it was resolved that the Parliament would meet to consider the better security of the revenues in those trades on March 14.[33]

As that day came nearer, the excitement throughout the country increased. Meetings continued to be held in the City against the proposed scheme, and a great many of the merchants went to St. Stephen's to solicit personally the members and urge them to oppose it.[34] On the morning of the great day, March 14, these merchants and other traders in tobacco, wines, coffee, tea, and other taxable merchandise, assembled before the Parliament doors. They were joined by numbers of other residents of London and Westminster, who crowded into the building and so filled the Court of Requests, Westminster Hall, the lobbies, and other rooms adjacent to the House of Commons that "the like was not seen in the Memory of Man."[35] To help prevent tumults and riots, and to preserve the peace, the reserves of Horse and Foot Guards were ordered in readiness at Whitehall, and the constables of Westminster were stationed all about.[36]

The personnel of this crowd was well known. A great many had come down because of their personal interest in the affair, but a great many more had been stirred up to go there, to influence and intimidate the members, and to make a great public show against what Walpole might propose. Walpole, himself, was well aware of the nature of this crowd and how it had been assembled:

There is now, Sir, a most extraordinary Concourse of People at our Door; I hope it will not be said, that all those People came there of themselves naturally, and without any instigation from others,

---

[33] *Journals of the House of Commons,* XXII, 77.

[34] *London Evening Post,* March 13, 1733.

[35] *Ibid.,* March 15, 1733; *Daily Journal,* March 15, 1733; *Craftsman,* March 17, 1733.

[36] *Daily Journal,* March 16, 1733; *Craftsman,* March 17, 1733.

for to my certain Knowledge, some very odd Methods were used to bring such Multitudes hither; circular letters, Sir, were wrote, and were sent by the Beadles, in the most publick and most unprecedented Manner, round almost every Ward in the City, summoning them upon their Peril to come down this Day to the House of Commons. This I am certain of, because I have one of those Letters in my Pocket, signed by a Deputy of one of the greatest Wards in the City of London, and sent by the Beadle to one of the Inhabitants of that Ward; and I know that such Letters were sent in the same Manner almost to every Liveryman and Tradesman in the Ward.[37]

In fact, Walpole was well aware of all the tricks of the Opposition in promoting the "Clamours which have been raised without Doors," and he added:

I am very far from taking them to be the sense of the Nation, or believing that the Sentiments of the Generality of the People were thereby expressed. The most Part of the People concerned in those Clamours did not speak their own Sentiments, they were plaid by others like so many Puppets: it was not the Puppets that spoke, it was those behind the Curtain that plaid them, and made them speak whatever they had in mind.[38]

Walpole was right in seeing Pulteney and Bolingbroke and their followers behind all this. The London merchants and men of influence there were in opposition mainly because they had come to believe that Walpole's measures would be to their hurt. The mob was for show, and it played its part effectively.

THE SCHEME AND ITS RECEPTION

In the House of Commons, on March 14, in a speech lasting two hours and a quarter, Walpole presented and defended his scheme to check the frauds in the tobacco trade and to give a square deal to the planters in America and the fair traders in England. It was aimed at smugglers, dishonest traders, and

[37] From Walpole's speech on March 14 in Boyer, *Political State*, XLVI, 409. Boyer (XLV, 339) prints a copy of a letter such as Walpole mentioned sent by the Deputy of Farringdon Ward Without. The *Craftsman* (March 17, 1733) reported that the Deputy and many citizens of that ward went in a body to Westminster on March 14.

[38] Boyer, *Political State*, XLVI, 409.

corrupt customs officials, and it was designed at increasing the revenues by insuring their collection. The plan, as Walpole outlined it, included the importation of tobacco free of duty, its storage in bonded warehouses, and the imposing of a tax or excise when the tobacco was brought out for sale in the domestic market, no charge being made for tobacco warehoused for re-exportation. By these means the trader's goods would be safely kept, and the payment and collection of duties assured. The warehouse scheme had been applied with considerable success to the tea, coffee, and chocolate trade since 1723; and Walpole felt that it should apply equally well now to tobacco, and later to wines. The frauds would be decreased, the revenues increased, and trade greatly benefited. Walpole envisioned London made a free port, and by consequence, the market of the world.[39]

It was an admirable plan, beneficial alike to both the commercial and landed interests, and would be approved by posterity. But the Opposition leaders in 1733 saw only an opportunity for an attack on the ministry, and their speakers arose to the occasion. Pulteney, Wyndham, Shippen, Sir Paul Methuen, Barnard, Perry, and George Heathcote were the most active. They declared that the accounts of the frauds had been exaggerated, and they denied that the planters and traders had been dealt with unfairly. Chiefly, however, they stressed the excise part of Walpole's scheme, for they knew they could make it the subject of popular animosity, and they depicted again the dangers which would arise from it, and how it would take away the liberties of the English people. All these charges Walpole ably refuted, both in his speech of presentation and in his rebuttal, and he showed that the people had nothing to fear. At the same time he warmly condemned the methods of the Opposition in stirring up popular unrest. He was seconded by Henry Pelham, Sir William Yonge, Sir Philip Yorke, and Sir Joseph Jekyll. The debate lasted until after midnight. When the question was finally put to a vote, Walpole was sup-

[39] The most complete account of Walpole's speech is in Coxe, *Sir Robert Walpole*, I, 385-399, compiled from the *Orford Papers*, *Political State*, and *Historical Register*.

ported by a majority of 61, the division showing 265 for the Excise Scheme and 204 against it.[40]

To the efforts of the Opposition the Londoners in Parliament gave full support. The records of the parliamentary debates at this time are very incomplete, but the speeches of three London merchants were important enough to be remembered. Sir John Barnard, representative of the City and a wine merchant, was the chief of these, and he combined his usual opposition to Walpole with his concern for restrictions on the wine trade.[41] Micajah Perry, also a representative of London and a tobacco merchant, who on other occasions was generally considered a Walpole supporter, was now alarmed for his business interests, and denied strongly the alleged frauds and irregularities of the tobacco trade.[42] The third of these was George Heathcote, a City wine merchant, who sat for the town of Hindon, in Witshire. A nephew of that old Whig, Sir Gilbert Heathcote, he had consistently been in opposition to Walpole, and he continued to be so on this occasion.[43] None of these speakers was really effective in replying to Walpole, except perhaps Barnard, but they were all voicing the opposition of the merchants of the City and the aroused citizens to the proposed scheme. On the division which followed the debate other City men in Parliament had a chance to register their dissent, and it is to be noticed that they were all numbered among the "Glorious Two Hundred and Four." Besides the four City representatives, Sir John Barnard, Sir John Eyles,

[40] See Boyer, *Political State*, XLVI, 376-425; H. M. C., *Carlisle MSS*, pp. 103-105 (Charles Howard to Lord Carlisle, March 15, 1733); and Coxe, *Sir Robert Walpole*, III, 129-131 (Charles Delafaye to the Earl of Waldegrave, March 15, 1733). Counting the tellers on each side, the figures on the division would be 266 to 205, which are given by some writers. The lists of those who voted on each side were published, and emphasis was attached to the number of those who voted for the Excise Scheme who held places, implying that they were "bought." The 204 who had voted in the negative received much commendation, their healths were drunk, and ballads about them were sung, one of them ending:

"Peace, Plenty, and Honour, with joy evermore,
Attend on the Glorious Two Hundred and Four."

—from "The British Merchant's Toast," Add. MSS, 31152, f. 12.
[41] Cobbett, *Parliamentary History*, VIII, 1291-1295, 1307.
[42] *Ibid.*, VIII, 1281-1285.
[43] *Ibid.*, VIII, 1296-1297.

Micajah Perry, and Humphrey Parsons, these also included Sir George Caswell (Leominster), Sir Francis Child (Middlesex), Sir John Williams (Aldborough), George Heathcote (Hindon), John Rudge (Evesham), Henry Furnese (Dover), and Sir Joseph Eyles (Southwark). Sir William Thompson, the Recorder of London, who sat for Ipswich, was evidently absent, since his vote is not recorded.[44]

The motion to bring in a bill, on March 16, reopened the debate, and it was carried on with all the intensity of the previous session. The administration's majority, however, was maintained, and a committee was ordered to prepare the bill.[45] Then followed a few days of calm for the House, while the members adjourned for the Easter holidays. But the clamor outdoors continued. In the City the merchants and tradesmen gathered in coffeehouse and tavern to voice their own opposition, to approve the latest pamphlet against the Scheme or the letters in the *Craftsman* or *Fog's*, and to condemn the offerings of the administration's writers. The *Daily Courant* came in for special censure, and the issue of March 15 was twice publicly burnt by the common hangman at Temple Bar, "for containing false and scandalous Reflexions on the Merchants and Traders of this City, for their Opposition to the Excise."[46] "It's inconceivable the clamour and spirit of opposition there is in this part of the world to this Scheme," wrote Charles Howard to Lord Carlisle on March 31.[47] Nevertheless, London was not alone, although the clamor was probably concentrated in greater intensity there. The same unrest and excitement were common throughout the kingdom.

The Excise Bill was brought in and given its first reading on April 4. Again the lobbies and rooms adjacent to the House of Commons were filled with the citizens of London and Westminster, including scores of merchants and traders in tobacco and wines and other commodities.[48] On this occasion the power

[44] For the lists on both sides, see Boyer, *Political State*, XLVI, 411 ff.
[45] Cobbett, *Parliamentary History*, VIII, 1314-1328.
[46] *London Evening Post*, March 27, 1733; *Craftsman*, March 31, 1733; *London Magazine*, II (1733), 159.
[47] H. M. C., *Carlisle MSS*, p. 105.
[48] *Daily Post*, April 5, 1733; *Craftsman*, April 7, 1733.

of the Opposition in the House was increasingly felt. On three successive divisions—on a motion that the bill be withdrawn, on a motion that the House adjourn, and on a motion for the second reading of the bill—the administration's wishes were upheld, but its majorities declined each time. This was plainly seen, and almost anything was to be expected at the second reading which was set for April 11.[49]

During the intervening week the clamor outdoors reached its height. Newspapers, pamphlets, and broadsheets spread the alarm far and wide, letters poured in to their members from cities and boroughs, and petitions and representations were sent to Parliament from all over England.[50] London itself "was in a great flame against the Excise."[51] On Sunday, April 8, Lord Perceval was informed that the City Fathers intended a march to the House to demonstrate against the bill. There was to be a great show of coaches, reaching from the Guildhall to Westminster, and the shops were to be closed so that "the apprentices may come down and make the greater crowd at the Parliament door."[52]

The City's action was considered the next day at another specially called meeting of the Common Council. The Lord Mayor, John Barber, opened the meeting:

Gentlemen,

There is a Bill depending in the House of Commons, (a Copy of which I have procured) laying an Inland Duty on Tobacco: which Duty, it is universally agreed, will prove extremely detrimental to the Trade and Commerce of this great City, as well as to that of the whole Nation. And as the high Station which I have the Honour to be in, obliges me to be watchful over every Thing that may affect the Interest of my Fellow-Citizens, I should think myself wanting in my Duty, if I neglected to call you together on this extraordinary Occasion, that you might have an opportunity to de-

[49] *Journals of the House of Commons*, XXII, 104; H. M. C., *Carlisle MSS*, p. 109; H. M. C., Eighteenth Report, *Manuscripts of the Earl of Egmont, Diary of Viscount Percival* (hereinafter cited as H. M. C., *Egmont Diary*), I, 347-354.
[50] *Weekly Register*, April 7, 1733; *Fog's Weekly Journal*, April 7, 1733; *Journals of the House of Commons*, XXII, 108-109.
[51] H. M. C., *Egmont Diary*, I, 356 (April 8, 1733).
[52] *Ibid.*

liberate on an affair of such Importance, wherin our Liberty and Property are so essentially concerned.[53]

The Excise Bill was then read and discussed, whereupon the aldermen and councilmen present unanimously agreed to petition the House of Commons against it. A committee (the same that had drawn up and presented the instructions of the Common Council to the City representatives in February) being appointed, it brought in the draft of a petition, which when read to the Council was also unanimously agreed upon, and ordered to be presented the next day at the Bar of the House by the Sheriffs.[54]

The petition was as follows:

> *To the Honourable the Commons of Great Britain in Parliament Assembled,*

The Humble Petition of the Lord Mayor, Aldermen, and Commons of the City of London in Common Council Assembled,

Sheweth,

That your petitioners observe in the Votes of the Honourable House, that a Bill hath been brought in, pursuant to the Resolutions of the Sixteenth Day of March last for repealing several Subsidies and an Impost now Payable on Tobacco of the British Plantations and for granting an Inland Duty in Lieu thereof.

That the Burthen of Taxes already imposed on every Branch of Trade however cheerfully born, is severely felt; but that Your Petitioners apprehend this Burthen will grow too heavy to be born, if it be increased by such Vexatious and oppressive Methods of levying and Collecting the Duty's, as they are Assured by Melancholy Experience, that the Nature of all Excises must necessarily produce.

That the Merchants, Tradesmen, and Manufacturers of this Kingdom have Supported themselves under the pressure of the Excise Laws in force by the comfortable Reasonable Expectation that Laws which nothing but publick necessity could be a Motive to Enact, would be repealed in favour of the Trade of the Nation,

[53] Journals of the Common Council, 57, f. 278b.

[54] *Ibid.*, 57, f. 279; *Daily Journal*, April 10, 1733; *London Evening Post*, April 10, 1733; Boyer, *Political State*, XLV, 436-438.

and of the Liberty of the Subject; whenever that Motive should be removed, as Your Petitioners presume it effectually is by undisturbed Tranquility at Home, and a General Peace so firmly established abroad.

That if this Expectation be entirely taken away, if the Excise Laws instead of being repealed, are Extended to other Species of Merchandise not yet Excised, and a Door opened for Extending them to all; Your Petitioners cannot, in Justice to themselves, to the Merchants, Tradesmen, and Manufacturers of the whole Kingdom and to the General Interest of their Country, conceal the Apprehension, that the most fatal Blow which ever was given, will be given on this occasion to the Trade and Navigation of Great Britain; that Great Spring from which the Wealth and prosperity of the Publick flows, will be Obstructed, the Mercantile part of the Nation will become, not only less able to trade to Advantage, but unwilling to Trade at all, for no Person who can Enjoy, all the Priviledges of a British Subject out of Trade, even with a small Fortune, will voluntarily renounce some of the most Valuable of those Priviledges, by subjecting himself to the Laws of Excise.

That Your Petitioners are able to shew that these their Apprehensions are founded both in Experience and in Reason. And therefore Your Petitioners must humbly pray, that this Honourable House will be pleased to Hear them by their Counsel against the said Bill.[55]

The next day, April 10, the petition was presented to the House of Commons, being carried there by "the Sheriffs of London, several Aldermen, and Common-Council, attended by most of the Merchants and eminent Traders of this City."[56] The more than two hundred coaches in the procession made a very impressive showing and brought forth the remark that "the Opposers of the Excise are not all Sturdy Beggars."[57] They were accompanied by the populace of London and Westminster; and as on the previous occasions, Westminster Hall was again filled, as were the lobbies and other halls, and the

[55] Journals of the Common Council, 57, ff. 279-279b.
[56] London Evening Post, April 10, 1733.
[57] Fog's Weekly Journal, April 14, 1733. "Sturdy Beggars" was the appellation used by Walpole in referring to the mob outside the Parliament door on March 14, and was taken up by the Opposition as pertaining to all the merchants and individuals opposed to the Excise.

near-by streets were crowded.[58]   The petition was presented in
due form.   Viscount Perceval's diary reveals the picture:

This morning I went earlier to the House than usual, expecting the
City petition against the Tobacco Bill.   Accordingly at one o'clock
it was presented by the Sheriffs of London.   It was handsomely but
strongly couched, and concluded with prayer it be heard by counsel
against it.   Alderman Parsons moved it might be received and read,
and that counsel might be heard according to the prayer of the
petition, which being seconded, Lord Malpas agreed to the receiving and reading it, but moved for an amendment to the motion
by leaving out the words, "to be heard by counsel".   This occasioned a debate till past ten o'clock, in which the great speakers on
both sides appeared.   On one side there spoke for allowing counsel:
Mr. Sands, Mr. Gibbons, Mr. Pulteney, Sr John Barnard, Alderman Perry, Sr Will. Wyndham, Counsellor Bootle, Sr Thomas
Ashton.   Against counsel: Mr. Winnington, Mr. Pelham, Sr Robert
Walpole, Attoney General, Sr Philip Yorke, Solicitor General, Mr.
Talbot, Sr Joseph Jekyl.[59]

Lord Perceval then gives the arguments of the debate, being
mainly over points of order—those opposed declaring that it
was unparliamentary for a petition to be received against money
bills, which they said the Excise Bill was, and those favoring
the City's petition quoting precedents, and urging that it warranted reception.   Continuing, however, Lord Perceval comments:

The true reasons why one side supported the petition was to delay
the Bill, and bring petitions against it from all parts of the kingdom,
for that had been the consequence of this if London had been heard
by counsel, and every petition praying the same we must have sat
all summer.

    The reason for opposing the petition was to preserve the Bill,
to give it despatch; wherefore, we who approved the Bill were
against allowing the City to be heard by counsel, and those who
disapproved it, voted against it.   On the division, we were but 214,
and the others 197, difference 17.[60]

    [58] *Post Boy*, April 12, 1733; *Craftsman*, April 14, 1733; *British Gazet-
teer*, April 14, 1733; *Weekly Miscellany*, April 14, 1733.
    [59] H. M. C., *Egmont Diary*, I, 358-359.
    [60] *Ibid.*, I, 359.

The City Petition thus failed in its object of obtaining a hearing against the bill to excise tobacco, but it proved to be successful in that it finally showed Walpole that he had better drop that bill.[61] For not only was it representative of the attitude of the citizens of London, and indeed the whole country, but the division on the motion to receive it showed once more the declining majorities of the administration in Parliament.[62] Walpole was thus convinced that even if the Bill should pass the Commons, he would have difficulties in enforcing the measure.[63]

The Minister, therefore, considered it strategic to retreat. "This dance it will no further go," he told his friends in the evening of the day that the City's petition was rejected,[64] and the next day (April 11) he moved that the second reading be postponed until June 12, a move "which you know is equivalent to dropping it entirely for the Session," as one correspondent wrote.[65] According to Viscount Perceval again:

His reasons for giving it up [he said] were three; first the declension of the majority, which showed itself the first day, being 61, which last night he saw reduced to 17; secondly, the clamours raised against it, which though artificially stirred up, yet it was not prudent to press a thing which the nation expressed so general a

[61] According to Hervey (*Memoirs*, I, 156), Walpole had become convinced on the night before to drop the Bill, but he had then decided to wait until after the City petition had been rejected "lest it should be thought to be done by the weight and power of the City."

[62] The voting on the bill had been as follows. On March 14, when the scheme was first introduced, it was upheld by a vote of 265 to 204. On March 16, in voting on the resolutions, the vote was 249 to 189. On April 4 the three divisions after the bill was read the first time showed votes of 232 to 176, 237 to 199, and 236 to 200. The next day, in a small House, a motion to print the bill was defeated 128 to 112. And on April 10 the City petition was defeated 214 to 197. The majorities were thus 61, 60, 56, 38, 36, 16, and 17.

[63] "Should the Bill pass, and the City of London resolve not to comply with it, as I hear they will not, then the Excise officers must call for the army to support them, and what consequences may not be apprehended from it," wrote Lord Perceval on April 7, and two days later he added: "I heard the City have declared, pass what Bill you will, they won't comply with it" (H. M. C., *Egmont Diary*, I, 355, 357).

[64] Hervey, *Memoirs*, I, 162.

[65] Add. MSS, 15868, f. 161 (Edward Weston to James Dayrolle, April 20, 1733).

dislike to, however they were deceived; and thirdly, which was with him of most moment, the apprehensions which many honest and sincere friends of the Government had entertained of danger to his Majesty's person and Government from the disaffection which they supposed this Bill, however mistaken, might create in the abused people's minds; which alone was reason sufficient to justify his parting with the Bill.[66]

Great rejoicings followed the postponement. The people had been so filled with alarm over an intended "General Excise" that the relief was unbounded when the imagined danger was removed. "Last Night Bonfires, Ringing of Bells, and other Demonstrations of Joy were shewn throughout the City."[67] The Monument and the Bank of England were illuminated, as were also many private houses. "The City seemed to be nothing but one continued Blaze of Light."[68] At Temple Bar, in front of the Guildhall, and in Smithfield, effigies of Walpole and the Queen were burnt. At other places the crowd treated figures of excise officers in the same manner. Cockades were worn bearing the motto of "Liberty, Prosperity, and no Excise." Taverns and coffeehouses rang with the shouts of the merrymakers, and healths were drunk to the King, to the Lord Mayor and Common Council of London, to the leaders of the Opposition in Parliament, and to the "Glorious Two Hundred and Four."[69] The same rejoicing was observed in many other cities and towns. "All our news for this Week as well as last, have been full of the great Rejoycings made throughout England, on account of the putting off of the late Excise Scheme."[70]

Nor was it all in good spirit. In the City the mobs inflicted much damage. They broke the windows of the Post Office and of many houses of people suspected of favoring the scheme.[71] Moreover, those who waited outside the Houses of Parliament

---

[66] H. M. C., *Egmont Diary*, I, 360.
[67] *Daily Journal*, April 12, 1733.
[68] *The Bee*, I, 431 (April 14, 1733).
[69] *Daily Journal*, April 12, 1733; *London Evening Post*, April 12, 1733; *London Magazine*, II (1733), 211; H. M. C., *Egmont Diary*, I, 362,
[70] *Fog's Weekly Journal*, April 28, 1733. See also *The Bee*, I, 475-476 (April 21, 1733).
[71] *Daily Post*, April 13, 1733.

were very tumultuous and menaced and insulted many of the Members who had favored the Excise, including Sir Robert Walpole himself. ". . . they enclosed him on all sides, crying 'Damn you! no Excise!' The mob bore him from one side of the Court of Requests to the other; numbers of sticks were held up over his head; and one fellow caught hold of his collar, and gave him a great pull, whether with a design to throw him off his feet, which if it had happened they would have trod him to death, or what, I can't tell. In this situation he was in for some time, till with great difficulty he got to his chariot, and got away."[72]

This action came in for much censure in the Commons the next day, and several resolutions were passed *nemine contradicente* condemning the use of mobs to promote or impede bills in the House as " a most outrageous and dangerous Violation of the Rights of Parliament, and an high Crime and Misdemeanor."[73] Proper indignation was expressed at the whole conduct of the City mobs, and the resolutions, which were ordered sent to the Lord Mayor of London and to the Sheriffs of London and Middlesex, were really a vote of censure of the City and its government.[74] The feelings of the latter, however, being far from penitent, were plainly perceived in the attitude of the Lord Mayor, John Barber, a few weeks later, when the Grand Jury was engaged in investigating the late tumultuous proceedings in the City, and he cautioned that body to distinguish properly between "Public Rejoicings" and "Riotous Mobbings."[75]

The City of London was happy upon the defeat of the Excise Bill, and on April 18 the Common Council expressed its gratitude to those of the Corporation who had aided in bringing it about. According to the Journals:

This Court doth unanimously Return Thanks to their Representatives in Parliament for the great Regard shown by them to

[72] H. M. C., *Carlisle MSS*, p. 108 (Charles Howard to Lord Carlisle). For similar accounts, see H. M. C., *Carlisle MSS*, p. 110; H. M. C., *Egmont Diary*, I, 362; and Hervey, *Memoirs*, I, 164.
[73] *Journals of the House of Commons*, XXII, 115.
[74] Hervey, *Memoirs*, I, 166-167; Boyer, *Political State*, XLVI, 517-518.
[75] *Gentleman's Magazine*, III (1733), 266.

the Representation of this Court and to the Trade and Liberty of their Fellow Citizens in steadily and Strenuously opposing any Extension of Excise Laws which by Melancholy Experience are found highly prejudicial to the Fair Trader and the Liberty of the Subject.

This Court doth unanimously Return Thanks to the Right Honourable John Barber, Esquire, Lord Mayor, for his Care and Vigilance for the Welfare and Prosperity of this City and particularly for so timely and seasonably calling us together, and Laying before us a Copie of a Bill then depending in Parliament for Laying an Inland Duty on Tobacco Whereby We had an Opportunity to Apply by Petition to the House of Commons against the said Bill which was attended with Success.

This Court doth return Thanks to Sir Frances Child, Knt, Sir John Williams, Knight Alderman, and Sir George Caswell, Knight, Members of the Court for their Steady and Strenuous Opposing the said Bill.[76]

The Bill was defeated, and all those who had worked against it rejoiced, but the victory for the Opposition in Parliament was short-lived. Only ten days after Walpole announced the postponement, Sir John Barnard presented a petition of the dealers in tea and coffee, asking that they be relieved of the excise laws on their commodities. They hoped to gain by the feeling in the Commons aroused by the tobacco bill. Such was the strength of the administration, however, that the petition was rejected by a vote of 250 to 150,[77] plainly showing that "although numbers went off the Court in the affair of the excising tobacco and wines, yet they had not deserted their party and become malcontents, as the minority flattered themselves."[78] The administration was still strong.

This was further proved on April 25, when the ministry succeeded, by a good majority, in naming all of the committee of twenty-one persons to examine into the frauds of the customs.[79] It was the turn of the leaders of the Walpole administration to be joyful. They had gained a "noble victory" as

[76] Journals of the Common Council, 57, f. 280b.
[77] Journals of the House of Commons, XXII, 123.
[78] H. M. C., Egmont Diary, I, 365.
[79] Journals of the House of Commons, XXII, 127; H. M. C., Egmont Diary, I, 365, 367; Hervey, Memoirs, I, 179-184.

Thomas Pelham wrote to Lord Waldegrave. "Our success in these two points, added to the King's declared support of the present ministry by the examples his majesty has already made of some who would obstruct their measures,[80] has effectively disappointed the views of the opposers in the progress of the session."[81] Nevertheless, the defeat of the Excise Bill had given the ministry a real scare, and as had been predicted, the subject was not brought up again during the session, which ended in June. The excitement aroused, however, did not immediately die. Throughout 1733 and into the following year newspapers and pamphlets kept up the flame, and it continued to be a topic of importance through the parliamentary elections of 1734.

Its Effect on London Elections, 1733-1734

In the local elections held in London during 1733 feeling over the Excise affair was especially noticeable. The Londoners seem to have been drawn together in their common opposition to what they felt was to be a restriction on their trade. This unanimity was seen in the election of sheriffs in June and of the Lord Mayor in September. Robert Westley, a Merchant-Taylor, and Daniel Lambert, a Mercer, were elected "unanimously" to the shrievalty;[82] and Sir William Billers, alderman of Cordwainer Ward, and the next below the chair, was chosen without opposition as successor to John Barber.[83]

The election of a Chamberlain for the City in March, 1734, upon the death of Colonel John Robinson is interesting, not only because there was a real contest, but also because John Bosworth, who was finally elected, had been the leader of the City tobacco merchants in their opposition to the Excise Bill.[84] The election "came on" at the Guildhall on March 21, and the

---

[80] Referring to the dismissal of Lord Chesterfield and Baron Clinton from their places on April 13, which was followed by the removal of Lords Cobham, Montrose, and Marchmont in June, and of Bolton in August.

[81] Coxe, *Sir Robert Walpole*, III, 132 (April 26, 1733).

[82] *London Magazine*, II (1733), 306, 369; *Gentleman's Magazine*, III (1733), 377.

[83] Boyer, *Political State*, XLVI, 338; *London Magazine*, II (1733), 475.

[84] See p. 141, n. 15, above.

candidates were Bosworth, William Selwin, and John Thomas.
Bosworth was declared by the sheriffs to have the majority of
hands, but a poll was demanded for Selwin. Then followed
what was termed "the greatest and most equal Struggle that
ever was known in this City."[85] Both candidates were "of that
Party which is now called the Country Party; but Mr. Selwin,
besides his own particular Friends, had the Court Interest entirely in his Favour," because of Bosworth's activities of the
year before.[86] Nevertheless, Bosworth won, although by a
very small majority, the poll showing a difference of only seven
votes (3,326 to 3,319), which was further reduced to four by
the scrutiny demanded for Selwin (3,312 to 3,308). Bosworth
was declared elected Chamberlain of the City on April 4.[87]

Two weeks later a proclamation was issued by the King dis-
solving the Parliament, the first of George II, and ordering
the election of a new one by the thirteenth of June.[88] The defeat of the Excise a year before and the growing strength of
the Opposition promised to make this general election a real
test for the administration. Yet, when the struggle was over,
the administration of Sir Robert Walpole still remained in
power, and the country as a whole had returned him a good
majority, although it was not as large as he had had previously.[89] To the casual observer it was amazing. Even Pulteney was puzzled. The English must be "slaves," he wrote
to Swift in the following year; otherwise how "would it have
been possible for the same Minister who had projected the
Excise Scheme, before the heats it had occasioned with the

[85] Boyer, *Political State*, XLVII, 331.

[86] *Ibid.*, XLVII, 332.

[87] Boyer, *Political State*, XLVII, 549. See also the *London Magazine*,
III (1734), 264-265; and the *Weekly Miscellany*, May 11, 1734. An interesting sidelight is noticed by John Entick, in his *History and Survey of
London, Westminster, and Southwark*. He says (II, 439): "The court party,
to shew their resentment to the city for so strenuous an opposition to a candidate set up by the ministry, would not indulge Mr. Chamberlain Bosworth
with the office of receiver-general of the land-tax, which had generally been
annexed to the chamberlainship; but gave that lucrative office to their disappointed friend Mr. Selwin."

[88] *Journals of the House of Commons*, XXII, 316.

[89] According to the *London Evening Post* of June 29, 1734, 308 members
for the Court, and 251 members for the Country, gave Walpole a majority
of 57 members.

nation were well laid, to have chosen a new Parliament again exactly to his mind, and though perhaps not altogether so strong in numbers, yet as well disposed in general to his purposes as he could wish."[90]

The answer lay in the power and influence which the administration controlled. The victory had been foreseen, and the reasons for it had been set down by George Dodington in writing to the Duke of Dorset on the previous January 15. "That there will be a Whigg Parliament, there is no doubt, and I think, considering the reall weight that the families, fortunes, and interest of them in the King's service naturally gives us, separate from the vast influence of the power and very great revenue of the Crown (if either should be made use of), I say I think there is no room to doubt but that it will be a Court Parliament."[91]

The administration still had sufficient weight throughout the country to swing a general election, even in the face of what appeared to be a contrary public opinion. For the opinion of the general public was not necessarily shared by the more limited number who held the franchise, and who were subject to the influence of members of the ruling classes. Nevertheless, it is significant that the Opposition did make important gains, and Walpole was made to realize the growing strength of those who comprised it.

In London they were very successful, and the Excise played an important role in the election of the City's four representatives. "The Voting for or against the Excise has been the chief (though not the sole) Guide for the members chosen," declared one writer.[92] Excitement had been further stirred up on this score on April 11, the anniversary of the day on which the Excise had been dropped. The citizens had planned

---

[90] Ball, *Correspondence of Jonathan Swift*, V, 280.

[91] H. M. C., Ninth Report, Appendix, Part III, *The Manuscripts of Mrs. Stopford Sackville, of Droyton House, Northamptonshire* (hereinafter cited as *Sackville MSS*), p. 35. For more light on the influence mentioned, and especially the part played by the Duke of Newcastle in elections in various parts of the country (not in London), see Basil Williams, "The Duke of Newcastle and the Election of 1734," *English Historical Review*, XLV (1897), 448-488.

[92] In the *London Evening Post*, June 8, 1734.

to make a great celebration, but the Lord Mayor, Sir William Billers, and the Court of Aldermen, not wishing to offend the national administration, published an order against all such public rejoicings. Nevertheless, the spirit of the people ran high; a number of "bonefires" were lit and houses illuminated to celebrate the occasion. In fact, the mob, as usual, got out of hand, the windows of the Lord Mayor's house and those of some of the aldermen being broken, and Sir William wounded in the head when he attempted to stop it.[93]

Advertisements for the candidates first appeared in the *Daily Journal* and the *London Evening Post* on April 18, and in the following days support was asked for Sir John Barnard, Micajah Perry, George Chapman, Robert Godschall, John Barber,[94] Robert Willimot, and Joseph Chitty. Single advertisements were the most common, but some grouped Barnard, Perry, Chapman, and Godschall together on one list. The election was held on Tuesday, the last day of April. The candidates were severally put up, and on the first show of hands Barnard, Barber, and Parsons received an overwhelming majority. The other candidates were then put up a second time, and Godschall was said to have the majority. Barnard, Barber, Parsons, and Godschall were therefore declared elected; but upon this being challenged by the friends of Perry and Willimot, a poll was granted.[95]

For eight days the voting was carried on. Advertisements appeared daily for each of the candidates, and the liverymen were urged to vote for the right men. Throughout the poll

[93] Boyer, *Political State*, XLVII, 437; H. M. C., *Egmont Diary*, II, 82.

[94] Viscount Perceval records (H. M. C., *Egmont Diary*, II, 67) that "great offense" had been taken in the City upon the presentation of an Address to his Majesty upon the marriage of the Princess Royal with the Prince of Orange (March 17) by the Lord Mayor, Aldermen, and Common Councilmen (Boyer, *Political State*, XLVII, 326-327) because they had not been given the honor of kissing the King's hand (really a blunder on the part of the Duke of Grafton, the Lord Chamberlain, according to Hervey, *Memoirs*, I, 281, but spread about as being a mark of the King's resentment at certain references in the Address), and therefore a group of the citizens had "met that very night and agreed to put up Alderman Barber in nomination for a member at the ensuing election, who is an acknowledged enemy of the Government."

[95] *London Evening Post*, April 30, 1734; *Daily Journal*, May 1, 1734; Boyer, *Political State*, XLVII, 547-548.

Barnard and Parsons maintained a comfortable lead, and Perry ran a close third. The contest was between Barber, Godschall, and Willimot. Barber was personally very popular in the City because of his leadership in opposing the Excise, but he was running as an independent candidate, while Barnard, Parsons, Perry, and Willimot were now being supported on a list. Moreover, he was the subject of many attacks by the administration's press writers,[96] and he was opposed by the Dissenters among the liverymen.[97] Then, on May 6, Godschall withdrew his candidacy; and Willimot forged ahead, receiving the votes of many who would have supported Godschall. Two days later, Wednesday, May 8, when the poll closed, the election was clearly decided: Sir John Barnard, Humphrey Parsons, Micajah Perry, and Robert Willimot were declared the representatives of the City in the next Parliament.[98]

Unlike previous contests at the City parliamentary elections, this was not really a struggle between the proadministration and antiadministration interests. Rather, the City at this time being so singularly united, the question of who was for or who was against Walpole was not the chief issue; and after the show of hands had limited the candidates to men, all of whom had been "zealous Opposers of the late Excise Schemes," the struggle during the poll was largely a personal one, Barber alone being singled out for opposition by supporters of the Court interests. Of the four men elected, Barnard and Parsons were

[96] See the *London Journal*, April 20, 1734; the *Free Briton* of May 4 and 16, 1734; and the *London Magazine*, III (1734), 215.

[97] *Daily Post*, May 4, 1734. Despite these handicaps Barber received a sizable vote, which, quoting the *London Evening Post* of May 11, "plainly shews what a Regard the Grateful Part of the City paid him for his eminent Services."

[98] *London Evening Post*, May 9, 1734; *Daily Journal*, May 9, 1734; *Craftsman*, May 11, 1734. The voting on the poll and the standing of each candidate each day were as follows:

	Thursday May 1	Friday May 2	Saturday May 3	Monday May 6	Tuesday May 7	Wednesday May 8
Barnard	276 (1)	577 (1)	974 (1)	2042 (2)	3033 (2)	3840 (2)
Parsons	267 (2)	556 (2)	930 (2)	2046 (1)	3070 (1)	3932 (1)
Perry	208 (3)	463 (3)	799 (3)	1850 (3)	2893 (3)	3725 (3)
Godschall	182 (4)	364 (4)	577 (4)	1078 (6)	....	....
Barber	157 (5)	311 (5)	478 (5)	1243 (5)	1877 (5)	2381 (5)
Willimot	100 (6)	273 (6)	477 (6)	1361 (4)	2214 (4)	2984 (4)

confirmed anti-Walpolians, while Perry and Willimot had gone into opposition when the Excise Scheme was proposed, and continued to act so until the fall of the Walpole administration in 1742.[99]

In the City, therefore, Walpole had suffered serious defeats as a result of the Excise Scheme of 1733 and the parliamentary election of 1734. During the following years he was to find the citizens increasingly at variance with his policies.

[99] Thomas Osborne, in the *London Journal* of July 6, 1734, admits that the London representatives could not be counted as "Court Members," but he pointed out that, unlike the "Patriots," they were not against the administration "in all Points." He had no doubt, he added, but that the London members "will prove themselves Friends to their Country; and therefore Friends to the Court."

CHAPTER VII

The London Scene, 1734-1738

THE MANSION HOUSE FUND "RACKET"

THE POLITICAL situation in London, during the next year or two, was marked by no unusual contests involving the interests of the national administration in the City. In fact, even in Parliament there was a quiet period in contrast with the storm aroused by the Excise Bill. During the two sessions that followed, after its hopes for a victory in the general election of 1734 had been frustrated, the Opposition remained in a "very languid" way. It needed time to recover from its disappointments and to gird its loins for the next battle. The session of 1736 was especially quiet. Bolingbroke had retired to France in the preceding year. Pulteney, discouraged and sick in body, absented himself a great deal from the House and in May left England to consult doctors on the Continent. Wyndham, thus deprived of both his "private prompter" and his "coadjutor in public action," proved incapable of formidable leadership.[1]

Effective opposition, in both the City and the nation, did not again arise until 1737, and it reached its height in the following year only when the grievances of the British merchants over the depredations of the Spaniards united all the anti-Walpole interests against that Minister. Meanwhile, the London scene unfolded.

During the intervening years the chief magistrates of the City continued to be chosen according to custom. Sir Edward Bellamy was the senior alderman below the chair in September, 1734, and was chosen Lord Mayor on Michaelmas Day to succeed Sir William Billers. In the following year Sir John Williams was elected to the mayoralty. In 1736, upon the deaths of the three aldermen next in line, the choice fell upon

[1] Mahon, *History of England, 1713-1783*, II, 178-180; Hervey, *Memoirs*, II, 529; Coxe, *Sir Robert Walpole*, II, 333 ff.; Ball, *Correspondence of Swift*, V, 333 ff.; *London Magazine*, V (1736), 278.

Sir John Thompson. He was followed by Sir John Barnard in 1737, and in 1738 Micajah Perry was given the honor. All of these men were chosen in the usual form and without opposition, according to the newspapers of the time, which was in striking contrast with the situation that developed in the following year, 1739, and which will be given full consideration in the next chapter. Even Sir John Barnard was not turned down, despite some unpopularity prior to his election.[2] In none of these elections did the issue of national politics have a part.

The same was true in the midsummer elections of sheriffs. In fact, in these elections, the chief concern of the liverymen seems to have been to elect, not men whom they wanted in office, but rather men whom they did not want and who did not want the office themselves. Peculiar as this seems, it nevertheless was true. The explanation lies in the fact that in 1728 the Corporation had definitely decided that the City should have a residence for its Lord Mayors, and on April 30, 1730, the Common Council passed a resolution that all fines paid in to the City Chamber for being excused the office of sheriff (amounting to 400 pounds and 20 marks each) were to be laid out in 3 per cent annuities, to be applied towards the building of a Mansion House.[3]

[2] This was on account of his introducing into Parliament early in 1737 a bill to lower the interest rate on the public debts from 4 to 3 per cent. He thereby incurred the enmity of "the Jews and the Stock-brokers," and on the night that the bill was defeated (249 to 134) he was burnt in effigy and had the windows of his house broken by the fickle mob, while the cry in the streets was "Long live Sir Robert Walpole!" Lord Percival comments: "This may be a lesson to men not to rely on popularity. A few years past Sir John was the darling of the City, for the opposition he gave to the Excise scheme . . . Sir Robert Walpole, for inventing and pressing it was burnt, as Sir John is now. But now the service of the one and the demerit of the other is forgotten" (H. M. C., *Egmont Diary*, II, 396, April 30, 1737). See also H. M. C., *Carlisle MSS*, pp. 182-184; Coxe, *Sir Robert Walpole*, I, 497-509; *Memoirs of the Late Sir John Barnard*, pp. 13-14; *A Letter to a Livery-Man* [Sir John Barnard] *Occasion'd by His Commencing Projector* (London, 1737); *Considerations upon a Proposal for Lowering the Interest of All Redeemable National Debts to Three Per Cent. per Ann.* (London, 1737).

[3] Journals of the Common Council, 57, f. 225; Boyer, *Political State*, XLVII, 324. There were several reasons for asking to be excused. Ill-health and age were common, also religious qualifications (see note on Dissenters below), but the chief one was financial. The office of sheriff was costly, because of the entertainment expected, and the holders really had to be men of wealth.

During the years immediately following this move party interests had continued to be the chief issue at the various shrievalty elections, but after the City opposition to the Walpole administration in 1733 had united, to a large degree, the different political elements in London, this issue became no longer paramount. Instead, the elections became regular occasions for the promotion of contributions to the increase of the Mansion House fund, and the citizens became so fond of the project that they waited "with no small Impatience" to hear each time whether those elected would accept the office or pay the fine.[4] A long list of names was put in nomination each year, a great many of them Dissenters,[5] by the process of being drunk to by the Lord Mayor;[6] and these had the privilege of "swearing off" and paying their fines, or standing election. If, in the latter case, they were elected and then should refuse to serve, they were subject to a fine of £600. It really became what in twentieth-century parlance is called a "racket."

At the beginning of 1734, as a result of these procedures, the Mansion House fund stood at £3,550.[7] However, such was the number of those who swore off before the Midsummer Day election of that year or after it, necessitating several more elections during the summer months, that by September (after thirty-seven men had been excused) the fund had swollen to nearly £18,000,[8] and by December it had risen to £19,655.[9] Incidentally, those who were finally chosen that year and who accepted the office (on September 13) were Aldermen Micajah Perry and John Salter.[10]

In the following year a number of those on the list paid their fines before the election, but the election itself was conducted very quietly, and Alderman Sir John Barnard and his

---

[4] Add. MSS, 27981, f. 158.

[5] Dissenters were really barred from holding city offices by the Corporation Act (13 Car. II, s. 2, c. 1), since most of them would not take the sacrament of the Church of England.

[6] It was the custom for the Lord Mayor to nominate one gentleman every Tuesday, from the fourteenth of April to the fourteenth of June. See Boyer, *Political State*, LVII, 394.

[7] Boyer, *Political State*, XLVIII, 10.

[8] *Daily Journal*, Sept. 6, 1734; *Weekly Miscellany*, Sept. 14, 1734.

[9] *London Magazine*, III (1734), 665.

[10] *Daily Courant*, Sept. 14, 1734.

brother-in-law Alderman Robert Godschall were chosen "almost unanimously," and agreed to serve.[11]   This situation was repeated in June, 1736, when two commoners, William Rous, a Salter, and Benjamin Rawlins, an Apothecary, were elected and accepted the office, six other citizens previously nominated having paid their fines.[12]

In June, 1737, Henry Benyon and Thomas Russell, Haberdashers, were chosen.   Benyon, however, swore off and paid his fine, on account of his health.   On July 19 John Marlowe, a wholesale Grocer, was chosen in his place; but he, too, paid his fine soon afterward.   Finally, on June 28, Alderman Sir George Champion was chosen "by a great majority."   In the meantime seven others had paid their fines to prevent being elected.[13]   Russell and Champion were sworn in on September 28, but Russell died soon after Christmas, and Alderman Robert Cater was chosen at a special election to serve the remainder of his term.[14]

Similar situations prevailed at the elections of 1738 and 1739.   In the former John Wightman, a Brewer, and James Brooks, a Stationer, were chosen on June 24; but Wightman could not qualify, being a Protestant Dissenter, and William Westbroke, a Goldsmith, was chosen and sworn in with Brooks to serve for the ensuing year.[15]   In 1739 William Townshend, Merchant-Taylor, and Robert Grosvenor, Leatherseller, were chosen, but both "swore off."   Grosvenor, who was a Dissenter, had at first refused to pay the fine, on the ground that the City resolution of 1730 was contrary to the Toleration Act of 1689,[16] but when taken up in the courts the case was decided against

[11] *London Evening Post*, June 24, 1735; *Daily Journal*, June 25, 1735; *Old Whig, or, Consistent Protestant*, June 26, 1735.

[12] *Daily Journal*, June 25, 1736; *London Evening Post*, June 26, 1736; *Gentleman's Magazine*, VI (1736), 354.

[13] *London Evening Post*, June 25 and July 28, 1737; *Old Whig*, June 30, 1737; *London Magazine*, VI (1737), 396, 397; *Gentleman's Magazine*, VII (1737), 370, 449.

[14] *London Magazine*, VII (1738), 48.

[15] *Ibid.*, VII (1738), 308, 360, 465; *Gentleman's Magazine*, VIII (1738), 325, 489; *Daily Advertiser*, June 26 and July 7, 1738.

[16] 1 W. & M., s. 1, c. 18.

him.[17] On July 3 Aldermen George Heathcote and Sir John Lequesne were elected sheriffs and agreed to serve.[18]

WALPOLE'S MAJORITY IN THE COURT OF ALDERMEN DECLINES

The elections of aldermen during the years between 1734 and 1738 continued to show the declining power of the Walpole administration among the members of the Court of Aldermen. Ten changes were made during this period, and while the majority of the new aldermen were theoretically of the same political belief as their particular predecessors, three anti-administration men were returned from wards which had formerly elected proadministration aldermen. The complexion of the Court thereby changed from fifteen to eleven in favor of the ministry to fourteen to twelve against it. Moreover, the effects of the Excise scheme and the feeling in the City which had developed against Walpole in the years following were such that he could not count regularly on even those twelve who were nominally for him. So by 1737 Walpole seems to have lost largely what influence he did have in the City, and the activities of the Londoners during the war with Spain contributed in a large way to his final overthrow.

The first of these changes came late in 1735. On October 12 of that year Sir John Tash, alderman of Walbrook Ward, died. He had been a strong Whig, as had been Sir Gilbert Heathcote, who served the ward before him. His successor, however, was

[17] In 1742 the Common Council made the resolution of the year 1730 into a bylaw, and then proceeded deliberately to nominate and choose Dissenters in order to fine them. Court proceedings were instituted by the Dissenters in 1754, but it was not until 1767, in the House of Lords, that judgment was finally given in favor of the Nonconformists, and henceforth they were excepted from office and the payment of fines. For Lord Mansfield's speech ("of classic eloquence") on the case, see Philip Furneaux, *Letters to the Honourable Mr. Justice Blackstone*, Appendix, pp. 249-284. See also Sir Walter Besant, *London in the Eighteenth Century*, pp. 22-23.

[18] Boyer, *Political State*, LVIII, 283; *Common Sense, or, The English-man's Journal*, July 7, 1739. In the same year (1739) work was begun on the Mansion House, on the site occupied by the Stocks Market since 1282, and the cornerstone was laid on October 25. The income from fines, at 3 per cent interest, proved ample for the construction and furnishing of the new building, and it was finished in 1752. Sir Crisp Gascoigne, elected in September of that year, was the first Lord Mayor to take up his residence there. The total cost of building the Mansion House was £42,639. See Sidney Perks, *The History of the Mansion House* (Cambridge, 1922).

Sir Gilbert's nephew, George Heathcote, who had been in the opposition to Walpole since his first entrance to Parliament in 1727 (he was now sitting for Southwark), being especially active at the time of the Excise Bill. Because of his uncle, as well as in his own right, he was very popular in the ward, and won his election "without a Negative." Then he "treated" all the good citizens of the ward "in a very elegant and Polite Manner."[19]

In the same month died Sir William Humphreys, alderman of Bridge Ward Without and a supporter of Walpole. The senior alderman, who would normally take his place as "Father of the City," was Sir Charles Peers, of Tower Ward; but Sir Charles was passed over for the next in line, and Sir Gerard Conyers, alderman of Broad Street Ward, was transferred to Bridge Without. It was given out that Peers was too old and infirm, but the "Country Interest" hinted that the real reason lay in the fact that the "Court" supporters knew that his successor would be an opposition man, while they thought that they had strength enough in Conyers' ward to elect an alderman favorable to them.[20] Be this as it may, the "Country" candidate, Deputy John Lequesne, gained the majority of votes over his opponent, Sir William Chapman, at the election on October 30 (191 to 103); and the declaration was "received with loud universal Acclamations, not only in the Hall, but thro' the Streets when he passed in the Ward."[21]

Following these two victories of the "Country" interest, which brought the balance of the Court of Aldermen to an even thirteen, the two following elections resulted in no further change. Going over into the next year (1736), on January 2, came the death of Sir Richard Hopkins of Lime Street Ward, the senior alderman below the chair. A warm contest followed at the Wardmote held three days later. The candidates were Robert Willimot, Cooper, and a member of Parliament for the City, who had the support of the pro-Walpole interests, and

[19] *London Evening Post*, Oct. 14 and 16, 1735; *Daily Journal*, Oct. 15, 1735; *London Daily Post, and General Advertiser*, Oct. 15, 1735.

[20] *Daily Journal*, Oct. 28, 1735; *London Evening Post*, Oct. 28, 1735.

[21] *London Evening Post*, Oct. 28, 30, and Nov. 1, 1735; *London Daily Post*, Oct. 28 and 31, 1735.

Thomas Pomeroy, a wholesale Linen Draper, and Deputy of the Ward, who was supported by the opposition. The show of hands was equal, and the poll itself extremely close, being 62 for Willimot and 61 for Pomeroy. A scrutiny, however, was granted, and increased the majority to nine, the good votes proving to be 56 for Willimot and only 47 for Pomeroy. Willimot was therefore declared on January 28 to be the next alderman.[22] A year later Sir Henry Hankey, alderman of Langbourn Ward, died. At the Wardmote on February 1 there was no contest at all, since his son, Joseph Hankey, also a Haberdasher, was proposed and elected "without opposition." Both the Hankeys were anti-Walpole in their political views.[23]

The next election, which definitely changed the balance of the Court of Aldermen away from the administration, was also held on February 1, 1737, following upon the death of Sir Charles Peers, alderman of Tower Ward. As had been predicted in the *London Evening Post* over a year before,[24] the "Country" interests were able to elect his successor. Their candidate was Daniel Lambert, a wine merchant, who had played an active part against the Excise scheme; he was opposed by Peter Burrel, a banker. The former was declared to have the majority of hands, but in a poll that followed it was charged that "Influence" was freely used for the "Court" candidate. Lambert, however, easily emerged the victor, the votes on the poll being 196 to 98. A writer in the *London Evening Post* commented: "These 196 deserve to have their Names wrote in Letters of Gold, and transmitted to Posterity as Supporters of Liberty and Property, scandalously attack'd by Menaces, Threats, and large offers of Gold. It is thought that if every Elector had been left to his own Choice, without any unfair Practices, Mr. Lambert would have had 250 Votes out of the 292. Last Night there were Bonfires, Illuminations, and great Rejoycings throughout the Ward."[25]

[22] *Daily Journal*, June 3, 6, and 29, 1736; *London Evening Post*, June 3, 6, and 29, 1736.
[23] *Daily Gazetteer*, Jan. 31 and Feb. 2, 1737; *London Evening Post*, Feb. 1, 1737.   [24] See p. 169, above.
[25] *London Evening Post*, Feb. 3, 1737. See also the issues of Jan. 29 and Feb. 1 of the same paper; the *British Gazetteer*, Jan. 31 and Feb. 5; and the

In consequence of this election, the balance of the Court of Alderman was, from February, 1737, definitely in the favor of the anti-Walpole interests. Moreover, although there were a number of other elections before the Walpole administration ended, this was the last one which resulted in a change of "party" power in the wards. Nevertheless, the feeling continued to be intense, the methods used by the "Court" adherents in some of these elections arousing pointed comments from some of the writers in the "Country" interest.

The year 1737 continued to take its toll of the older aldermen. Robert Alsop, alderman of Queenhithe Ward, and next the chair, died on March 12. His successor, Robert Westley, Merchant-Taylor, was quickly chosen, and elected without the least opposition. It was even stated that "no Courtier could be chosen in that Ward if they spent 10,000 pounds."[26]   In July, however, the opposite was the case; and the "Court" maintained its hold in two wards when, upon the death of Sir Gerard Conyers, of Bridge Ward Without, he was succeeded as senior alderman and "Father of the City" by Sir John Eyles, who in turn was succeeded as alderman of Vintry Ward by Sir William Rous, a Druggist, for whom no opposition was raised on July 22, when the Wardmote was held.[27]

There was a real contest in Farringdon Ward Within upon the death of Richard Brocas, on November 7.[28] The candidates were Henry Marshall, Draper, a member of Parliament for Aversham, in Buckinghamshire, who stood "in the Country Interest," and William Selwin, a Government "place" man,

---

Craftsman, Feb. 5, 1737. Typical of the electioneering, the following verses were printed and posted in various parts of the ward:

> Rouse, Citizens, be on your Guard,
>   If Courtiers cringe into you;
> Their Views are not to serve the Ward
>   But fleece and quite undo you.
>
> Then if you would our Trade retain,
>   Let Lambert be your Choice;
> Brave Lambert will your Rights maintain
>   Secure from Party Noise.

[26] *London Evening Post*, March 12 and 15, 1737.
[27] *Ibid.*, July 21 and 23, 1737.
[28] *Ibid.*, Nov. 8, 1737.

being Receiver-General of the Land Tax for London and Middlesex. At the Wardmote Marshall had the majority of hands, and succeeded in gaining the majority of votes on the poll which followed, although only after a struggle. The final count showed 383 for Marshall and 327 for Selwin.[29] The "Country" interests were extremely pleased; one of their writers reported that the declaration of Marshall's election was received by "the most universal Acclimation of Joy ever heard at a Wardmote, it being look'd upon that the Court Interest will never be able to make a Head any more in that Ward."[30]

But such was not the case in Cheap Ward a year and a half later, following the death of Sir Robert Cater on the last day of 1738.[31] Great interest developed in this election, the "Court" supporting Sir Joseph Eyles, brother of Sir John, and the "Country" backing Richard Hoare, a grandson of the famous banker of the same name. On January 4, 1739, at the Wardmote, the show of hands was so equal that a poll was demanded and agreed upon by both sides. While it was being taken, charges flew freely, the supporters of Eyles receiving the more blame. Typical of these was the report that a number of men had been "given Half a Crown each and a good Dinner and Drink, to huzza at the Bonfire in Cheapside for Sir Joseph Eyles, where two Barrels of Beer were given away amongst the Mob."[32] "Bank-Bills" were "plentifully thrown about," another writer charged; and still another reported that "towards the Close of the Poll, Turkies and Quarters of Lamb fetch'd a most extravagant Price in a neighboring Market; they were sold for above two Guineas a Pound."[33] When the poll ended,

[29] Ibid., Nov. 10, 1737; Craftsman, Nov. 12, 1737.
[30] London Evening Post, Nov. 12, 1737.
[31] Daily Advertiser, Jan. 1, 1739; London Evening Post, Jan. 2, 1739. Sir Robert was a Kendall (see p. 137, above), but changed his name in order to inherit the estates of his brother-in-law, Sir John Cater, in Bedfordshire. See Boyer, Political State, LVII, 86.
[32] London Evening Post, Feb. 1, 1739; Boyer, Political State, LVII, 105-106.
[33] London Evening Post, Jan. 4, 1739; Craftsman, Jan. 6, 1739; Gentleman's Magazine, IX (1739), 45; Boyer, Political State, LVII, 17. The opposition newspapers of this period were full of charges against the electioneering methods used on behalf of "Court" candidates. No doubt there was some truth in the charges, but they were as applicable to one side as the other. And it is to be noticed that despite the outcries of these newspapers, it was the "Country" candidates who at this time won most of the elections.

Eyles led, but by only one vote (137 to 136); and the closeness is more apparent when we read that "the Minute the Books were clos'd, two Persons came in to Poll for Mr. Hoare, which would have made a Majority for him."[34] But it was too late, and the scrutiny which his friends demanded likewise did not help him, for when it ended on January 29 Sir Joseph Eyles was declared elected, with a majority of nine votes (125 to 116).[35] To celebrate his election, Eyles then gave a "grand entertainment" at the Bedford-Head Tavern in the Poultry, "where all the Gentlemen of the Ward were invited."[36]

It is interesting to note that this same intense activity by the "Court Interest," so prevalent in the aldermanic elections, was also to be seen in the Common Council elections during these years—according to reports in the Opposition organ, the *London Evening Post*, which seems to have been the only newspaper considering the results of these elections of enough interest to print. Nevertheless, this activity availed nothing, and the Common Council continued, as it had been all through Walpole's administration, to be strongly opposed to him. The report of the 1736 election very plainly stated that the election was carried by a great majority against "those that have for many Years vainly attempted to bring the Common-Council of the City of London, under the Influence of the Court, and be (like themselves) the Creatures of the Ministry."[37] In 1739 the "Court Party" was charged with greater use of bribery than ever before, especially in Bishopsgate and Bridge Within Wards, where several taverns were said to have been "open'd," and where "luxurious Living has prevail'd."[38] Notwithstanding this, there was no better success; and after the election it was stated that "the Majority of True Friends to their Country is larger than ever . . . notwithstanding the flattering Promises, Corruptions and Menaces" of the friends of the ministry.[39]

[34] Boyer, *Political State*, LVII, 17; *Common Sense*, Jan. 6, 1739.
[35] *London Evening Post*, Jan. 30, 1739; *Gentleman's Magazine*, IX (1739), 46.
[36] Boyer, *Political State*, LVII, 96.
[37] *London Evening Post*, Dec. 21, 1736.
[38] *Ibid.*, Dec. 18, 21, and 22, 1739.
[39] *Gentleman's Magazine*, X (1740), 91.

Such abuse of their opponents was typical of all these elections, but to the end of the period of the Walpole administration common councilmen in the "Country Interest" were regularly returned a majority over the "Courtiers."[40]

FREDERICK, PRINCE OF WALES

It was during these years after the middle of the decade that the City came to be on good terms with Frederick, Prince of Wales,[41] and thereby came in closer contact than before with the parliamentary Opposition of which the Prince had become the center.[42] On April 29, 1736, upon the occasion of his marriage, the Lord Mayor and members of the Court of Aldermen went to St. James's and presented addresses of congratulations and good wishes, first to the King and Queen, and later to the Prince and Princess.[43] All four of the royal family received the Londoners very graciously, but the Prince is reported to have received them "with peculiar Marks of Condescension and Goodness."[44] One part of the interview is particularly entertaining:

[40] See the *London Evening Post* for Dec. 22, 1737; Dec. 21, 1738; and Dec. 24, 1740. Also *Champion*, Dec. 25, 1739; and Boyer, *Political State*, LVII, 1-3; LVIII, 519-539; and LIX, 3-7.

[41] Frederick Louis, son of George II and Queen Caroline, was born in Hanover, came to England in 1728, and died there in 1751. The Prince did not get along with his father or his mother. They were constantly at odds on a number of points, but Frederick was particularly vexed by the fact that he had no income of his own, and was forced to submit to the generosity of his parsimonious sire. This point was aggravated after the Prince's marriage, in April, 1736, to the Princess Augusta of Saxe Gotha, and it led to his demand for a permanent income of £100,000 a year, a demand which was taken up by the Opposition as a possible means of embarrassing Walpole by infuriating the King. Fortunately for Walpole, however, the bill proposed was defeated, on February 22, 1737. In September of that year, because of his conduct at the time of the birth of his first child, the Prince was ordered from St. James's, and took up his residence at Norfolk House. See Hervey, *Memoirs*, III, 661 ff., 806 ff.; Coxe, *Sir Robert Walpole*, pp. 519 ff. See also the Appendix to the *Diary of George Bubb Dodington* (London, 1785). For a recent study of the Prince, see Sir George Young's *Poor Fred: The People's Prince* (London, 1937).

[42] Lord Bolingbroke, early after the Prince's arrival in England, had paid court to him; and he was soon joined by Pulteney, Wyndham, Carteret, Chesterfield, Swift, and Pope. After 1733 they were joined by Cobham and his "Boys," namely, Pitt, Lyttleton, and the Grenvilles.

[43] Repertories of the Court of Aldermen, 140, f. 254; Journals of the Common Council, 57, ff. 375-377.

[44] *London Magazine*, V (1736), 275.

Among other obliging Things he told them, that he was sorry the Princess was not so well versed in the English Language, as to return an Answer to them in it; but that he would be answerable for her, that she should soon learn it, and inquir'd of Sir John Barnard, if he understood French, to speak to her Royal Highness in that Tongue. Sir John handsomely excusing himself, referr'd to Alderman Godschall, who, with Alderman Lequesne made short and agreeable Compliments to the Princess, and received gracious Answers from her Royal Highness.

At the invitation of the Prince, the City Fathers were then invited to dinner with Lord Baltimore, the Prince's first Lord of the Bedchamber, at his home in Grosvenor Square.[45]

This gesture made a great impression on the Londoners. In the fall of the year (November 18) the Sadlers made him free of their Company,[46] while a month later, December 17, the Lord Mayor and Court of Aldermen waited on the Prince again and presented him with the Freedom of the City—the first time a Prince of Wales had been so honored.[47] Frederick was very pleased at this action of the Londoners and assured them that he would always have the interest of the City at heart and would endeavor to promote their welfare and trade. He then gave them all "a grand Entertainment and fine Desert" at Carlton House, in Pall Mall.[48] Shortly afterward, he gave a further mark of his favor by sending £500 to the Lord Mayor "to be apply'd to the releasing poor Freemen of the City of London out of Prison."[49]

Frederick took a great interest in the City and its affairs and made frequent visits there. On one occasion he proved very helpful. It was the occasion of a dreadful fire in the Inner Temple, which burned all night (January 4, 1737) and did great damage. The Prince came down and "by directing the soldiers and encouraging the firemen to work, both by his

---

[45] *Ibid.*; H. M. C., *Egmont Diary*, II, 322.
[46] *Gentleman's Magazine*, VI (1736), 682.
[47] Repertories of the Court of Aldermen, 141, ff. 48, 75; *London Magazine*, V (1736), 699. It was written in gold letters on fine vellum, and enclosed in a gold box forty ounces in weight and of £200 value, on the top of which was engraved the arms of the City.
[48] *Weekly Miscellany*, Dec. 25, 1736; H. M. C., *Egmont Diary*, II, 321.
[49] *London Magazine*, VI (1737), 50.

presence and his money, 'tis said he did great service."[50]

All this did much to make him very popular in the City, and the citizens were "exceedingly pleased and said to one another they had now a Prince of their own."[51] In September of that year (1737) following upon the birth of their first child, a daughter, in July, the City presented a formal address of congratulations to the Prince and Princess,[52] and in June of the next year the same was done upon the birth of a son (George III to be), the Lord Mayor, Court of Aldermen, and members of the Common Council going to Norfolk House "in a great Cavalcade of 84 Coaches."[53]

On November 20, 1737, Queen Caroline died.[54] While an occasion of sorrow to the nation, it put the leaders of the Opposition in high spirits. The downfall of the Minister could now be expected, they thought. Lord Chesterfield had presented the situation in a letter to George Lyttleton on November 12, when he wrote: "In case the Queen dies, I think Walpole should be looked upon as gone too . . . and if the Opposition are wise, instead of treating with him, they should attack him most vigorously and personally, as a person who has lost his chief support. Which is indeed true, for though he may have more power with the King than any other body, yet he will never have that kind of power which he had by her means."[55]

[50] H. M. C., *Carlisle MSS*, pp. 175-176 (Lady Irwin to Lord Carlisle, Jan. 11, 1737); Hervey, *Memoirs*, II, 643-644.

[51] H. M. C., *Egmont Diary*, II, 322.

[52] *Weekly Miscellany*, Sept. 30, 1737.

[53] *Ibid.*, June 30, 1738.

[54] *London Evening Post*, Nov. 21, 1737. See Hervey, *Memoirs*, III, 877 ff., for the story of her last days.

[55] *The Letters of Philip Dormer Stanhope, 4th Earl of Chesterfield*, ed. Bonamy Dobrée (London, 1932), II, 308. It is interesting to compare Chesterfield's opinion with that of the Duke of Newcastle at this time. Writing to the Duke of Devonshire on November 26 (Add. MSS, 32690, ff. 445-446), Newcastle commented on the friendliness between the King and Walpole and then said: "If any are so vain, as to flatter Themselves, with any Hopes of a Change, from the fatal Incident, upon a Supposition of the King's Sentiments being different from Those of the Queen, I can venture to Affirm, that They will find Themselves extremely Mistaken." This was echoed in a letter of Francis Hare, Bishop of Chichester, to his son, a month later (H. M. C., Fourteenth Report, Part IX, *The Manuscripts of Theodore J. Hare, Esq., of*

Frederick was to figure in all this. A few days later Chesterfield wrote: "Nothing will more hasten his [Walpole's] retreat, nor his ruin, if he is resolved to stand it out, than the part which the Prince may, ought, and therefore I am persuaded will act."[56] And he added in a postscript: "If the Prince would play the rising sun, he would gild it finely; if not, he will be under a cloud, which he will never be able hereafter to shine through."[57] An increased energy, therefore, was soon apparent, after the Queen's death, among those who gathered around the heir-apparent, and during the two following months frequent meetings were held at Norfolk House to arrange the campaign for the next session and for what they considered would be the final drive to overthrow the Minister.[58]

Borden Wood, Hants., hereinafter cited as H. M. C., *Hare MSS*, p. 237) : "The enemies of the ministry flatter themselves that Sir Robert in her death has lost his support, and that now they shall soon be able to supplant him. But I think I may say so with confidence, that they will find themselves greatly Mistaken, and that the King is more firmly than ever attached to him."

[56] *Letters of the Earl of Chesterfield* (Dobrée), II, 312 (Nov. 15, 1737).

[57] *Ibid.*, II, 314.

[58] "After much deliberation, it was resolved that Walpole was to be thwarted in every measure he introduced; his past policy was to be nightly attacked; the King was to be poisoned against him by those in the confidence of the Court; the divisions in the Cabinet, which intrigue and ambition had been busy in creating, were to be widened and encouraged by promises of support in the future; principles, patriotism, the honour of English gentlemen, were all to be sacrificed, if necessary, provided by such means the hated Minister could be overthrown. Such was the programme of the Opposition on the eve of the parliamentary session of 1738." See Ewald, *Sir Robert Walpole*, p. 323.

CHAPTER VIII

The War of Jenkins' Ear and the End of the Walpole Administration

Promoting the War with Spain

In 1738 Parliament was opened on January 24. A week later the Opposition began its attack on Walpole, when Shippen, in the House of Commons, called for a reduction in the standing army.[1] This move was typical of the continually thwarted minority. Walpole had consistently stood for peace throughout his administration. The Opposition, just as consistently, because this was his policy, had attacked him for it and advocated a bold front toward the other nations. Yet, at the same time the Opposition had inconsistently opposed the maintenance of a military force capable of upholding the prestige of England on the Continent, which Walpole favored. To such an extreme did hatred of the Minister bring these leaders of faction. The move to reduce the standing army, in February, 1738, was but one more of a number of such moves to provide embarrassment to the ministry; like the others, it came to naught.[2]

This was but a preliminary skirmish to the great subject of the session—the treatment of British merchants and sailors by the Spaniards—feeling concerning which the Opposition worked up and spread throughout the country with all the zeal and prejudice that party tactics in this period could muster. It was not a new subject, for there had been friction of one sort or another between English and Spanish seamen since the days of Elizabeth. Of late years, however, the disputes had become particularly keen, most of them arising from the interpretation to be put upon the various treaties between England and Spain, which regulated their commerce in the New World.[3] There

[1] Cobbett, *Parliamentary History*, X, 379 ff.
[2] *Ibid.*, X, 467.
[3] By one of these, in 1667, Spain had recognized the British possessions in America and the right of the British merchantmen to trade with them, but,

were many grievances on both sides. The British merchants on the one hand objected to the "Right of Search," while the Spaniards on the other became more and more angry at the smuggling which was increasingly continued.[4] If, at times, the *guardacosta* captains treated those whom they caught with especial severity, they may only have felt it was in just retribution. But the British merchants raised a loud cry,[5] which was taken up by the Opposition in Parliament and echoed by the nation.[6]

The whole story of this affair, its history and its diplomatic background; its introduction anew into Parliament in 1738, when complaint was again raised by the merchants and traders against the depredations which had reached a new height in the year before; the warm debates which followed, during which the ministry was soundly denounced for its policies; the consideration of the evidence presented at the Bar of the House of Commons, including that said to have been offered by Captain Robert Jenkins, after whose oft-discussed ear historians have named the war which followed; the efforts of Walpole to consider the whole affair in a rational manner and to nego-

---

by the same treaty and another in 1670, British merchants were forbidden to trade with the Spanish colonies, and British vessels sailing near the ports or in the seas of New Spain were liable to be searched and all goods of a contraband nature seized and confiscated. To carry out the provisions of these treaties, the Spanish established a fleet of *guardacostas*, or guardships, to overhaul and inspect the cargoes of British ships found in Spanish waters. Thus the disputes arose.

[4] The British were very much to blame. By the Treaty of Utrecht in 1713, the South Sea Company had been allowed to send once a year a ship laden with British goods to the Spanish colonies. The British soon, it is said, arranged to have this vessel accompanied by others which, anchored at a distance, supplied the South Sea ship with fresh goods. British ships pretending to put into Spanish ports for refitting managed to dispose of great quantities of British wares. Also, the merchants arranged secret meetings with smugglers from the mainland who stole out to sea in their long-boats to obtain cargoes of British goods duty free.

[5] "Off the Spanish Main it was largely a question of give and take, of hand-to-hand fights between British smugglers and Spanish preventive officers. When the former succeeded, sleek merchants [in England] rubbed their hands; when the latter succeeded, these same sleek merchants squealed and angrily petitioned Parliament." See Pemberton, *Carteret*, p. 155.

[6] See Mahon, *History of England*, II, 267-269. To the complaints of the merchants were added the quarrels respecting the British right to cut logwood in Campeachy Bay (Honduras), and the boundaries of Georgia and Carolina.

tiate a peaceful settlement with Spain, resulting in the Convention of the Pardo in January, 1739; the latter's reception in the session of Parliament following; the growing spirit among the people of both England and Spain which finally led to a declaration of war in October, 1739; and the war itself which followed—all this has been studied generally and in detail, and written about as an epoch in Britain's national history as well as in that of Europe and America.[7] By such writers the British Government and the parliamentary Opposition have been given their full share in the proceedings. What, however, was the part played by the Londoners? What influence did the national situation have in the City? How were politics in the metropolis affected? A study of these questions gives a side of the story not so well known.

As in the case of the Excise scheme of 1733, it was the London merchants who, in 1738, took the first steps which led to the "War of Jenkins' Ear."[8] During the preceding winter reports of seizures of British vessels by the Spaniards and their usual harsh treatment of the crews had increased amazingly. Many of these, and letters purporting to come from sailors

[7] See Coxe, *Sir Robert Walpole*, I, 556 ff.; Mahon, *History of England*, II, 267 ff.; Leadam, *Political History of England, 1702-1760*, pp. 385 ff.; Briscoe, *Economic Policy of Robert Walpole*, pp. 198 ff.; W. M. Torrens, *History of Cabinets, from the Union with Scotland to the Acquisition of Canada and Bengal* (London, 1894), I, 482 ff. For special studies see Harold W. V. Temperley, "The Causes of the War of Jenkins' Ear, 1739," *Transactions of the Royal Historical Society*, 3d ser., III, 197-236; J. K. Laughton, "Jenkins' Ear," *English Historical Review*, IV, 741-749; John Tate Lanning, *The Diplomatic History of Georgia: A Study of the Epoch of Jenkins' Ear* (Chapel Hill, 1936), pp. 124 ff.; Paul Vaucher, *Robert Walpole et la politique de Fleury, 1731-1742* (Paris, 1924), pp. 228 ff.; and Ernest G. Hildner, "The Role of the South Sea Company in the Diplomacy Leading to the War of Jenkins' Ear, 1729-1739," *Hispanic American Historical Review*, XVIII (1938), 322-341, and "The Caribbean in Anglo-Spanish Diplomacy, 1720-1762" (unpublished thesis in the University of Michigan Library). For the debates in Parliament, see Cobbett, *Parliamentary History*, X, 561 ff., and XI, 1 ff.

[8] They had previously petitioned Parliament in 1729, complaining of the Spanish depredations, along with merchants of Bristol and Liverpool who had petitioned again in 1731. The resulting diplomatic correspondence failed to remedy the situation. In October, 1737, the merchants of London presented a similar petition to the King and were given a hearing before a meeting of the Privy Council. See *Journals of the House of Commons*, XXI, 233, 631, and 646; XXIII, 53-54; H. M. C., *Egmont Diary*, II, 440-441, 442; Add. MSS, 9130, f. 165; *London Magazine*, VI (1737), 576.

languishing in Spanish prisons, were printed in the newspapers; and the Opposition writers, especially "Caleb D'Anvers" in the *Craftsman*,[9] made political capital from them, enlarging upon the awfulness of the Spanish depredations and attacking the ministry for its lack of a determined policy against the Spanish government. Nevertheless, it was not all talk, and many of the West India merchants had suffered real losses at the hands of the Spanish *guardacostas*. On February 24, therefore, a large number of them gathered at the Ship Tavern, behind the Royal Exchange, resolved to apply again to Parliament for the redress of the grievances under which they labored.[10] This was done, and on March 3 their petition was presented by Alderman Micajah Perry, representative of the City, to the Commons.[11] It called attention to their previous petitions, emphasized the fact that the depredations had continued with greater effect than ever, being especially severe in 1737 (when a number of vessels had been seized, their goods confiscated, and their crews "inhumanely treated"); pointed out that their trade with America was gradually being destroyed; and prayed that the House would provide a timely and adequate remedy for the situation and relief for the sufferers.[12]

Then followed the session in Parliament in which the Opposition, led by Pulteney, Wyndham, Barnard, and the rest, made the issue a matter of real consequence.[13] Spain had challenged the right of the British to the Seven Seas, and the Opposition took up the challenge—but for political rather than for patriotic reasons. To arouse the nation, they produced evidence to show the enormity of the indignities heaped upon British seamen and merchants.[14] A long list of the English

[9] For examples, see issues of Nov. 5, Dec. 10 and 24, 1737; and Jan. 28 and Feb. 11, 1738.

[10] *London Evening Post*, Feb. 25, 1738; H. M. C., Fourteenth Report, Appendix, Part IX, *The Manuscripts of the Earl of Buckingham* (correspondence of Robert Trevor) (hereinafter cited as H. M. C., *Trevor MSS*), p. 13 (Horatio Walpole to Robert Trevor, Feb. 28, 1738).

[11] *London Evening Post*, March 4, 1738; *Journals of the House of Commons*, XXIII, 53.

[12] *Journals of the House of Commons*, XXIII, 53-54.

[13] See Cobbett, *Parliamentary History*, X, 569 ff.

[14] Sir George Young, in his *Poor Fred: The People's Prince*, p. 146, writes that in the Windsor Castle muniment room are preserved great quantities of

ships taken and plundered by the Spaniards since 1728 (fifty-
two of them, meaning a loss of some £140,000 to their owners)
with the names of their captains, value, places taken, barbarous
usage, and so forth, was produced.[15]   Many of the captains and
members of crews of ships harshly treated were examined personally, the most notorious of those summoned being Captain
Robert Jenkins.[16]   Their testimony, full of Spanish ill-treat-

---

materials which the Prince and the "Patriots" had gathered—depositions of
British captains and crews concerning their maltreatment by the Spaniards,
and dispositions of the British fleet for the restoration of their rights—all
being propaganda for making war.

[15] *British Gazetteer*, March 11, 1738; *London Evening Post*, March 11
and 23, 1738; *Gentleman's Magazine*, VIII (1738), 163-164.

[16] Jenkins did not appear personally in the House in 1738, but his story
was used effectively by Pulteney: in March, 1731, Jenkins and his ship, the
Rebeccah, had been taken by a Spanish *guardacosta* near Jamaica.   The ship
had been plundered, the crew treated rather badly, and Jenkins himself deprived of one of his ears.   With great difficulty they had then managed to
return to London early in June.   The first report of the affair, with no
details, appeared in the *Daily Journal* of Saturday, June 12, 1731.   In the
following days the story grew, and the details became more and more sadistic.
By the end of the next week Jenkins had been tortured, threatened with
scalping, hung up to the mast three times; and finally one of the officers, it was
said, "took hold of his left Ear, and with his Cutlass slit it down, and then
another of the Spaniards took hold of it and tore it off, but gave him the
Piece of his Ear again, bidding him carry it to his Majesty King George."
All this Jenkins had reported to Walpole at Chelsea and to the King at
Hampton Court, and shortly after he had been given a new commission and
had sailed away to the East Indies.   (See *Daily Journal*, June 12, 14, 16,
and 17; *British Gazetteer*, June 19; *Daily Courant*, June 18; and *Craftsman*,
June 19, all of 1731.)
   According to Archdeacon Coxe (*Sir Robert Walpole*, I, 573 ff.) Captain
Jenkins, in March, 1738, was the prize exhibit of the Opposition, even to the
severed ear which he carried wrapped in cotton in a box.   His story, which
is said to have been told with great feeling, and his famous answer when
asked to describe his reaction at the moment of the outrage ("I recommended
my soul to God, and my cause to my country"), were taken up, and spread
like wildfire throughout the country.   Coxe's account, derived from a footnote
in the *Gentleman's Magazine* of July, 1738 (VIII, 336), was accepted by
later historians.   Recent research, however, has shown that Jenkins' appearance
before Parliament was but a journalistic tale.   It is true that he was summoned to appear, but it seems that he "was otherwise engaged and did not
go."   See Laprade, *Public Opinion and Politics in Eighteenth Century England*, pp. 394, 397.
   The truth is that Jenkins was not in London nor even in England at the
time of the investigation (March, 1738).   He was aboard his ship, the *Harrington*, homeward bound from a voyage to the West Indies; and he did not
arrive in London until May 25, which was five days after Parliament had
been prorogued for the summer (*General Evening Post*, May 27, 1738).
Nor did he tarry long in England.   On June 15 he was given new orders

ment and cruelty, had a great effect. In the House several of the members, if we can believe a contemporary journalist, "could scarce restrain from Tears."[17] Outdoors, restated, enlarged, and commented upon in newspaper and pamphlet, it aroused popular resentment to the extent that there was a clamor for war. "Revenge on the Spanish Devils!" was heard on all sides, and the cry of "No Search!" became as loud and as frequent as that of "No Excise!" had been formerly.[18]

In April, a writer in *Common Sense* wrote: "The Nation calls loud for War, all Ranks of Men have a Feeling of the Losses and Sufferings of our Merchants, and the very common People are enraged at the Insults and Indignities that have been offered the Nation."[19] In July it was reported that "there appear'd an universal Joy among the generality of the People, upon the Hope of a War with the Spaniards."[20] In August, D'Anvers, writing in the *Craftsman,* was said to have "justly express'd the Sentiments of the Nation":[21]

The general Cry is War, Revenge on the Spaniards, Restitution for our past Losses, Satisfaction to our National Honour, and above all, ample Security to our Future Trade and Navigation. The Country Gentleman and Farmer who are distress'd with peaceable Taxes, pray for an honourable and vigorous War. The Merchant, who is always the greatest Sufferer upon such Occasions, is in the same Disposition, and ready to sacrifice his present Profit to the future Interest of his Country. The poor Tradesman, Mechanick, and Husbandman, who can hardly supply their Families with the Necessities of Life, seem willing to part with their last Mite in this glorious Cause. Our Sailors, both officers and private

---

by the East India Company, and late in July he set sail bound for India and China (*General Evening Post,* June 15, July 22, and Aug. 1, 1738; *Daily Advertiser,* July 22, 1738). He returned two years later after an adventurous voyage and was given a present of 300 Guineas for his courage in defending his ship when it was attacked by pirates (*Daily Advertiser,* Dec. 15, 1740).

The war which carries his name began while he was far away in the China seas.

[17] *London Evening Post,* March 25, 1738.
[18] H. M. C., *Hare MSS,* p. 243.
[19] *Common Sense; or, the Englishman's Journal,* April 22, 1738.
[20] *Gentleman's Magazine,* VIII (1738), 379.
[21] *London Evening Post,* Aug. 19, 1738.

Men, are alert, and want nothing so much as an Opportunity of avenging themselves on their cruel Enemies. . . . What can any Minister desire more in his Favour?"[22]

But Walpole, attacked on all sides and even criticized by members of his own cabinet, did not want war. He sympathized with the complaints of the British merchants, but he also realized that the Spaniards had their proper claims.[23] He was rather for compromise. War could not bring about the desired results. It was too "dangerous and destructive . . . especially to a trading and industrious nation."[24] Besides, knowing of the secret "Family Compact" between France and Spain, he feared that war at this time could not be isolated.[25] He therefore exerted his utmost to negotiate a settlement with Spain, with the result that the Convention of the Pardo was arranged with the Spanish envoy in London, Don Tomás Geraldino, signed on August 29, 1738, and concluded on January 14, 1739, in Madrid by Benjamin Keene, the British minister to Spain, and Don Sebastian de la Quadra, the Spanish secretary of state, as a preliminary step to what Walpole hoped would be the adjustment of a lasting peace.[26]

On February 1 the Convention was laid before Parliament for approval. No sooner were its clauses examined, however,

[22] *Craftsman*, Aug. 19, 1738.

[23] "If the Spaniards had the liberty of making speeches in the presence of their sovereign, they would not want eloquence to prove the justice of their cause. Your merchants, by studied declamations and artful discourses, represent the excesses of our guarda costas to be much greater than they are: but they conceal, dissemble, or diminish the abuses they are guilty of in our commerce." See Coxe, *Sir Robert Walpole*, III, 529 (letter of a Spanish minister to Benjamin Keene).

[24] Cobbett, *Parliamentary History*, X, 581.

[25] What is known as the first of the three famous *pacte de famille* had been signed on November 7, 1733; and Article IV provided that France would undertake to aid Spain with all her forces if England resorted to hostilities should Spain suspend England's enjoyment of commerce in American waters. See J. R. Seeley, "The House of Bourbon," *English Historical Review*, I (1886), 86-104, who shows that Walpole knew of this in 1738.

[26] It was agreed that plenipotentiaries would meet within six weeks to regulate the rights of trade of the two kingdoms and to settle the boundaries of Carolina and Florida, eight months being allowed for the proceedings; and that Spain, as a compensation for the damages sustained by British commerce, should pay the sum of £95,000 within four months after the ratification of the Convention. See Add. MSS, 35875, f. 403 ff. (copies in French, Spanish, and English).

than the bitterest criticisms were showered upon it by the Opposition members.[27]   The question of "Right of Search" had been carefully avoided, they charged.   There was not one word about the British claims to the cutting of logwood in Campeachy Bay or the settling of the boundary of Georgia.   On the question of punishing the Spanish captains guilty of cruelty to English seamen, the Convention was silent.   In both Houses the Opposition speakers severely denounced it.[28]   Finally, Walpole arose to reply upon the whole debate.   He admitted that it was not a definitive treaty, but he declared that it laid the foundation to procure one.   It promised peace thereby, and he was proud to feel that he had had a part in preventing a war which, on England's part, would have been unjust and dishonorable.   He realized, of course, by what means the popular clamor had been raised; nevertheless, he declared: "I am resolved while I have the honour to serve his Majesty in the station I am in, to let no popular clamour get the better of what I think is for my country's good . . . I shall never be for sacrificing our real interests for the pursuit of military glory."[29]   The divisions which followed were close, but favorable to the ministry, and on March 9 the Convention was ratified.[30]

It was during this period, when the Convention was being considered in Parliament, that the City Fathers at last felt compelled to take a part and express their views on the question which was now arousing the whole nation.   Through the year 1738 it had been primarily a concern of the merchants, because they were most vitally affected, but now it was made a concern of the general citizenry through the campaign of the Opposition to stir up public opinion and clamor against the Spaniards and against the ministry.   It became at the beginning of 1739 a concern of the governing bodies of the Corporation.

[27] "The Convention was condemned before its contents were known. After it was published it was grossly vilified and misrepresented."   See Etough Papers, Add. MSS, 9200, f. 63.
[28] Cobbett, *Parliamentary History*, X, 940 ff.
[29] *Ibid.*, X, 1290-1292.
[30] *Journals of the House of Commons*, XXIII, 277; *Journals of the House of Lords*, XXV, 308.   See H. M. C., *Egmont Diary*, III, 29, 31-32; and Coxe, *Sir Robert Walpole*, III, 515 ff.

On February 20 the Lord Mayor, Sir John Barnard, called a meeting of the Common Council to consider it, and such was the interest that nearly the entire body of the aldermen and common councilmen turned out.[31] The matter was presented by Alderman Sir Robert Godschall, who called attention to the Convention then being debated in Parliament and moved that a committee be appointed to draw up a petition to both Houses setting forth "the fatal Consequences that must attend the Trade and Navigation of Great Britain, on the American Seas, if the pretensions of the Spaniards . . . be admitted of, in any Degree or manner whatsoever."[32] This was readily agreed to, the committee was chosen,[33] and after some deliberation presented the following petition for the approval of the Council:

The most humble Petition of the Lord Mayor, Aldermen, and Commons of the City of London, in Common Council assembled, to both Houses of Parliament,

Sheweth,

That the Citizens of London are too deeply interested in whatever affects the Trade of this Nation, not to express the utmost Anxiety for the Welfare and Prosperity, of that only Source of our Riches; And it is with a Concern Your Petitioners are unable to Express, that they perceive the Trade to his Majesty's American Colonies still continues Exposed to the Insults of the Spaniards, who under unwarrantable and injurious Pretences continue to Stop Search and make prizes of British Vessels navigating the American Seas, in manifest Violation of the Treaties subsisting between the two Crowns.

Your Petitioners most humbly Apprehend, that the Trade from these his Majesty's Kingdoms, to his American Colonies, is of the utmost Importance, and almost the only profitable Trade this Nation now enjoys, unrivaled by others; And they were induced to hope from his Majesty's Known Goodness, and Paternal Care of his

[31] *London Evening Post*, Feb. 20, 1739.
[32] Journals of the Common Council, 58, f. 121.
[33] The committee consisted of Aldermen Godschall, Barber, Lambert, and Westley, and Councilmen Ayliffe, Sandford, Benn, Parker, Roberts, Heywood, and Sedgwick.

Subjects supported by the vigorous Resolutions of both Houses of Parliament and the Equipment of a very powerful Fleet, that his Majesty's trading Subjects in the Seas of America, as well as in all other parts of the Ocean, would not only have received a full satisfaction for their losses occasioned by the Depredations of Spain, but also an undoubted security for their Commerce for the Time to come; And that a reasonable and adequate Reparation would likewise have been Obtained for the Barbarities and inhumen Cruelties exercised by that Nation on the English Seamen, who have had the Unhappiness of falling into their merciless hands.

Your Petitioners most humbly beg Leave to testify their great Concern and Surprise to find by the Convention lately concluded between his Majesty and the King of Spain, that the Spaniards are so far from giving up their (as we humbly apprehend) Unjust Pretensions of a Right to Visit and Search our Ships on the Seas of America, that this pretension of theirs is amongst others, referred to the future Regulation and Decision of Plenipotentiaries appointed on each side, whereby We apprehend it is in some Degree admitted.

We humbly conceive we have too much Cause to fear, If the Right pretended to by Spain, of Searching Brittish Ships at Sea be admitted in any Manner or Degree whatsoever, That the Trade of his Majesty's Subjects to America will become so precarious, as to depend in a great Manner upon the Indulgence and Justice of the Spaniards, of both which they have given us for some Years past such Specimens, as we humbly think this Nation can have no Cause to be Satisfied with.

Your Petitioners beg leave further to Express their humble Apprehensions that such a precarious Situation as this must inevitably expose the Trade to the American Seas to Continual Interruptions and perpetual Alarms as well as to Severe Losses: That to these unhappy Causes, they humbly apprehend the present low State of the British Colonies in America may in a great Measure be Attributed, And if the Cruel Treatment of the English Sailors, whose hard Fate has thrown them into the Hands of the Spaniards, should be put up, without any Reparation, Your Petitioners humbly Apprehend it may be the Means of Deterring Seamen, from undertaking Voyages to the Seas of America, without any Advance of Wages, which that Trade or any other will not be able to support.

Your Petitioners therefore having laid before the Honourable House, the high Importance this Trade is of, to the Kingdom in General, and this City in particular, thought it their Indispensible Duty to represent in the most humble and respectful Manner to this Honourable House, fatal Consequences of Leaving the Freedom of Navigation, any longer in suspense, and uncertainty, They therefore humbly hope this Honourable House will take it into their Mature Deliberation, and do therein so to their great Wisdom as shall seem meet.[34]

This petition was agreed upon almost unanimously by the Council, "there being only four Spaniards against it";[35] and the sheriffs were ordered to present copies to both Houses of Parliament on Friday, February 23.[36] This was done, and the City petition along with petitions from various groups of merchants of London, Bristol, Liverpool, Edinburgh, Glasgow, and other cities was considered by the Lords and the Commons.[37] By the Opposition members they were well received, but they brought forth much criticism from the ministerial supporters, who were determined that the Convention should be approved. In the Lords the petitions were accepted, but in the Commons they were rejected, although by a small majority.[38]

For their action at this time the Londoners were criticized by the ministerial writers in the press, who made fun of them for assuming to give advice to the Government. Among other things—"to take off the Weight of the Application in Matters of a National concern, and lessen them in the Esteem of the Members of both Houses, by representing them as an insig-

[34] Journals of the Common Council, 58, ff. 121b-122b.

[35] London Evening Post, Feb. 22, 1739. These were Alderman Sir John Eyles, Sir Joseph Eyles, Sir Robert Baylis, and Sir George Champion—all loyal Walpolians. At a Court of Aldermen held afterward, Sir Joseph Eyles tried to stop the petition by moving that the Court put their negative to it. Such was the feeling against Walpole at this time, however, that the motion was overwhelmingly defeated (16 to 4).

[36] Journals of the Common Council, 58, f. 122b.

[37] Journals of the House of Commons, XXIII, 247 ff.; Craftsman, Feb. 24, 1739.

[38] Cobbett, Parliamentary History, X, 1090. This majority of nineteen (227 to 208), and that of twenty-eight (242 to 214) upon the division to approve the Convention on March 9, show the formidable strength of the Opposition, which was becoming increasingly noticeable. See also Boyer, Political State, LVII, 164-165, 185-187.

nificant Body of Tradesmen and Mechanicks, who could not be expected to be well-informed of, nor reason concerning Matters of State"[39]—lists of the members of the Common Council, with their respective trades or companies, to which was appended a Biblical text to the effect that however useful such men might be in a city "they shall not be sought for in Public Counsel," were printed and distributed.[40] Men of trade had not yet attained the prestige of those who held the land; nevertheless, this action was keenly resented by the Londoners, who were naturally very conscious of their own power and wealth and felt that they should have a proper place in the councils of the nation. Therefore the move only added fuel to the fire of their antagonism against the Walpole government, an antagonism which was growing ever stronger in the City.

On the part of the Opposition, printed lists were distributed of the members of Parliament who had voted for and against the Convention, emphasis being centered on the large majority of place-men among those who voted in its favor.[41] These lists also reveal how the Londoners in Parliament voted on this question. Although not unanimous, the majority were clearly opposed to it. Of these, the four City representatives had been the most active in the debate, Sir John Barnard, Micajah Perry, Robert Willimot, and Humphrey Parsons all taking part. They were joined on the division by Sir Francis Child, sitting for Middlesex, Edward Gibbon, for Petersfield, Sir Richard Lockwood, for Worcester, Henry Marshall, for Agmondesham, and George Heathcote, for Southwark. Voting with the Government majority for the Convention were three—Sir George Caswell, sitting for Leominster, Sir Joseph Eyles, for Devizes, and Sir George Champion, for Aylesbury; the latter two, it will be remembered, having opposed the City petition against the Convention while it was in Common Council. All these came in for much abuse and condemnation by the City, and Champion's vote actually cost him the Lord Mayorship.

[39] Maitland, *History of London*, I, 599.

[40] *Daily Gazetteer*, March 2, 1739; Boyer, *Political State*, LVII, 222-230.

[41] Boyer, *Political State*, LVIII, 21-42; *London Magazine*, VIII (1739), 299-303, 336-340.

THE ELECTION OF LORD MAYOR IN 1739

By the summer of 1739 the London citizens were thoroughly aroused over a peace with Spain and against the national administration and all those who supported it. Now it happened that Sir George Champion was the senior alderman next the chair,[42] and according to the custom which had grown up in recent years he would be chosen Lord Mayor in the September election. Yet, as early as July 7 there was talk among the liverymen of setting aside this custom of rotation, because of Champion's vote, and reverting to the older method of free election.[43] In August the following letter from "A Liveryman" was circulated among the members of the Common Hall:

You will soon have an Opportunity in your collective Body, to declare in a public Manner your Sentiments of the late memorable Convention; by your representatives both in Parliament and Common Council, you have shewn your dislike to it; convince the World therefore, Brethren, whether those that voted for it, have acted agreeable to your Sentiments or not, by conferring your highest Honour on one that voted for it, or setting him aside.[44]

A month later a similar letter was printed in the press signed by "A Citizen," who came out strongly against Champion's voting for the Convention contrary to the City's opposition as expressed in the petition to Parliament, saying that if Champion should be chosen, "it will show so great a Supineness and Disregard to your Liberties, that the whole Nation (who have always cast their Eyes on you in all great Events) can have no Hope of your succeeding on future Occasions."[45] And to show the importance of this election, a "puff," inserted two days later in the same newspaper (the *London Evening Post*),

[42] He had become so upon the death of Sir Thomas Lombe, alderman of Bassishaw Ward, on January 3, 1739, whose place in the ward had been taken by William Baker, an East India merchant. See *London Evening Post*, Jan. 4, 1739; and Boyer, *Political State*, LVII, 18.
[43] *London Evening Post*, July 7, 1739. "C. T.," in the *Daily Advertiser* of September 27, remarks: "When Sir George Champion acted with Vigour against the Excise Scheme, he was the Darling of the City; but now that he has been so Unfortunate as to vote for the Peace of the Kingdom, he is become the Object of their Resentment."
[44] *London Evening Post*, Aug. 18, 1739.
[45] *Ibid.*, Sept. 20, 1739.

reported that letters had been received from other cities and trading corporations mentioning the great expectation they had "of hearing, that the Citizens of London will act consistent with themselves in their Election of Lord Mayor on Saturday next; and [they] doubt not as the Citizens of London were so unanimous in petitioning against the Convention, they will be unanimous in setting Him aside who voted for it."[46]

During the last week in September a number of pamphlets were written, and advertisements and letters appeared daily in the newspapers either urging that Champion be set aside or maintaining that he should be elected.[47] Sir George still had many friends. On September 25 a large number of them (the *London Evening Post* reported that there were "about 500") met at the Crown Tavern, behind the Royal Exchange, and "unanimously" agreed to support him for Mayor. That same night, however, another group of citizens met at the Bull-Head and Three Tuns Tavern, in Cheapside, and proposed to set aside Champion, putting in nomination the next two aldermen below him in seniority; namely, Sir John Salter and Sir Robert Godschall. This step was again proposed, on the following day at another meeting held at Vintners' Hall; and the liverymen assembled there agreed, "for the Peace of the City," to support Salter and Godschall.[48]

Because of the interest thus aroused, a great assembly was held at the Guildhall on Saturday, September 29, when the Court of Common Hall was called to order by the Lord Mayor in office, Micajah Perry.[49] Sir William Thompson, the Re-

[46] *Ibid.*, Sept. 22, 1739. Also in *Common Sense*, Sept. 29, 1739.

[47] Sir George, himself, wrote a letter in the *Daily Advertiser* of September 24, justifying his conduct and appealing for support. See also all issues of the *London Evening Post, Daily Post*, and *Daily Advertiser* from September 20 to 29, 1739. Boyer, *Political State*, LVIII, 226-227, 238-242, and 296-310, contains many of these and other letters. For pamphlets, see *The Reasons For and Against the Seclusion of Sir G. C. from Being Lord Mayor of London* (London, 1739); *A Letter to Sir G—— C—— Shewing the Reasons of Setting Him Aside at the Approaching Election* (London, 1739); and *Serious Considerations on the Ensuing Election of a Lord-Mayor* (London, 1739).

[48] *London Evening Post*, Sept. 27, 1739; *London Magazine*, VIII (1739), 465.

[49] The reporter for the *Gentleman's Magazine* (IX, 495) estimated the number to be 7,776 persons, "nearly the whole livery." According to Boyer,

corder, then made his customary speech of instructions on procedure and concluded by saying "that it was their undoubted Right to return to the Court of Aldermen, two fit and able Persons of that Court, who had served the office of Sheriff, out of whom they were to chuse one of them to be Lord Mayor for the Year ensuing; and that he would not take upon him to dictate to them, in their present Choice, well knowing their Prudence would direct them, to act in the best Manner for the Good, Peace, and Welfare of this great City." The Lord Mayor and the aldermen present then withdrew, and the election was conducted by the sheriffs, George Heathcote and Sir John Lequesne.[50]

All the aldermen eligible were voted on, as was the custom; but Champion, Salter, and Godschall received the most hands. After consulting with each other the sheriffs declared the two latter candidates to have the majority. But a poll was demanded for Champion, and it was immediately begun. After a short time Sir George and his friends, realizing that they had no chance, gave it up. On the following Tuesday (October 2) a meeting of the Court of Aldermen was held, the two aldermen returned by the Common Hall were voted on, and Sir John Salter, the senior of the two, was chosen to be Lord Mayor for the ensuing year. He was at once proclaimed upon the Hustings, and the choice was "approved of by the Citizens with the Loudest Acclamations."[51]

Before the Common Hall was dismissed, two other matters were considered. Upon the sponsorship of Richard Glover, one of the City merchants and a poet of some repute,[52] the

---

Political State, LVIII, 310, three thousand was nearer the figure. The report in *Common Sense* (Oct. 6, 1739) states that "a greater Number of Liverymen appear'd at Guildhall . . . than was ever known on a like Occasion. The Hall was quite full by Eleven o'Clock."

[50] *London Magazine*, VIII (1739), 499; Boyer, *Political State*, LVIII, 310; *The Proceedings of the Court of Hustings and Common Hall of the Liverymen of the City of London at the Late Election for Lord Mayor* (London, 1739), p. 9.

[51] *London Magazine*, VIII (1739), 500. See the Book of Common Hall, 7, ff. 277-277b; *London Evening Post*, Oct. 2 and 4, 1739; Boyer, *Political State*, LVIII, 311-312, 317; *Common Sense*, Oct. 6, 1739; *Proceedings . . . at the Late Election for Lord Mayor*, pp. 10-11, 19.

[52] Richard Glover (1712-1785), the son of a Hamburgh merchant, was

liverymen approved of a "Representation" to be sent to the four representatives of the City (Barnard, Perry, Parsons, and Willimot), thanking them for their late endeavors against the Convention and urging them to promote a bill for reducing the number of place-men in Parliament.[53] An attempt was also made, while the liverymen were in a mood of unanimity, to get them to instruct the City members in Parliament to obtain the repeal of the clause in the City Elections Act of 1725 which upheld the Court of Aldermen's negative power over the Court of Common Council. Lord Mayor Perry, however, ruled that the presentation of such a matter was out of order, and the Common Hall was dismissed before any further action could be taken.[54]

Both of these moves reflected the spirit of the citizens at this time. The first showed their opposition to the power of the Walpole administration, which they had been led to believe was founded on bribery and jobbery; and the second arose from the fear which had also been stirred up, that control of the City government would rest with a national administration which could corrupt a majority of the aldermen. Nevertheless, although the City might wish a Place Bill, the members of the parliamentary Opposition, now feeling that their day was at hand, were not willing to pass a bill which would deprive them of privileges which they could make use of while in power; and the time was not ripe to repeal the "negative." The most important act of the Common Hall, therefore, was the setting aside of Champion because of his having voted against the

---

engaged in his father's business, but had a passion for writing poetry, most of which was of a rather dull sort. His best known poems are *Leonidas*, an epic poem published in 1737, and *London, or the Progress of Commerce*, and *Admiral Hosier's Ghost*, both published in 1739. The Prince of Wales was his patron, and he was intimate with George Lyttleton and Bubb Dodington. He took an active, though not altogether successful, interest in politics throughout his long life (Leslie Stephen, in *D. N. B.*, XXII, 6-7).

[53] *Craftsman*, Oct. 6, 1739; *London Magazine*, VIII (1739), 500; Boyer, *Political State*, LVIII, 313-315.

[54] *London Evening Post*, Oct. 4, 1739; *London Magazine*, VIII (1739), 501; Boyer, *Political State*, LVIII, 316-321; *Proceedings . . . at the Late Election for Lord Mayor*, pp. 13 ff.

Convention.[55] By this act it was shown that the City was united in its opposition to the peaceful and conciliatory policies of the Walpole administration and that its citizenry was resolved on a continuation of that belligerent spirit which demanded revenge and just retribution for the depredations of the Spanish—indeed, a war if necessary.[56]

Nor were they disappointed. For war with Spain, despite Walpole's earnest efforts, was forced upon the country. Spain had made no move to honor the Convention or to pay the £95,000. The Spanish *guardacostas* had continued to stop British ships. British indignation had grown increasingly. His Majesty's Government was finally forced to accede to the popular clamor.[57] On October 19 the declaration of war was made, and four days later it was proclaimed with appropriate ceremonies in front of St. James's, at Charing Cross, within Temple Bar, in Cheapside, and at the Royal Exchange. At each place the "greatest crowds of people" gathered, and all "expressed their great Satisfaction by loud Acclamations of Joy."[58] That night celebrations were held throughout the City, and "it was observ'd, that a general Joy sat smiling in each British Face."[59]

[55] Bishop Hare wrote to his son (Oct. 13, 1739): "There might be other reasons with respect to his character in private life for setting him aside, but the reason given is his voting for the Convention, and private character could not be very decently insisted on anyway after their choice of J. Barber, who is far from being a saint." See H. M. C., *Hare MSS*, p. 252.

[56] See the *Craftsman*, Oct. 13, 1739; *Proceedings . . . at the Late Election for Lord Mayor*, p. 31. The City's action evidently met with approval outside, for it was reported in *Common Sense* on October 13 that "the Merchants and Wholesale Tradesmen about Town have receiv'd many Letters from their Correspondents in most of the Counties in the Kingdom, highly applauding the conduct of the City, with regard to their late Election of a Lord Mayor."

[57] "Sir Robert Walpole was forced into the war by the people, who were influenced to this measure by the most leading politicians, by the first orators, and the greatest poets of the time. For that war, Pope sang his dying notes. For that war, Johnson, in more energetic strains, employed the voice of his early genius. For that war, Glover distinguished himself in the way in which his muse was the most natural and happy. The crowd readily followed the politicians in the cry for war, which threatened little bloodshed, and which promised victories that were attended with something more solid than glory." See Edmund Burke, *Two Letters Addressed to a Member of the Present Parliament, on the Proposals for Peace with the Regicide Directory of France* (London, 1796), pp. 71-72.

[58] *London Gazette*, Oct. 23, 1739; *Daily Gazetteer*, Oct. 23, 1739; *London Evening Post*, Oct. 23, 1739; H. M. C., *Trevor MSS*, p. 35; *Hare MSS*, p. 253.

[59] *London Evening Post*, Oct. 25, 1739.

Tavern and coffeehouse rang with good cheer, and "every brave Subject's Glass was crown'd with Success to the Arms of Great Britain."[60] Even the Prince of Wales, attending upon the procession, stopped at the door of the Rose Tavern, near Temple Bar, to drink with the rest.[61] In Walpole, however, war aroused soberer thoughts, and upon hearing the bells of the London churches pealing he is said to have remarked: "They now ring the bells, before long they will be wringing their hands."[62]

The conduct of the war during the remainder of Walpole's administration, from the opening victory on November 22 with Admiral Edward Vernon's capture of Porto Bello, on the Isthmus of Darien (Panama), the port in which the *guardacostas* had been fitted out, which was followed by a period when failures were more common than victories, is a subject beyond the scope of this study.[63] Nevertheless, it all had its effect on the London scene, the victories giving the Londoners a time to rejoice, and the failures making them murmur, especially when the prices of stocks tumbled sharply.[64]

Unlike the election of Lord Mayor in 1739, the other local elections in London during the following year were little, if at all, affected by the war with Spain. Nor were any of them contested. The death of Sir Joseph Eyles, on February

[60] *Ibid.*, Oct. 25, 1739.

[61] Coxe, *Sir Robert Walpole*, I, 618.

[62] *Ibid.*, I, 618 n.

[63] The "War of Jenkins' Ear" continued beyond the period of Walpole's administration; after the death of the Emperor Charles VI, followed by Frederick the Great's move to enlarge Prussia at the expense of Maria Theresa's possessions, it merged into the War of the Austrian Succession. It was temporarily halted by the Treaty of Aix-la-Chapelle in 1748, but the Seven Years War and the War of American Independence owed their origins to this beginning in 1739, so that the war which then started really did not end until the Peace of Versailles in 1783.

[64] Admiral Vernon's victory at Porto Bello was received with great joy, although the news did not arrive in England until March 13, 1740, nearly four months after the event. On March 25 the members of the Common Council agreed upon an address to the King, congratulating him upon the "Glorious Success" of British arms, and assuring him of their continued financial support; they voted to give Admiral Vernon the Freedom of the City, "out of the grateful Sense of the Services he has done to the Trading Part of this Nation." See the Journals of the Common Council, 58, ff. 167-168b; *London Evening Post*, March 29, 1740.

8, after serving Cheap Ward for only one year, was followed by a very quiet election at the Wardmote of the ward; and George Arnold, a Linen-Draper and Eyles' Deputy, was chosen in his room.[65]   In April, Sir Francis Child, who had served the ward of Farringdon Without for nearly twenty years (as "a true Patriot, an upright Magistrate, and a sincere Friend"), was succeeded by Richard Hoare, another banker, who had previously contested unsuccessfully against Sir Joseph Eyles in Cheap Ward. This time Hoare was elected "without his spending one Shilling, or asking one Man for his Vote (he being at Bath)," which was considered "very rare and uncommon."[66]   In November Alderman Richard Levett, of Aldersgate Ward, passed on and was succeeded by William Benn, "an eminent Soap-Boiler," who was "unanimously" chosen.[67]   At the election of sheriffs in June this unanimity was also apparent.   As in the previous years, a number of those drunk to by the Lord Mayor "swore off" and paid their fines; but on Michaelmas Day, by "a great Majority," the choice fell on Alderman Henry Marshall and Richard Hoare, who both accepted and agreed to serve.[68]

THE LORD MAYOR'S ELECTION OF 1740

The Lord Mayor's election of 1740 was different from and even more unusual than that of the year 1739.   Whereas in that election Sir George Champion had been set aside because of his support of the Convention to which the City was opposed, in the 1740 election Sir Robert Godschall, the brother-in-law of the popular Sir John Barnard and a leader in the City's opposition to the Convention, was twice set aside by the Court of Aldermen after being returned by the Court of Common Hall, and for no given reasons.   The election of 1739 is understandable.   The election of 1740 has always been a puzzle.

There was no advance indication of what would happen. On September 25, as had become the custom of late years, the

[65] London Magazine, IX, (1740), 100; Boyer, Political State, LIX, 140, 261.
[66] London Evening Post, April 22, 1740; Common Sense, April 26 and 28, 1740.
[67] Common Sense, Nov. 15; 1740; Daily Advertiser, Nov. 13, 1740; Boyer Political State, LX, 392.
[68] Daily Advertiser, June 25, 1740; London Magazine, IX (1740), 299.

liverymen assembled in a preliminary meeting at Vintners' Hall
to consider whom they would support on Michaelmas Day at
Guildhall.   On this occasion Richard Glover was made the
chairman.   In his opening speech, referring to the rejection of
Sir George Champion in the previous year and the unanimity
displayed by the City at that time, he urged that a Mayor be
chosen who would again meet the approval of the great majority of the citizens.   A discussion followed, and it was determined once more to pass over Sir George.   The liverymen
then agreed that Sir Robert Godschall and George Heathcote,
who were next in line below the chair, should be supported at
the election.[69]

Accordingly, on Monday, September 29, when the full body
of the livery assembled in Common Hall, Godschall and Heathcote were given a great majority of the votes and were duly
returned to the Court of Aldermen for one of them to be
chosen Lord Mayor.[70]   Godschall was the senior of the two
and, according to custom, was expected to be chosen.   The
Court of Aldermen "thought proper," however, to pass over
him, for by a vote of eleven to eight they chose George Heathcote to be Lord Mayor.[71]   Alderman Godschall at once spoke
up and expressed to the Court his suprise "that he should be
put aside, without any reason alledged against him."

Sir John Eyles upon this said, that the Court had, in this affair,
only exercised a right, which they might at any time use; and they
thought it expedient to make use of it now, and were not obliged to
give their reasons.

Then Sir John Barnard replied, that he thought none could be
well justified in the exercise of a power, but when they had a good
reason for it; that for his part he should always vote for the Senior

[69] *London Magazine*, X (1741), 37-38; *Daily Advertiser*, Sept. 26, 1740.
[70] The Book of Common Hall, 7, f. 284b.
[71] Repertories of the Court of Aldermen, 144, ff. 389, 400.   Those who
voted for Heathcote were Eyles, Baylis, Billers, Thompson, Master, Champion,
Rous, and Arnold (all Walpolians) and Williams, Hankey, and Baker (nominally anti-Walpole).   Those who voted for Godschall were Barber, Barnard,
Godschall, Heathcote, Lambert, Lequesne, Marshall, and Hoare (all nominally
anti-Walpole).   Six (Parsons, Perry, Bellamy, Levett, Willimot, and Westley)
were absent, and the Lord Mayor, Sir John Salter, did not vote.

in rotation, unless some objection should arise against him as improper.[72]

The Court of Aldermen was then adjourned; the members returned to the Common Hall, where George Heathcote was declared on the Hustings to be duly elected.[73]

This outcome was entirely unexpected. The liverymen at once "were thrown into general Consternation. Every Man seemed surprised and shocked . . . all treated it with a becoming Displeasure and Resentment."[74] There was a great uproar, and "the noise and tumult and hissing, etc., lasted for some time."[75] Finally, quiet was restored. Then Alderman Godschall, who seems to have taken the affair in an affable manner, addressed the liverymen and thanked them for the honor they had done him in returning him to the Court; but at the same time he expressed his concern that his brother aldermen, without giving any reason, had denied him the office which had been intended for him. He was followed by Alderman Heathcote, who also thanked the liverymen for the honor that had been so surprisingly betowed upon him, but pleading ill-health and the fact that he had so lately served the tiring and costly office of sheriff, he asked to be excused, especially so, he concluded, since not the least objection, in point of honor, ability, or integrity, had been given by the Court of Aldermen against his senior colleague, Godschall.[76] The liverymen, of course, could do nothing then about the situation. They received, however, Heathcote's modest request very favorably and referred it to the consideration of the Common Council, which, on October 10, after considerable argument, finally voted

[72] *A Journal of the Shrievalty of Richard Hoare, Esq., in the Years 1740-1741* (London, 1815), p. 8.

[73] *London Evening* Post, Sept. 30, 1740; *London Magazine*, IX (1740), 506; Boyer, *Political State*, LX, 289; *Journal . . . of Richard Hoare*, pp. 7-8; *An Impartial Relation of the Proceedings of the Common Hall and Court of Aldermen . . . at the Election of a Lord Mayor* (London, 1740), pp. 5-6.

[74] *An Impartial Relation of . . . the Election of a Lord Mayor*, p. 7.

[75] *Journal . . . of Richard Hoare*, p. 9.

[76] *London Evening Post*, Sept. 30, 1740; Boyer, *Political State*, LX, 289; *Journal . . . of Richard Hoare*, p. 18; *An Impartial Relation of . . . the Election of a Lord Mayor*, p. 6.

upon it and excused him from serving the office of Lord Mayor and from paying any fine.[77]

This then necessitated another election, and the liverymen were summoned to meet again on October 14. As before, a preliminary meeting was held at Vintners' Hall with Glover in the chair. In his opening speech he denounced the failure of the aldermen to choose Godschall. He declared this action of the "eleven Gentlemen of the Court of Aldermen against the whole of the Livery of London" to be wholly unjustifiable, and charged that it was done merely out of spite for the Common Hall having refused to nominate Champion the year before. The livery thereupon agreed to support Godschall again at the second election.[78]

This was done, and at the Common Hall meeting, all of the aldermen who had already served the office of sheriff being put up, Godschall was chosen by a very great majority to be returned to the Court of Aldermen. Since it was necessary to return two names, they also chose Humphrey Parsons, who had already served the office of Lord Mayor in 1731, feeling certain that the Court would not choose him again.[79] What was their surprise, however, when the Court of Aldermen, after a debate which lasted over three hours, by a majority of one again passed over Godschall and named Humphrey Parsons for a second time, and again disclosed no reason for the action.[80]

On October 22 at another Court of Common Council Alderman Parsons told the members that if they so desired he was willing to accept the office of Lord Mayor again, "let the Ex-

[77] Journals of the Common Council, 50, f. 182b; Daily Advertiser, Oct. 11, 1740; London Magazine, IX (1740), 506.
[78] London Magazine, X, (1741), 39.
[79] The Book of Common Hall, 7, f. 285; London Evening Post, Oct. 14, 1740.
[80] Boyer, Political State, LX, 342-343; London Magazine, IX (1740), 507; Journal . . . of Richard Hoare, p. 24. Parsons received twelve votes to eleven for Godschall. Those voting for Parsons were the same who had voted for Heathcote in the Michaelmas Day election with the addition of Sir Edward Bellamy, an absentee on that day. Godschall was again supported by the eight who had voted for him in the first election, with the addition of three absentees on that occasion, namely, Aldermen Parsons, Willimot, and Westley. Perry, Levett, and Salter were absent on the occasion of this second election.

pense be what it would."[81]   The Court being highly pleased,
a motion was made that thanks be given to Parsons for accepting
the office a second time "and thereby endeavouring in some
Measure to restore the Peace and Tranquility of this City which
has been greatly Disturbed by a late extraordinary and unusual
Proceeding."[82]   To this the Common Council readily agreed,
but, some of the aldermen present objecting to the part here
quoted (as containing ambiguous matter which would only renew the disturbances), insisted on a separate vote by the Court
of Aldermen.   There was a long debate, and the power of
that Court of putting a negative on the proceedings of the
Common Council was disputed "with great warmth."   Finally,
Sir John Barnard, Humphrey Parsons, and the other aldermen
who had voted for Godschall, along with a large number of
the common councilmen, left the meeting, after which the remaining aldermen sat as a Court and negatived, by twelve votes
to one, the words objected to.[83]

On this same day a letter was published from Alderman
Godschall, again thanking the liverymen for their support of
him.   He began:

I have been, 'tis true, depriv'd of the great Office, for which
you design'd me, by a Majority of One Vote, amongst my Brethren
Aldermen; but the repeated Honour of so Unanimous a Choice of
my Fellow-Citizens, conferr'd on me in two very numerous Com-
mon-Halls, sufficiently Recompenses me for that Slight.   And as
the Honour you have done me cannot be taken from me by any
Persons whatever, I shall always prize it infinitely beyond the splen-
dour of any Post, how eminent soever it may be.

He then concluded by expressing the hope that this affair would
not "in any Manner disunite the City, and thereby lessen the
Weight it receives for Unanimity" and promised his continued
zeal and attachment to the welfare of the metropolis.[84]

[81] *London Magazine*, IX (1740), 508.
[82] *Ibid.*; Boyer, *Political State*, LX, 343.
[83] *Journals of the Common Council*, 58, ff. 190-191; *Daily Gazetteer*,
Oct. 23, 1740; *Weekly Miscellany*, Oct. 25, 1740; Boyer, *Political State*, LX,
343-344; *Journal . . . of Richard Hoare*, p. 27.
[84] *Common Sense*, Oct. 25, 1740; *London Magazine*, IX (1740), 508;
Boyer, *Political State*, LX, 345-346.

The objection to Sir Robert Godschall for Lord Mayor in 1740 is not stated anywhere. The resentment of some of the aldermen at the rejection of Sir George Champion in the previous year may have been a factor, but there was no personal objection to Godschall. It seems most likely that he was the victim of circumstances. Godschall's time came just when the feeling of enough of the aldermen to dominate the Court was aroused to show their superior position over the Common Council. It was a swing back to the days before the City Elections Act had been passed, when the two Courts were continually at odds with each other. It was not a situation in which the war with Spain had a leading part, although the spirit engendered by that war was undoubtedly important; nor even one in which the friction between the City and the national administration was a feature, although it was suggested by one writer that Walpole was back of it.[85] The fact that all the pro-Walpole aldermen were each time in the group voting against Godschall seems to point to that possibility. Nevertheless, while two or three Walpolians (possibly Eyles, Baylis, and Champion) may have particularly resented the opposition of the City to the administration's policies, not enough of them in the court composed a majority, and on each of the votes against Godschall they were joined by aldermen who were strongly antiadministration. Moreover, it is well to note that

[85] "I am confident there is but one man in the Kingdom, who could have been capable of advising such an extraordinary step . . . and I cannot think that even he would have done it, if his Destiny had not been nigh at hand, for *quem perdere vult Jupiter, dementat prius.*" See *An Impartial Relation of . . . the Election of a Lord Mayor*, p. 9. This letter was also printed in *Common Sense*, Oct. 4, 1740 (unsigned).

Milton Percival, in his notes to "Walpole Ballads" (Vol. VIII, *Oxford Historical and Literary Studies*), echoes this thought when he says (p. 148) that "it was this time Walpole's turn to thwart the natural order of election. Godschall's defeat was desired by Walpole, not only because he had been influential in the setting aside of Sir George Champion the year before, but also—if the partial testimony of *The Daily Gazetteer* may be accepted—because he had 'notoriously been the chief promoter and fomenter of all disturbances and divisions that have happened in the City' (October 3, 1740). The Common Hall was too large and popular a body to be controlled or greatly influenced by Walpole; but in the Court of Aldermen he had considerable power, which he used on this occasion quietly but effectively. The citizens were taken entirely off their guard."

the two men chosen, Heathcote and Parsons, were both strongly anti-Walpole.

The whole crux of the matter is that the Court of Aldermen was slowly losing its control over the government of the Corporation, and the majority in that Court, most of them older men who had been aldermen since the disturbing times before the City Elections Act had been passed, determined in this 1740 election to prove that they still had the deciding voice. Naturally, the junior aldermen, with shorter memories but with longer vision, such as Barnard, Heathcote, Willimot, Lambert, and the others, resented this, not only because they were very good friends of Godschall, but also because they preferred the interest of the City above that of the Court of Aldermen as such. The whole incident of the election of 1740 is an interesting study in human nature, and like the Mansion House fund activities in connection with the sheriff's elections, it shows how personal interest, self-indulgence, and even greed sometimes ruled in matters of a political nature.

This feeling, moreover, was carried over into the spring of 1741, when, on March 21, Humphrey Parsons died and the necessity of electing a Lord Mayor for the remainder of his term arose. At the Common Hall two days afterward, Godschall was again returned to the Court of Aldermen, and with him Sir John Barnard, who had served as Mayor in 1737-1738. Again the aldermen refused to name Godschall, and Barnard obtained the majority of votes. He declined, however, on account of his health. Then the Common Hall returned Godschall and Daniel Lambert. For the fourth time within the year, Godschall was passed over by the Court of Aldermen, and by a vote of thirteen to ten Lambert was chosen to be Lord Mayor and agreed to serve out Parson's term of office.[86]

By the following September, however, there was a change.

[86] *London Evening Post*, March 23, 1741; *Common Sense*, March 28, 1741; *London Magazine*, X (1741), 152. Lambert was supported by Eyles, Baylis, Billers, Thompson, Master, Champion, Salter, Rous and Arnold (Walpolians), and Williams, Perry, Hankey, and Baker (anti-Walpole), all but Perry and Salter, who were then absent, having voted in the 1740 elections for Heathcote and Parsons. Godschall again received the votes of Barnard, Godschall, Heathcote, Willimot, Lambert, Westley, Marshall, and Hoare, and also Benn and Ladbroke, who had succeeded Barber and Levett, respectively.

Perhaps the older aldermen were getting tired of the dissension, or perhaps they had been finally convinced, by the continued support of Godschall by the liverymen and by his election in April as one of the City's four representatives to Parliament,[87] that Godschall was the popular choice for Lord Mayor. Anyway, following upon his nomination again (with George Heathcote) at a preliminary meeting held at Joiners' Hall on September 25, and their return by the Common Hall on Michaelmas Day, Alderman Godschall was chosen by the Court of Aldermen to serve as Lord Mayor of London. On October 29, 1741, he was invested with that honor with the usual ceremonies and pageantry.[88] The following poem, published shortly afterward, although not to be considered for its literary merits, expresses the thought of the final triumph of the citizens:

> The Proverb is antient, altho' it seems odd,
> That the Voice of the People's the Language of God:
> Tho, dubious by some the Assertion is held,
> Yet the Honour of London the Truth has fulfill'd,
> And now 'tis a Point that needs no Vindication,
> That Godschall is Mayor to the Wish of the Nation.[89]

THE LONDON PARLIAMENTARY ELECTION OF 1741

Meantime, while the war with Spain was being carried on in foreign waters, Walpole at home was waging a losing fight against the parliamentary Opposition; and the succeeding sessions showed clearly the growing weakness of his power.[90] By the end of 1740 the Opposition had felt strong enough to make a direct attack on the Minister, and in February, 1741, Carteret in the Lords and Sandys in the Commons each moved that an Address be made to the King asking that Sir Robert be re-

[87] See pp. 204-207, below.

[88] *London Evening Post*, Sept. 29 and Oct. 29, 1741; *London Magazine*, X (1741), 465, 515; *Gentleman's Magazine*, XI (1741), 499, 552.

[89] *Common Sense*, Oct. 31, 1741.

[90] Moreover, the ministry itself was not united. Newcastle, Hardwicke, Harrington, and Wilmington, all had been for war with Spain in contrast to Walpole's peaceful policy, and differed with him in its conduct. The King wanted war more than any of them. Walpole at this time was sick and dejected. He was troubled with recurring attacks of the "stone," and he had suffered the loss of his first wife in August, 1737, and his second in July, 1738.

moved "from his Majesty's presence and counsels for ever."[91]
The Opposition, however, had at this time miscalculated its
strength.   In the Lords the motion was defeated by a vote
of 81 to 54, while in the Commons, aided by the withdrawal
of Shippen and his Jacobite and Tory friends, who refused
to vote, the Minister was victorious by 290 votes to 106.[92]
Nevertheless, notwithstanding this seemingly large majority,
Walpole and his administration were actually losing control;
and in the general election which followed the dissolution
of Parliament on April 27, the administration suffered severe
reverses throughout the nation, especially in Scotland and the
Prince of Wales' Duchy of Cornwall, and its strength very
noticeably diminished.[93]

In the London election the Opposition won a complete victory, although not without a contest.   As early as mid-October,
1740, there had been talk of the City's candidates; and Barnard,

[91] For an account of the debates, see Cobbett, *Parliamentary History*, XI,
1047 ff., 1223 ff.; Add. MSS, 6043, ff. 72b-86b; 9200, ff. 140 ff.; H. M. C.,
Egmont Diary, III, 191-192; and Coxe, *Sir Robert Walpole*, III, 559 ff.
There were many accusations, a statement of the details of which would be
only to repeat the history of his administration as his opponents interpreted
it.   Walpole made a brilliant defense, and in scathing yet truthful words,
pointed out the real crux of the situation: "My great and principle crime is
my long continuance in office, or, in other words, the long exclusion of those
who now complain against me.   This is the heinous offense which exceeds all
others: I keep from them the possession of that power, those honours and
those emoluments to which they so ardently and pertinaceously aspire. . . .
They have laboured the point for twenty years unsuccessfully. . . .   They
clamour for a change of measures, but mean only a change of ministers."
See Cobbett, *Parliamentary History*, XI, 1284-1285.

[92] *Journals of the House of Commons*, XXIII, 648; Cobbett, *Parliamentary
History*, XI, 1223, 1388.   Since the death of Wyndham, the year before, the
Tories and the Whigs in Opposition had not been so friendly, and many of
the former like Shippen withdrew or stayed and voted for the Minister.
Among those who withdrew were the Lord Mayor, Humphrey Parsons, and
Alderman Henry Marshall, while Alderman Micajah Perry stayed and voted
for Sir Robert.   See H. M. C., *Egmont Diary*, III, 192.

[93] "The loss of rank and file to the Administration was palpable and great,
though not so definable as party writers chose to name—not so measurable as
anybody could tell who did not know how it had been individually got, kept,
or lost" (Torrens, *History of Cabinets*, p. 527).   For the General Election
of 1741, see Torrens, I, 522 ff.; Mahon, *History of England*, III, 88 ff.;
Add. MSS, 9200, 74b, 138-140.   For the Duke of Newcastle's influence and
methods in this election, see Clarence Perkins, "Electioneering in Eighteenth
Century England," *Quarterly Journal of the University of North Dakota*,
XIII, 103-134.

Parsons, and Perry, of the sitting members for the City in Parliament were mentioned for renomination, with Heathcote, Godschall, Champion, Hankey, and Baker all coming in for considerable support.[94] The first formal nominations were made on November 19 at a meeting of the Livery at Vintners' Hall. Sir John Barnard was nominated first, but immediately asked to be excused from serving again, pleading ill-health.[95] Richard Glover, who was still busily taking advantage of all opportunities to make himself heard, arose and extolled, however, the virtues of Sir John; then, setting aside the latter's excuses, he insisted that his name be included in the list of nominees.[96] Barnard was therefore nominated over his objections, and with him were suggested the Lord Mayor, Humphrey Parsons, and Aldermen John Barber, Micajah Perry, Sir Robert Godschall, George Heathcote, and Daniel Lambert. Upon a vote being taken, the majority fell on Barnard, Parsons, Godschall, and Heathcote, and these were agreed upon as the men to be supported.[97] During the winter they were kept before the public with advertisements, which appeared from time to time. In March, upon the death of Lord Mayor Parsons, and the election of Lambert in his room, the liverymen, at another meeting, likewise agreed to support Lambert in Parson's place on the list of parliamentary candidates.[98]

Two days before the Parliament was dissolved (April 27, 1741) another group of the Livery met at the Fleece Tavern, in Cornhill, to nominate a list. Aldermen Perry, Barnard, Sir Joseph Hankey, Sir George Champion, Sir William Billers, William Baker, and Sir Edward Bellamy were all nominated, as well as Admiral Edward Vernon, absent in the West Indies, but still a very popular figure in London. Of these, Perry, Barnard, Bellamy, and Vernon were chosen to run against the

[94] *London Evening Post,* Oct. 16, 1740.
[95] *London Magazine,* X (1741), 41-43.
[96] *Ibid.,* IX (1740), 560; H. M. C., *Trevor MSS,* p. 61 (Horatio Walpole to Robert Trevor, Nov. 29, 1740).
[97] *London Evening Post,* Nov. 20, 1740; *London Magazine,* IX (1740), 560; Boyer, *Political State,* LX, 387-398.
[98] *Daily Advertiser,* March 27, 1741; *London Evening Post,* March 28, 1741; *London Magazine,* X (1741), 153.

previously nominated list.[99] These men were approved by another meeting on April 29 held at the Merchant-Taylors' Hall.[100] This list had the support, though not a very active one, of the friends of the ministry in the City; and since Vernon was a nominal Opposition member, it was readily charged that the addition of his name to this second list was purely a move for vote-getting. Writers in the Opposition press termed it a "Shallow Artifice" and warned the citizens to beware of "a snake in the Grass."[101]

The election was held on Tuesday, May 5. After the usual formalities, approval was given by the Common Hall to the two lists which had been previously named and advertised. Then came the voting. One of the Sheriffs in office, Richard Hoare, has left us a brief account of the events of this period:

> Then the common cryer put up the names of the two above-mentioned lists, and my brother sheriff [Henry Marshall] and I, having duly attended and observed the number of hands held up for each candidate, and consulting thereon, did agree and publickly declare, that the majority of hands were held up for Daniel Lambert, Lord Mayor, Sir John Barnard, Sir Robert Godschall, and George Heathcote. But a poll being demanded for the other list, it was granted and begun that afternoon.[102]

The poll was carried on "with great heat" at first, the "ministerial party" again being charged with using underhand methods;[103] but it was soon seen that the Vintners' Hall list (Lambert, Barnard, Godschall, and Heathcote) would have the majority. By Saturday, Perry and Bellamy were willing to concede the election; but since they could not get Admiral Vernon's assent to drop the poll, he being in the West Indies, the balloting had to go on for the full eight days.[104] On Tuesday, May 12, the poll closed and the numbers were given out. Barnard, who was on both lists, had the most votes (3,769);

[99] *London Evening Post*, April 25, 1741; *Journal . . . of Richard Hoare*, p. 77.
[100] *Daily Advertiser*, April 30, 1741.
[101] *London Evening Post*, April 25 and May 2, 1741.
[102] *Journal . . . of Richard Hoare*, p. 78.
[103] *London Evening Post*, May 9, 1741; *Craftsman*, May 23, 1741.
[104] *Daily Advertiser*, May 11, 1741; *London Evening Post*, May 12, 1741.

and he was followed in order by Heathcote (3,322), Lambert (3,217), and Godschall (3,143), who were the next day declared duly elected.[105] All four of them were known to be against the Walpole administration, and it was a gratifying victory for the Opposition. "Such a Glorious Majority shows at what a low Ebb his Honour's [Walpole's] Interest is in this great City, and should be an example to the whole Kingdom," was the joyful comment of one writer.[106]

Before the Common Hall adjourned, it was suggested that the liverymen present a "Paper of Instructions" to the four newly elected representatives, which was readily drawn up and approved. It began with a short preamble:

We, the Citizens of London, who have cheerfully elected you to serve us in Parliament, and thereby committed to your Trust the Safety, Liberty, and Privileges of ourselves and Posterities, think it our Duty, as it is our undoubted Right to acquaint you with what we desire and expect from you, in discharge of the great Confidence we repose in you, and what we take to be your Duty as our Representatives.

It then listed in some detail what was expected. It urged the City's representatives to maintain "a constant and vigorous Opposition to all standing Armies in Times of Peace"; to oppose the extension of all laws of excise, and to promote if possible the repeal of the existing laws; to work for the repeal of the Septennial Act, and the restoration of Triennial Parliaments; to insist on the procuring of a proper bill for reducing and limiting the number of placemen in the House of Commons; to support his Majesty in the granting of supplies for the war, and to insist on a "glorious" peace; and to persist "until you shall prevail" in getting a bill or bills passed to procure the repeal of the hated "negative" of the Court of Aldermen.[107]

[105] Book of Common Hall, 7, f. 288; *London Evening Post*, May 14, 1741; *London Magazine*, X (1741), 252; *Journal . . . of Richard Hoare*, p. 84. Of the other three, Perry received 1,710 votes, Bellamy 1,311, and Vernon 1,175. Vernon's victory at Porto Bello, which the populace still applauded, made him a potential candidate for other constituencies. He was beaten in Westminster, but was elected from Rochester, Ipswich, and Penryn.
[106] In the *London Evening Post*, May 14, 1741.
[107] *London Magazine*, X (1741), 253.

THE END COMES TO THE WALPOLE ADMINISTRATION

Whether or not the City's instructions to its representatives were carried out is not to be considered within the limits of this study, for with the opening of the new Parliament, the third of George II, on December 1, 1741, the days of the Walpole administration were numbered. It had been readily agreed that the Opposition would soon control a majority, and the results of the first trials of election petitions proved it so. On December 9 a division on the contested Bossiney election gave the ministry a majority of only seven votes (222 to 215).[108] Upon the choice of a chairman for the parliamentary committee on elections, on December 16, the Opposition candidate, Dr. George Lee (Devizes), defeated the Ministerial candidate, Giles Earle (Malmesbury), by four votes (242 to 238),[109] while six days later the contested election of Westminster, where the ministerial candidates had been returned, was voided by majorities of four and five votes (220 to 216, and 220 to 215).[110] These were real victories for the Opposition, and Walpole found it harder and harder to fight back. Not only was his numerical majority in Parliament depleted, but his own physical strength was not what it had been in his earlier years, and he suffered much from repeated attacks of the "stone."[111]

"But even a sick and rather heartless lion was still a match for a terrier," as his latest biographer has written,[112] and Pul-

[108] *Journals of the House of Commons*, XXIV, 14.

[109] *Ibid.*, XXIV, 9; H. M. C., *Egmont Diary*, III, 232-233.

[110] *Journals of the House of Commons*, XXIV, 37; H. M. C., *Egmont Diary*, III, 233.

[111] Horace Walpole wrote to Horace Mann on October 19, 1741, that his father, who before "was asleep as soon as his head touched the pillow . . . now never sleeps above an hour without waking; and he, who at dinner always forgot that he was Minister, and was more gay and thoughtless than all his company, now sits without speaking and with his eyes fixed for an hour together. Judge if this is the Sir Robert you knew." See *Letters of Horace Walpole* (Cunningham), I, 78.

[112] G. R. Sterling Taylor (*Robert Walpole*, p. 315). Walpole seemed to find new vigor for the struggle of the last days. Lord Morton, writing to Duncan Forbes, on January 5, 1742 (*Culloden Papers*, p. 172), to tell him of the difficulties of his old friend, observed that "considering what up-hill work 'tis like to be, I'm astonished to see the spirit, the intrepedity, and cheerfulness w^t wch he bears it out. . . . I find he intends to fight every inch in S^t St——n's Ch——l."

teney found this out when he attacked the Minister on January 21 and demanded an investigation of the conduct of the war by a secret committee. Pulteney made one of the best speeches of his career, but "Sir Robert exceeded himself; he particularly entered into foreign affairs and convinced even his enemies that he was thoroughly master of them. Mr. Pelham with the greatest decency cut Mr. Pulteney into 1,000 pieces. Sir Robert actually dissected him and laid his heart open to the view of the House."[113] The result was a vote of approval for the administration, although by a close margin; on the division the motion was rejected by 253 to 250.[114]

Nevertheless, it was but a final gallant stand. On February 2, on a division over the contested election in Chippenham, the Opposition won a decided victory by a vote of 241 to 225, a majority of sixteen votes.[115] It was clear now that the Minister could not continue to lead the administration. A week later Sir Robert was created Earl of Orford, and on February 11, 1742, he resigned his offices and retired from active public service.[116]

So, at long last, the period of Walpole's administration came to an end. It had been the longest continuous period that any chief minister had directed, or would in the future direct, the destinies of the British nation. During that period the House of Hanover had been firmly set upon the British throne, and, until the last two years, the country had been at peace,

[113] Sir Robert Wilmot to the Duke of Devonshire, Jan. 23, 1742 (Coxe, *Sir Robert Walpole*, III, 588). See also Horace Walpole's letter to Horace Mann, on January 22, in *Letters of Horace Walpole* (Cunningham), I, 119-121.

[114] *Journals of the House of Commons*, XXIV, 53. See Mahon, *History of England*, III, 100-101.

[115] *Journals of the House of Commons*, XXIV, 80. See H. M. C., *Egmont Diary*, III, 247.

[116] *Daily Post*, Feb. 9, 1742; *London Gazette*, Feb. 12, 1742. Lord Wilmington (Sir Spencer Compton) took Walpole's place as First Lord of the Treasury, with Samuel Sandys as Chancellor of the Exchequer; but Lord Carteret, who, with the Duke of Newcastle, was made a Secretary of State, was the chief figure in the new administration. Pulteney accepted a title as Earl of Bath and discovered that he had thereby lost any opportunity he might have had to retain his leadership. Walpole, now Earl of Orford, continued to have some influence, behind the scenes, on the Government, but in his last days he preferred the quiet of his Norfolk home. He died, four years after the close of his long ministry, on March 18, 1745.

making possible sound economic progress and a foundation for the larger and world-wide development of the British Empire that followed. In all of this the City of London had its part. Being the center of England's commercial interests, it reaped great rewards from the years of peace and the wise economic measures of the Walpole administration. Nevertheless, throughout the period the City never wholly accepted the leadership of the chief minister and increasingly worked in opposition to him, finally contributing in a large way to his overthow.

CHAPTER IX

In Summary

LONDON during the administration of Sir Robert Walpole, just as it had been through the preceding centuries, was a power in the nation. Its position, its size, and its wealth made it a factor to be reckoned with. It was natural, therefore, that Walpole should seek to gain its friendship and to avoid its enmity. That he never did accomplish the former and seemed increasingly to provoke the latter explains the almost constant opposition by the City throughout his period as chief minister. Support was given him for the greater part of the period by the executive body of the Corporation, the Court of Aldermen; but the legislative group, the Court of Common Council, as well as the more voluble mass of citizens which it represented, looked with disfavor on nearly everything he did. Perhaps the City's attitude should not be attributed to the citizens entirely; for their moments of greatest opposition came only when aroused by those who belonged to the Opposition group in Parliament, who came to use the London mob as a pawn in the great game they were playing, the object of which was the overthrow of the Minister.

This was clearly seen in 1721, when the City was stirred up against the seemingly harmless clauses of the Quarantine Act. It was likewise true of the opposition to the proposed bridge over the Thames at Westminster. The political enemies of Walpole seized upon both of these occasions to work on the fears of the citizens for their economic and political liberties and privileges, and produced such a clamor that Walpole was obliged to repeal or withdraw both the matters protested. These setbacks did not overthrow the Ministry; nevertheless, the results showed definitely the power that the City could exert upon occasion and spurred the leaders of both the Ministry and the parliamentary Opposition to greater efforts to gain its favor and support.

The opposition to the Excise Bill in 1733 and the outbreak of the Spanish War in 1739 were also examples of occasions when the City was aroused by the opponents of the Minister to aid them in their efforts to overthrow him. By the Excise Bill Walpole had in mind to aid the country in general by increasing its revenues, and the City merchants in particular by protecting their goods. That he failed may be laid to the power of a vocal public opinion which was strong enough to make Walpole believe the withdrawal of the bill to be necessary for the continued peace of the country. The war with Spain resulted from a similar demonstration, and the popular opposition to the administration's efforts to obtain in a peaceful manner satisfaction from Spain for the depredations committed on British ships and sailors was sufficient to bring on the conflict.

In all these matters London played an important role in national affairs. Likewise the national administration played its part in City politics. At nearly every election in the City—of common councilmen, aldermen, sheriffs, lord mayors, or parliament men—the question of support of or opposition to the Walpole ministry was an important factor, and in some of them the leaders or representatives of one or both of the national parties took a personal and active part.

The City Elections Act of 1725 was an example of ministerial interference. Intended in part to settle the disputes and bring about order among the citizens at election times, it was also an effort by the ministry to check the activities of the hostile-minded Common Council and insure the predominance of the more favorably inclined Court of Aldermen. The Act proved successful in bringing about order at elections and in contributing to the peace of the City, but the dominance of the aldermen, while insuring support to the administration for a time, only added in the end to the resentment of the councilmen and the citizens and thus contributed to their increased opposition.

Nor did the support of the aldermen continue. Although Walpole could count on a large majority in 1721, repeated changes in the personnel of the court throughout the period gradually resulted, because of the ever-growing opposition of the Londoners to Walpole, in the election of enough ward leaders contrary-minded politically to change the favorable majority to one unfavorable to the Minister. Thus in the latter years of his administration, the City—aldermen, common councilmen, and citizens—was almost wholly united against him.

National affairs also had their part in the local political scene. The unrest following upon the South Sea failure, the clamor over the Quarantine and Westminster Bridge bills, abhorrence of Jacobite plottings, resentment of foreign encroachments, the opposition to the Excise scheme, the demand for war with Spain, all appeared as issues at one time or another in the varied and sundry London elections. In the choosing of City representatives to Parliament it was to be expected that national issues would be important, but throughout the period they constantly appeared at both the ward and Common Hall meetings, this being just as apparent at the elections of common councilmen in December, 1721, as it was in the choice of the City Chamberlain in 1733, of the Lord Mayor in 1739, or of any one of a dozen aldermen during the course of the period.

Thus the City and the national government were in close contact at all times, the influence of the one being felt in the conduct of the other, and a keen interest being taken by both in the affairs of each. The City could not be overlooked by those connected with the Walpole administration—whether as friends or as enemies—and the interests of the nation were so bound up with the City's interests that the policies and activities of the national government could but be a matter of the deepest concern to the citizens and government of the metropolis. Sir Robert Walpole held the leadership of his Majesty's government for a longer continuous period than any of his predecessors did before him or his successors have done since, but his administration would have been far more peaceful and he would have suffered far less from the Opposition if he had been successful in his efforts to win and hold the friendship of the City of London.

Bibliography

I. Unpublished Manuscripts

BRITISH MUSEUM

Stowe MSS
  251. Transcripts of State Letters, 1724-1748.

Egerton MSS
  1721. Correspondence of William, Count Bentinck, 1730-1765.
  2543. Miscellaneous Historical Papers of Sir Edward Nicholas, and his Son, 1661-1722.

Additional MSS
  9130. Political Papers, 1723-1737.
  9132. Papers by Horatio, Lord Walpole.
  9153-9178. Letters and Papers Relative to the Political History of Great Britain, 1720-1742.
  9199-9201. Papers and Correspondence of the Rev. Henry Etough, Relative to Political Affairs, 1733-1757.
  27980-27981. Newsletters on Public Affairs, Addressed to Viscount Perceval, London, March, 1723, to March, 1724; January, 1729, to December, 1730.
  31152. Political and Other Pieces in Verse, Chiefly Relating to the Early Period of the Eighteenth Century.
  32096. State Papers, Historical Documents, etc., 1700-1762.
  32686. Newcastle Papers—General Correspondence, 1697-1723.
  32687-32699. Newcastle Papers—Home Correspondence, 1724-1742.
  32738-32802. Newcastle Papers—Foreign Correspondence, 1724-1742.
  33051-33052. Newcastle Papers—Miscellaneous Papers, 1704-1751.
  34712-34713. Collections, Historical, Antiquarian, etc., Made by Thomas Astle, 1711-1763.
  35335. Original Letters and Miscellaneous Papers, Chiefly Relating to Robert Walpole, 1700-1783.
  35406-35407. Hardwicke Papers—Political Correspondence with the Duke of Newcastle, 1723-1743.

35423. Hardwicke Papers—Political Correspondence with Henry Pelham, 1724-1753.

35584-35586. Hardwicke Papers—General Correspondence, 1704-1741.

35875-35876. Hardwicke Papers—Parliamentary Correspondence, 1720-1749.

CITY OF LONDON GUILDHALL LIBRARY (RECORD OFFICE OF THE CORPORATION).

Repertories of the Court of Aldermen. Vols. 125-146 (1720-1742).

Journals of the Court of Common Council. Vols. 57-59 (1717-1751).

Books of Common Hall. Vols. 6-7 (1710-1751).

PUBLIC RECORD OFFICE

State Papers Domestic, George I (for years 1720-1727).

State Papers Domestic, George II (for years 1727-1742).

II. NEWSPAPERS AND PERIODICALS

(The majority of the newspapers listed are in the Burney Collection at the British Museum. Dates listed are inclusive of the issues examined. Abbreviations: d.—daily; m.—monthly; s.w.—semiweekly; t.w.—triweekly; w.—weekly.)

Applebee's Original Weekly Journal. w. 1720-1733.

Bee: or, Universal Weekly Pamphlet. w. 1733-1735.

Brice's Weekly Journal. w. 1725-1726.

British Gazetteer (see *Weekly Journal; or, British Gazetteer*).

British Journal. Continued as *British Journal; or, the Censor* from January 20, 1728. w. 1723-1731.

Champion; or Evening Advertizer. t.w. 1739-1740, 1742.

Common Sense; or the Englishman's Journal. w. 1737-1741.

Craftsman. Continued as *Country Journal; or, the Craftsman* from May 13, 1727. w. 1726-1742.

Daily Advertizer. d. 1731, 1738-1742.

Daily Courant. d. 1720-1735.

Daily Gazetteer. d. 1735-1737, 1740.

Daily Journal. d. 1721-1737.

Daily Post. d. 1720-1742.

Daily Post-Boy (see *Post-Boy*).

Evening Post. t.w. 1723.

Exeter Mercury; or Weekly Intelligence. w. 1722.

Flying Post; or, the Postmaster. t.w. 1722.

Fog's Weekly Journal (see *Weekly Journal; or, Saturday's Post*).

Free Briton. w. 1733-1734.

General Evening Post. t.w. 1738.

Gentleman's Magazine; or Monthly Intelligencer. Continued as *Gentleman's Magazine and Historical Chronicle,* from 1736. m. Vols. I-XII, 1731-1742.

Grub Street Journal. w. 1730-1737.

Historical Register, Containing an Impartial Relation of All Transactions, Foreign and Domestic. With a Chronological Diary of All the Remarkable Occurrences, etc., That Happen'd in This Year. Vols. V-XXIII, 1720-1738.

Independent London Journal. w. 1735-1736.

Independent Whig. w. 1720-1721.

London and Country Journal. w. 1739-1743.

London Daily Post and General Advertizer. d. 1736, 1738-1741.

London Evening Post. d. 1729-1742.

London Gazette. s.w. 1720-1742.

London Journal. w. 1720-1734.

London Magazine; or Gentleman's Monthly Intelligencer. Continued as *London Magazine and Monthly Chronologer,* from 1736. m. Vols. I-XI, 1732-1742.

Ludlow Post-Man; or, the Weekly Journal. w. 1725.

Mist's Weekly Journal (see *Weekly Journal; or Saturday's Post*).

Monthly Chronicle. m. 1728-1732.

Old Whig; or, the Consistent Protestant. w. 1735-1738.

Political State of Great Britain: Being an Impartial Account of the Most Material Occurrences, Ecclesiastical, Civil and Military in a Monthly Letter to a Friend in Holland. Author and compiler, Abel Boyer (to October, 1729). Vols. XIX-LX, 1720-1740.

Post-Boy. Continued as *Daily Post-Boy,* from November 19, 1728. d. 1720-1723, 1728, 1733, 1737.

Post-Master; or, the Loyal Mercury. w. 1724-1725.

Present State of Europe, or, the Historical and Political Monthly Mercury, Giving an Account of All the Publick and Private Occurrences, etc. m. Vols. XXXII-XLIII, 1720-1731; XLVI-XLVII, 1734-1735.

Read's Weekly Journal (see *Weekly Journal; or British Gazetteer*).

St. James's Post. t.w. 1725.

True Briton. s.w. 1723-1724.

Weekly Journal; or British Gazetteer, Being the Freshest Advices

Foreign and Domestick. Continued as *Read's Weekly Journal;
or British Gazetteer,* from August 15, 1730. *w.* 1720-1739.

*Weekly Journal; or Saturday's Post, with Fresh Advices Foreign
and Domestic.* Continued as *Mist's Weekly Journal,* from May
1, 1725; as *Fog's Weekly Journal,* from September 28, 1728.
w. 1720-1731.

Weekly Miscellany [sometimes called *Hooker's Miscellany*]; *Giving
an Account of the Religion, Morality, and Learning of the Present
Times. w.* 1732-1741.

Weekly Register; or Universal Journal. w. 1733-1734.

Whitehall Evening Post. t.w. 1721-1722.

III. PAMPHLETS

(All pamphlets were published in London.)

*An Appeal to the Landholders concerning the Reasonableness and
General Benefit of an Excise upon Tobacco and Wine.* 1733.

*A Brief State of the Several Disputes and Grievances at Present
Complain'd of in the City of London with Some Observations
Thereupon, and upon the Bill Now Depending in Parliament,
for Regulating Elections in the City of London, or for Preserving
the Peace, Good Order, and Government of the Said City.* 1724.

*A Candid Answer to a Letter, from a Member of Parliament to His
Friends in the Country, Concerning the Duties on Wine and
Tobacco.* 1733.

*The Case of the Levant Company, in Relation to the Bill Now De-
pending before This Honourable House for Performing Quarantine.* 1721.

*The Case of the Planters of Tobacco in Virginia as Represented by
Themselves, To Which Is Added, a Vindication of the Said Presentation.* 1733.

*The City Struggle: A Satire, Occasion'd by the Late Election of a
Lord Mayor.* 1740.

*Three Clauses in the Quarantine Act of VII George I, the Petition
of the City of London to the House of Lords, Their Lordships
Protest on Rejecting the Said Petition, and, Another Protest of
Their Lordships.* 1721.

*The Conduct of the Late Administration, with Regard to Foreign
Affairs, from 1722 to 1742; Wherein That of the Right of the
Honourable the Earl of Orford (Late Sir Robert Walpole) Is
Particularly Vindicated.* 1742.

The Conduct of the Liverymen at the Late Election of a Lord-Mayor, and Their Proceedings in the Common Hall Justified. 1739.

Considerations upon a Proposal for Lowering the Interest of All the Redeemable National Debts to Three Per Cent. per Ann. 1737.

Cowper, William. *An Account of What Sums of Money Have Been Paid by the Chamberlain of London, Concerning Any Causes or Suits at Law, Relating to the Elections of Aldermen or Common-Council Men, Since the Eighth Day of November, 1711, and by What Warrant.* 1719.

The D'Anverian History of the Affairs of Europe, for the Memorable Year, 1731. 1732.

A Further Report from the Committee of Secrecy, Appointed to Enquire into the Conduct of Robert, Earl of Orford; During the Last Ten Years of His Being First Commissioner of the Treasury, and Chancellor and Under-Treasurer of His Majesty's Exchequer. 1742.

[Gordon, Thomas.] *A Compleat History of the Late Septennial Parliament, Wherein All Their Proceedings Are Particularly Enquired into, and Faithfully Related.* 1722.

[Gordon, Thomas.] *A Short View of the Conspiracy, with Some Reflections on the Present State of Affairs. In a Letter to an Old Whig in the Country.* 1723.

An Impartial Relation of the Proceedings of the Common-Hall and Court of Aldermen on Monday the 29th of September, 1740, at the Election of a Lord Mayor for the Year Ensuing; in Which Is Inserted a List of the Aldermen Who Voted for, and against Setting aside Sir Robert Godschall. 1740.

A Letter from a Citizen to a Member of Parliament, against the Bill Now Depending for Regulating the Elections in the City of London, and for Preserving the Peace, Good Order, and Government of the Said City. 1725.

A Letter from an Absented Member to a Friend at Westminster, Showing His Reasons for Retiring into the Country upon the Present Situation of the Affairs of Great Britain. 1739.

A Letter to a Livery-Man [Sir John Barnard], *Occasion'd by His Commencing Projector.* 1737.

A Letter to Sir George Champion, Shewing the Reasons of Setting Him Aside at the Approaching Election. 1739.

A Letter to Mr. William Timms, of Cripplegate Within; Contain-

ing an Answer to the Report of a Committee of Aldermen, in
Affirmance of the Right of the Mayor and Aldermen to Put a
Negative to Bills or Acts of Common Council. 1724.

A List of the Members Who Voted for and against the Late Convention with Spain. 1739.

The Livery-Man: or Plain Thoughts on Publick Affairs; in Which
the Present Situation of Things, the General Disposition of the
People, the Insults Offer'd the City of London, etc., Are Consider'd and Explain'd. 1740.

The London Merchants Triumphant: or Sturdy Beggars Are Brave
Fellows. A New Ballad Proper to Be Sung on the 12th of June.
Humbly Inscribed to the Worthy Merchants and Citizens of Lon-
don. 1733.

The Lord Mayor's Speech and the City Petition about the Excise.
1733.

The Lords Protests in the Late Session of Parliament: To Which
Is Added, Britannia Excisa, or Britain Excised, with an Alpha-
betical List of All the Members Who Voted for and against the
Excise Bill, etc. 1733.

The Opposition Made by the Citizens of London against the Scheme
for an Excise of Wine and Tobacco. 1733.

The Poll of the Livery-Men of the City of London, at the Election
for Members of Parliament, Begun Tuesday, April the 10th,
1722, and Ended Saturday Following. 1722.

Popular Prejudices against the Convention and Treaty with Spain,
Examin'd and Answer'd. 1739.

The Principle Reasons Assign'd for Excising of Wines Consider'd;
in a Letter to a Member of Parliament. 1733.

The Proceedings at the Court of Hustings and Common Hall, of the
Liverymen of the City of London, at the Late Election of a Lord-
Mayor. By a Liveryman Who Was Present. 1739.

[Pulteney, William.] The Budget Opened: Or, an Answer to a
Pamphlet Intitl'd, a Letter from a Member of Parliament to His
Friends in the Country Concerning the Duties on Wines and To-
bacco. 1733.

[Pulteney, William.] The Case of the Revival of the Salt Duty,
Fully Stated and Considered; with Some Remarks on the Present
State of Affairs. In Answer to a Late Pamphlet, Intitl'd a Letter
to a Freeholder on the Late Reduction of the Land-Tax to One
Shilling in the Pound. 1732.

[Pulteney, William.] *An Enquiry into the Conduct of Our Affairs, from the Year 1721, to the Present Time.* 1734.

[Pulteney, William.] *A Review of the Excise Scheme; in Answer to a Pamphlet, Intitled, the Rise and Fall of the Late Projected Excise, Impartially Considered. With Some Proper Hints to the Electors of Great Britain.* 1733.

[Pulteney, William.] *A Short View of the State of Affairs, with Relation to Great Britain, for Four Years Past; with Some Remarks on the Treaty Lately Published and a Pamphlet Intitled, Observations upon It.* 1730.

Reasons against Subjecting Any Other Traders of Great Britain to the Laws of Excise. 1733.

The Reasons for and against the Seclusion of Sir G. C. from Being Lord Mayor of London. Now First Collected from the Papers in Which They Were Occasionally Printed. 1739.

The Reply of a Member of Parliament to the Mayor of His Corporation. 1733.

The Report of a Committee of Aldermen, in Affirmance of the Right of the Mayor and Aldermen to Put a Negative to Bills or Acts Depending in the Common-Council of London. Confirmed by the Court of Lord-Mayor and Aldermen, and Published by Their Authority on March 10, 1723. 1724.

A Review of the Whole Political Conduct of a Late Eminent Patriot, and His Friends; for Twenty Years Last Past: In Which Is Contained a Complete History of the Late Opposition: And a Full Answer to a Pamphlet, Entitled, Faction Detected by the Evidence of Facts, &c. 1743.

[Robins, Benjamin.] *An Address to the Electors, and Other Free Subjects of Great Britain; In Which Is Contain'd a Particular Account of All Our Negociations with Spain, and Their Treatment of Us, for Above Ten Years past.* 1739.

[Robins, Benjamin.] *A Narrative of What Passed in the Common Hall of the City of London, Assembled for the Election of Lord-Mayor, on Saturday the 29th of September, on Monday the 1st, and on Tuesday the 2nd of October.* 1739.

Rome Excis'd: A New Tragi-Comic Ballad-Opera of Three Acts: As It Is Now Acting with General Applause by a Polite Company of Courtiers. 1733.

Serious Considerations on the Ensuing Elections of a Lord-Mayor. 1739.

Some Observations upon a Paper, Intitled, the List. That Is, of Those Who Voted for and against the Excise-Bill. 1733.

The State Juggler: or Sir Politik Ribband. A New Excise Opera. 1733.

The Sturdy Beggars: A New Ballad Opera, Humbly Dedicated to the Lord Mayor, Aldermen, Common-Council, and the Merchants and Citizens of London. 1733.

The Thoughts of an Impartial Man upon the Present Temper of the Nation; Offer'd to the Consideration of the Freeholders of Great Britain. 1733.

[Vyner, Rev. Robert.] *A Very Long, Curious and Extraordinary Sermon Preached on Wednesday, March 14, 1733, at a Noted Chapel in Westminster, from These Words of St. Luke, c. II, v. 1: And It Came to Pass in Those Days That a Decree Went Out, That All the World Should Be Taxed. With Some Practical Observations and Uses Suited to the Present Time.* 1733.

[Walpole, Horace.] *The Convention Vindicated from the Misrepresentation of the Enemies of the Peace.* 1739.

[Walpole, Horace.] *The Grand Question, Whether War, or No War, with Spain, Impartially Consider'd: In Defense of the Present Measures against Those That Delight in War.* 1739.

[Walpole, Sir Robert.] *A Letter from a Member of Parliament to His Friends in the Country concerning the Duties on Wines and Tobacco.* 1733.

[Walpole, Sir Robert.] *Some General Considerations concerning the Alteration and Improvement of Publick Revenues.* 1733.

IV. OTHER PRINTED WORKS

(The place of publication is London, unless otherwise indicated.)

ACRES, W. MARSTON. *The Bank of England from Within, 1694-1900.* 1931. 2 vols.

ALLEN, THOMAS. *The History and Antiquities of London, Westminster, Southwark, and Parts Adjacent.* 1827-1828. 4 vols.

ANDREADES, A. *History of the Bank of England, 1640-1903.* 1924.

BADDELEY, JOHN JAMES. *The Guildhall of the City of London.* 1899.

―――. *The Aldermen of Cripplegate Ward, from 1267 to 1900.* 1900.

BALLANTYNE, ARCHIBALD. *Lord Carteret: A Political Biography, 1690-1763.* 1887.

BEAVEN, REV. ALFRED B. *The Aldermen of the City of London.*
1908-1913. 2 vols.

BEECHING, H. C. *Francis Atterbury.* 1909.

BESANT, SIR WALTER. *London in the Eighteenth Century.* 1903.

BIRCH, WALTER DE GRAY. *Historical Charters and Constitutional
Documents of the City of London.* rev. ed. 1887.

BOURNE, H. R. FOX *English Newspapers: Chapters in the History
of Journalism.* 1887. 2 vols.

————. *Famous London Merchants.* 1869.

BRISCOE, NORRIS ARTHUR. *The Economic Policy of Robert Walpole.* New York, 1907.

CALAMY, EDMUND. *An Historical Account of My Own Life, with
Some Reflections on the Times I Have Lived in, 1671-1731.*
Edited by John Towill Rutt. 2 vols. 1829.

Cambridge Modern History, The. Volume VI, *The Eighteenth
Century.* Edited by Sir A. W. Ward, G. W. Prothero, and
Stanley Leathes. Cambridge, 1909.

CAMPBELL, R. *The London Tradesman, Being an Historical Account of All the Trades, Professions, etc., Now Practised in the
Cities of London and Westminster.* 1757.

CARPENTER, WILLIAM. *The Corporation of London, As It Is
and As It Should Be.* 1847.

Catalogue of Additions to the Manuscripts of the British Museum.
1817-1933. 21 vols.

CHAMBERLAYNE, JOHN. *Magna Britannia Notitia: or, the Present
State of Great Britain; with Divers Remarks upon the Ancient
State Thereof.* 25th edition. 1718.

CHANCE, JAMES FREDERICK. *The Alliance of Hanover: A Study
of British Foreign Policy in the Last Year of George I.* 1923.

————. *George I and the Northern War: A Study of British-
Hanoverian Policy in the North of Europe in the Years 1709 to
1721.* 1909.

CHANCELLOR, EDWIN BERESFORD. *The Eighteenth Century in
London; an Account of Its Social Life and Arts.* 1920.

CHANDLER, RICHARD. *The History and Proceedings of the House
of Commons from the Restoration to the Present Time.* 1741-
1744. 14 vols.

CHESTERFIELD, LORD. *The Letters of Philip Dormer Stanhope,
4th Earl of Chesterfield.* Edited by Bonamy Dobrée. 1932.
6 vols.

City Biography; Containing Anecdotes and Memoirs of the Rise, Progress, Situation, & Character, of the Aldermen and Other Conspicuous Personages of the Corporation and City of London. 1799.

City Liberties: or, the Rights and Privileges of Freemen. Being a Concise Abridgement of All the Laws, Charters, By-Laws, and Customs of London, down to This Time. 1732.

COBBETT, WILLIAM. *Parliamentary History of England. From the Norman Conquest, in 1066, to the Year 1803.* 1806-1820. 36 vols. Volumes VII-XII, 1714-1743 were used.

COMMONS, HOUSE OF. *Members of Parliament, 1213-1874.* 1878.

COXE, WILLIAM. *Memoirs of the Life and Administration of Sir Robert Walpole, Earl of Orford. With Original Correspondence and Authentic Papers, Never Before Published.* 1798. 3 vols.

———. *Memoirs of Horatio, Lord Walpole, Selected from His Correspondence and Papers, and Connected with the History of the Times, from 1678 to 1757.* 1820. 2 vols.

CRANE, RONALD S., AND F. B. KAYE. *A Census of British Newspapers and Periodicals, 1620-1800.* Chapel Hill, 1927.

Culloden Papers: Comprising an Extensive and Interesting Correspondence from the Year 1625 to 1748, Including Numerous Letters from the Unfortunate Lord Lovat, and Other Distinguished Persons of the Time with Occasional State Papers of Much Historical Importance. The Whole Published from the Originals in the Possession of Duncan George Forbes, of Culloden. Edited by H. R. Duff. 1815.

DAVEY, RICHARD. *The Pageant of London.* 1906. 2 vols.

DEFOE, DANIEL. *A Tour thro' the Whole Island of Great Britain.* Reprinting of the first edition, 1724-1726. Edited by G. D. H. Cole. 1927. 2 vols.

Dictionary of National Biography. Edited by Sidney Lee and Leslie Stephens. 1885-1900. 63 vols.

DODINGTON, GEORGE BUBB. *The Diary of George Bubb Dodington, Baron of Melcombe Regis, from March 8, 1749, to February 6, 1761.* With Appendix. Edited by Henry Wyndham. 1785.

DONNAN, ELIZABETH. "Eighteenth Century English Merchants, Micajah Perry," *Journal of Economic and Business History,* IV (1931), 70-98.

DORAN, JOHN. *London in the Jacobite Times, 1715-1775.* 1877.

DOTTIN, PAUL. *The Life and Strange and Surprising Adventures of Daniel De Foe.* Translated from the French by Louise Ragan. New York, 1929.

DUPUY-DEMPORTES, JEAN BAPTISTE. *Histoire du ministère du chevalier Robert Walpole.* Amsterdam, 1764. 3 vols.

ENTICK, REV. JOHN. *A New and Accurate History and Survey of London, Westminster, and Southwark.* 1766. 4 vols.

EWALD, ALEXANDER CHARLES. *Sir Robert Walpole: A Political Biography, 1676-1745.* 1878.

FURNEAUX, PHILIP. *Letters to the Honourable Mr. Justice Blackstone, Concerning His Exposition of the Art of Toleration, and Some Positions Relative to Religious Liberty, in His Celebrated Commentaries on the Laws of England.* 2d edition, with additions, and an Appendix. 1771.

GEORGE, M. DOROTHY. *London Life in the Eighteenth Century.* New York, 1925.

GIUSEPPI, M. S. *A Guide to the Manuscripts Preserved in the Public Record Office.* 1924. 2 vols.

GOUGH, JOHN. *A History of the People Called Quakers.* Dublin, 1790. 4 vols.

GREGO, JOSEPH. *A History of Parliamentary Elections and Electioneering in the Old Days, from the Stuarts to Queen Victoria.* 1886.

GROSE, CLYDE L. "Thirty Years Study of a Formerly Neglected Century of British History, 1660-1760," *Journal of Modern History,* II (1930), 448-471.

HARRIS, GEORGE. *The Life of Lord Chancellor Hardwicke, with Selections from His Correspondence, Diaries, Speeches, and Judgements.* 1847. 3 vols.

HAYDN, JOSEPH. *The Book of Dignities Containing Lists of the Official Personages of the British Empire, Civil, Diplomatic, Heraldic, Judicial, Ecclesiastical, Municipal, Naval, and Military, from the Earliest Periods to the Present Time, etc. Remodelled and Brought down to 1851, by the Late Joseph Haydn, Continued to the Present Time, with Numerous Additional Lists, and an Index to the Entire Work by Horace Ockerbey.* 1894.

HAZLITT, WILLIAM CAREW. *The Livery Companies of the City of London.* New York, 1892.

HEATH, JOHN BENJAMIN. *Some Account of the Worshipful Company of Grocers of the City of London.* 1854.

HERBERT, WILLIAM. *The History of the Twelve Great Livery Companies of London.* 1837.

HERVEY, JOHN, LORD. *Some Materials towards Memoirs of the Reign of King George II.* Edited by Romney Sedgwick. 1931. 3 vols.

HILDNER, ERNEST G. "The Role of the South Sea Company in the Diplomacy Leading to the War of Jenkins' Ear, 1729-1739," *Hispanic American Historical Review,* XVIII (1938), 322-341.

HISTORICAL MANUSCRIPTS COMMISSION.

Ailesbury MSS. *The Manuscripts of the Marquis of Ailesbury.* Fifteenth Report, Part VII. 1898.

Bagot MSS. *The Manuscripts of Captain Josceline F. Bagot, of Levens Hall.* Tenth Report, Part IV. 1885.

Carlisle MSS. *The Manuscripts of the Earl of Carlisle, Preserved at Castle Howard.* Fifteenth Report, Appendix, Part VI. 1897.

Clements MSS. *The Manuscripts of M. L. S. Clements, Esq., Preserved at Ashfield Lodge, Cootehill, Co. Cavan.* Fifteenth Report. Various Collections, Volume VIII. 1913.

Egmont Diary. *The Manuscripts of the Earl of Egmont. Diary of Viscount Percival, Afterwards First Earl of Egmont.* Eighteenth Report. 1920-1923. 3 vols.

Hare MSS. *The Manuscripts of Theodore J. Hare, Esq., of Borden Wood, Hants.* Fourteenth Report, Appendix, Part IX. 1895.

Hodgkin MSS. *The Manuscripts of J. Eliot Hodgkin, Esq., of Richmond, Surrey.* Fifteenth Report, Appendix, Part II. 1897.

Marlborough MSS. *The Manuscripts of His Grace the Duke of Marlborough, at Blenheim, Co. Oxford.* Eighth Report, Appendix, 1881.

Onslow MSS. *The Manuscripts of the Earl of Onslow.* Fourteenth Report, Appendix, Part IX. 1895.

Polwarth MSS. *The Manuscripts of Lord Polwarth. Formerly Preserved in Mertoun House, Berwickshire.* Seventeenth Report. 1931. Volume III.

Portland MSS. *The Manuscripts of His Grace the Duke of Portland. Preserved at Welbeck Abbey.* Fifteenth Report. 1893-1923. Volumes V-VII.

Sackville MSS. *The Manuscripts of Mrs. Stopford Sackville, of Droyton House, Northamptonshire.* Ninth Report, Appendix, Part III. 1884.

Sutherland MSS. *The Manuscripts of His Grace the Duke of Sutherland, at Trentham, Co. Stafford.* Fifth Report, Appendix. 1876.

Trevor MSS. *The Manuscripts of the Earl of Buckinghamshire. Correspondence of Robert Trevor.* Fourteenth Report, Appendix, Part IX. 1895.

Underwood MSS. *The Manuscripts of Charles Fleetwood Weston Underwood, Esq., of Somerby Hall, Lincolnshire.* Tenth Report, Part I. 1895.

Wood MSS. *The Manuscripts of the Hon. Frederick Lindley Wood, Preserved at Temple Newsom, Leeds.* Fifteenth Report. Various Collections, Volume VIII. 1913.

HOARE, RICHARD. *A Journal of the Shrievalty of Richard Hoare, Esq., in the Years 1740-1741. Printed from a MSS. Copy in His Own Handwriting.* 1815.

An Impartial History of the Life, Character, Amours, Travels, and Transactions of Mr. John Barber, City-Printer, Common-Councilman, Alderman, and Lord Mayor of London. Written by Several Hands. 1741.

IRVING, WILLIAM HENRY. *John Gay's London.* Cambridge, 1928.

JENKS, EDWARD. *Walpole: A Study in Politics.* 1894.

JESSE, JOHN HENEAGE. *London and Its Celebrities.* 1850.

———. *Memoirs of the Court of England from the Revolution in 1688 to the Death of George the Second.* 1843. 3 vols.

Journals of the House of Commons. Vols. XIX-XXIV, 1718-1745.

Journals of the House of Lords. Vols. XXI-XXVI, 1718-1746.

KING, PETER, LORD. "Notes of Domestic and Foreign Affairs during the last Years of the Reign of George I and the Early Part of the Reign of George II," in *The Life of John Locke*, II, Supplement. 1830.

LAMBERT, B. *The History and Survey of London and Its Environs, from the Earliest Period to the Present Time.* 1806. 4 vols.

LANNING, JOHN TATE. *The Diplomatic History of Georgia: A Study of the Epoch of Jenkins' Ear.* Chapel Hill, 1936.

LAPRADE, WILLIAM THOMAS. "The Power of the English Press in the Eighteenth Century," *South Atlantic Quarterly*, XXVII (1928), 426-434.

―――. "The Present State of the History of England in the Eighteenth Century," *Journal of Modern History*, IV (1932), 581-603.

―――. *Public Opinion and Politics in Eighteenth Century England, to the Fall of Walpole.* New York, 1936.

LAUGHTON, J. K. "Jenkins' Ear," *English Historical Review*, IV (1889), 741-749.

Laws and Customs, Rights, Liberties, and Privileges of the City of London, The. 1765.

LEADAM, I. S. *The History of England, from the Accession of Anne to the Death of George II, 1702-1760.* 1909.

LECKY, WILLIAM H. *A History of England in the Eighteenth Century.* New York, 1878-1890. 8 vols.

LEE, WILLIAM. *Daniel Defoe: His Life, and Recently Discovered Writings, Extending from 1716 to 1729.* 1869. 3 vols.

The Life and Character of John Barber, Esq; Late Lord-Mayor of London, Deceased. 2d ed. (n. d.)

LOFTIE, REV. WM. JOHN. *London.* "Historic Towns Series." 1887.

KNIGHT, CHARLES. *London.* 1841-1844.

MAHON, LORD (PHILIP HENRY, FIFTH EARL STANHOPE). *History of England from the Peace of Utrecht to the Peace of Versailles, 1713-1783.* 1836-1854. 7 vols.

MALCOLM-SMITH, E. *British Diplomacy in the Eighteenth Century, 1700-1789.* 1937.

MAITLAND, WILLIAM. *The History and Survey of London from Its Foundation to the Present Time.* 1756. 2 vols.

MARCHMONT PAPERS. *A Selection from the Papers of the Earls of Marchmont in the Possession of the Right Hon. Sir George Henry Rose, Illustrative of Events from 1685 to 1750.* 1831. 3 vols.

MEADE, RICHARD. *The Medical Works of Richard Meade, M.D.* Dublin, 1767.

MELVILLE, LEWIS (LEWIS J. BENJAMIN). *The South Sea Bubble.* 1921.

―――. *The Life and Writings of Philip, Duke of Wharton.* 1913.

Memoirs of the Late Sir John Barnard, Knt. and Alderman of the City of London; together with Notes Furnished by Wm. H. Overall, Librarian of the City of London Guildhall Library; with a Preface by Thomson Hankey. 1820. Reprinted, 1885.

Memoirs of the Life and Character of Philip, Late Duke of Wharton, by an Impartial Hand. 1731. 2 vols.

MEREWETHER, HENRY A. *A History of the Buroughs and Municipal Corporations of the United Kingdom.* 1835. 3 vols.

MICHAEL, WOLFGANG. *English Geschichte im achtzehnten Jahrhundert.* Berlin, 1920-1937. 4 vols. ("Das Zeitalter Walpoles," III-IV, 1720-1742.)

MIEGE, GUY. *The Present State of Great Britain and Ireland.* 6th ed. 1728.

MILDMAY, SIR WILLIAM *The Method and Rule of Proceeding upon All Elections, Polls, and Scrutinies, at Common Halls, and Wardmotes within the City of London.* 1743.

MORISON, STANLEY. *The English Newspaper; Some Account of the Physical Development of Journals Printed in London between 1622 and the Present Day.* Cambridge, 1932.

MORLEY, JOHN. *Walpole.* 1896.

NORTON, GEORGE. *Commentaries on the History, Constitution, and Chartered Franchises of the City of London.* 1829.

NULLE, STEBELTON H. *Thomas Pelham-Holles, Duke of Newcastle: His Early Political Career, 1693-1724.* Philadelphia, 1931.

————. "The Duke of Newcastle and the Election of 1727," *Journal of Modern History,* IX (1937), 1-22.

OLDFIELD, THOMAS H. B. *An Entire and Complete History, Political, and Personal of the Buroughs of Great Britain; together with the Cinque Ports.* 1794. 2 vols.

————. *The Representative History of Great Britain and Ireland: Being a History of the House of Commons, and of the Counties, Cities and Buroughs, of the United Kingdom, from the Earliest Period.* 1876. 6 vols.

OLDMIXON, [JOHN]. *The History of England, During the Reigns of King William and Queen Mary, Queen Anne, and George I.* 1735.

OLIVER, FREDERICK SCOTT. *The Endless Adventure.* 1930-1935. 3 vols.

Orrery Papers, The. Edited by Emily C. Boyle, Countess of Clark and Orrery. 1903. 2 vols.

ORRIDGE, BENJAMIN B. *Some Account of the Citizens of London and Their Rulers, from 1060 to 1867.* 1867.

PARES, RICHARD. *War and Trade in the West Indies, 1739-1763.* Oxford, 1936.

PEMBERTON, W. BARING. *Carteret: The Brilliant Failure of the Eighteenth Century.* 1936.

PERCIVAL, MILTON. *Political Ballads, Illustrating the Administration of Sir Robert Walpole.* Oxford, 1916.

PERKINS, CLARENCE. "Electioneering in Eighteenth Century England," *Quarterly Journal of the University of North Dakota,* XIII (1923), 103-124.

PERKS, SIDNEY. *History of the Mansion House.* Cambridge, 1922.

PHILLIMORE, ROBERT JOSEPH. *Memoirs and Correspondence of George, Lord Lyttelton, from 1734 to 1773.* 1845. 2 vols.

PORRITT, EDWARD, AND ANNIE G. *The Unreformed House of Commons; Parliamentary Representation before 1832.* Cambridge, 1909. 2 vols.

PRICE, F. G. HILTON. *A Handbook of London Bankers, with Some Account of Their Predecessors, the Early Goldsmiths.* 1890-1891.

PULLING, ALEXANDER. *Practical Treatise on the Law, Customs, and Regulations of the City and Port of London.* 1842.

RALPH, JAMES. *A Critical History of the Administration of Sir Robert Walpole.* 1743.

————. *Of the Use and Abuse of Parliaments: In Two Historical Discourses.* 1744. 2 vols.

REALEY, CHARLES BECHTOLD. *The Early Opposition to Sir Robert Walpole.* Philadelphia, 1931.

————. "The London Journal and Its Authors, 1720-1723," *Bulletin of the University of Kansas Humanistic Studies,* V (1936), No. 3.

Report of the Commissioners Appointed to Inquire into the Municipal Corporations. Second Report, Dealing with London and Southwark. 1837.

ROBERTSON, J. M. *Bolingbroke and Walpole.* 1919.

ROBINSON, JOHN ROBERT. *Philip, Duke of Wharton, 1698-1731.* 1896.

ROGERS, J. E. THOROLD. *A Complete Collection of the Protests of the Lords, with Historical Introductions, 1624-1874.* Oxford, 1875. 3 vols.

SAUSSURE, CESAR DE. *A Foreign View of England in the Reigns of George I and George II.* Translated and edited by Madame Van Muyden. 2d ed. 1902.

SCOTT, WILLIAM ROBERT. *The Constitution and Finance of Eng-*

lish, Scottish, and Irish Joint-Stock Companies to 1720. Cambridge, 1911. 3 vols.

SEELEY, J. R. "The House of Bourbon," *English Historical Review,* I (1886), 86-104.

SEYMOUR, ROBERT. *A Survey of the Cities of London, and Westminster, Burough of Southwark, and Parts Adjacent.* 1734-1735. 2 vols.

SHARPE, REGINALD R. *London and the Kingdom.* 1894-1895. 3 vols.

SICHEL, WALTER S. *Bolingbroke and His Times.* 1901-1902. 2 vols.

Statutes at Large, The, from Magna Charta to the End of the Eleventh Parliament of Great Britain, Anno, 1861. Carefully Collated and Revised, with References, a Preface, and a New Accurate Index to the Whole by Danby Pickering. Continued by Others. Cambridge, 1762-1869. 109 vols.

STEVENS, D. H. *Party Politics and English Journalism, 1702-1742.* Menasha, Wisconsin, 1916.

SWIFT, JONATHAN. *The Correspondence of Jonathan Swift.* Edited by F. E. Ball. 1910-1914. 6 vols.

SYKES, NORMAN. *Edmund Gibson, Bishop of London, 1669-1748: A Study in Politics and Religion in the Eighteenth Century.* 1926.

TAYLOR, GEORGE ROBERT STERLING. *Robert Walpole: And His Age.* 1931.

TEMPERLEY, HAROLD W. V. "The Causes of the War of Jenkins' Ear, 1739," *Transactions of the Royal Historical Society,* Third Series, III, 197-236.

Times, The. Tercentenary Handlist of English and Welsh Newspapers, Magazines, and Reviews, 1620-1920. 1920.

TINDAL, NICHOLAS. *The History of England by Mr. Rapin de Thoyras, Translated from the French, and Continued from the Revolution to the Accession of King George II.* 1732-1747. 4 vols.

TORRENS, W. M. *History of Cabinets, from the Union with Scotland to the Acquisition of Canada and Bengal.* 1894. 2 vols.

TRELOAR, SIR WM. PURDIE. *A Lord Mayor's Diary, 1906-1907; to Which Is Added the Official Diary of Micajah Perry, 1738-1739.* 1920.

True State of England, The. Containing the Particular Duty, Business, and Salary of Every Officer, Civil and Military, in All the Publick Offices of Great Britain. 1729.

TURBERVILLE, ARTHUR STANLEY. *English Men and Manners in the Eighteenth Century.* Oxford, 1926.

————. *The House of Lords in the Eighteenth Century.* Oxford, 1927.

TURNER, E. R. "Early Opinion About English Excise," *American Historical Review,* XXI (1915), 314-318.

————. "The Excise Scheme of 1733," *English Historical Review,* XLII (1927), 34-57.

UNWIN, GEORGE. *The Gilds and Companies of London.* 1925.

VANBRUGH, SIR JOHN. *The Complete Works of Sir John Vanbrugh.* Edited by Bonamy Dobrée and Geoffrey Webb. 1928. 4 vols. (Volume IV, *The Letters.*)

VAUCHER, PAUL. *La crise du ministère Walpole en 1733-1734.* Paris, 1924.

————. *Robert Walpole et la politique de Fleury, 1731-1742.* Paris, 1924.

WADDINGTON, JOHN. *Congregational History, 1700-1800, in Relation to Contemporaneous Events, Education, the Eclipse of Faith, Revivals, and Christian Missions.* 1876.

WALPOLE, HORACE. *The Letters of Horace Walpole, Fourth Earl of Orford.* Edited by Peter Cunningham. 1891. 9 vols.

WARD, NED. *The London Spy: The Vanities and Vices of the Town Exposed to View.* Edited by Arthur L. Hayward. 1927.

WEBB, SIDNEY AND BEATRICE. *English Local Government from the Revolution to the Muncipal Corporations Act: The Manor and the Borough.* Part II. 1908.

Wentworth Papers, 1705-1739. Selected from the Private and Family Correspondence of Thomas Wentworth, Lord Raby, Created in 1711 Earl of Strafford, of Stainborough, York. With a Memoir and Notes by James J. Cartwright. 1883.

WHITE, JAMES G. *History of the Ward of Walbrook in the City of London.* 1904.

WILLIAMS, BASIL. "The Duke of Newcastle and the Election of 1734," *English Historical Review,* XII (1897), 448-488.

————. "The Foreign Policy of England Under Walpole," *English Historical Review,* XV (1900), 251, 479, 665; XVI (1901), 67, 308, 439.

————. *Stanhope: A Study in Eighteenth Century Diplomacy.* 1932.

————. *Carteret and Newcastle.* Cambridge, 1943.

WILKINS, W. H. *Caroline the Illustrious, Queen Consort of George II: A Study of Her Life and Times.* 1901. 2 vols.

WILLIAMS, FOLKESTONE. *Memoirs and Correspondence of Francis Atterbury, D.D., Bishop of Rochester.* 1869. 2 vols.

WILLIAMSON, ADAM. *The Official Diary of Lieutenant-General Adam Williamson, Deputy-Lieutenant of the Tower of London, 1722-1747.* Edited by John Charles Fox. Royal Historical Society, Camden Third Series, Volume XXII. 1912.

WRIGHT, THOMAS. *Caricature History of the Georges; or Annals of the House of Hanover.* 1867.

YORKE, PHILIP C. *The Life and Correspondence of Philip Yorke, Earle of Hardwicke, Lord High Chancellor of Great Britain.* Cambridge, 1913. 3 vols.

YOUNG, SIR GEORGE. *Poor Fred: The People's Prince.* 1937.

INDEX

Abney, Sir Thomas, senior alderman, 21; South Sea, 30; death, 60

Aislabie, John, 9, 10, 26

Aldermen, Court of, description, 18; members in 1721, 21-22; London representatives in parliament, 24; changes in attitude toward Walpole administration, 20-21, 32 and n., 60, 81, 134, 136-137, 168-171, 211-213; Jacobite Plot, 68 ff.; veto power (see Aldermanic veto); 1723 Cripplegate election contest, 83-84; 1723 sheriffs' election, 90-92; City Elections Act, 102-104, 107, 109; friction with Common Council, 4, 78, 104-105, 134; Frederick, Prince of Wales, 174-175; 1740-41 mayoralty elections, 197-202

Aldermanic veto, 19; report on (1724), 75-76; City Elections Act, 103, 105, 108-109 and n.; repeal urged, 193, 207; used, 200

Alsop, Robert, South Sea, 27; alderman, 112-113; sheriff, 133; death, 171

Amhurst, Nicholas, opposition writer as "Caleb D'Anvers," 125; on 1727 election, 128; on Spanish depredations, 181, 183

Applebee's Original Weekly Journal, opposition paper, 25 n.; cited, 27, 33, 44, 48

Arbuthnot, Dr. John, 38, 124, 142

Arnold, George, alderman, 196, 197 n., 202 n.

Arnall, William, 125 n.

Atterbury, Francis, Bishop of Rochester, leader of Opposition, 40 and n.; Quarantine Act, 40 and n., 42, 43; Quakers' Bill, 56, 57; Jacobite leader, 67, 72; arrested, 71; exiled, 72 and n., 122

Baillie, George, 11

Baker, William, alderman, 190 n., 197 n., 202 n., 205

Barber, John, South Sea, 27; alderman, 61, 117 n.; early career, 61 n.; City Elections Act, 102, 103 n.; Lord Mayor, 133, 137, 158; sheriff, 133; Excise Scheme, 142, 150, 156-157; 1734 parliamentary election, 161-162; Convention, 186 n.; 1740-1741 mayoralty elections, 197 n., 202 n.; 1741 parliamentary election, 205

Barnard, Sir John, career, 60 n.; 1722 parliamentary election, 60, 62-65; City Elections Act, 107, 109; of "new" opposition, 123, 181; 1727 parliamentary election, 127, 129-130; alderman, 135, 136; Excise, 141, 147-148, 153, 157; knighted, 141 n.; 1734 parliamentary election, 161-162; Lord Mayor, 165 and n.; sheriff, 166; Convention, 186, 189; M. P. for London, 193; 1740-1741 mayoralty elections, 196-197, 200, 202 and n.; 1741 parliamentary election, 204-206

Bathurst, Allen, 1st Earl Bathurst, 40 n., 123

Baylis, Sir Robert, alderman, 22; election, 79; unsuccessful for sheriff, 32; supporter of Feast, 82; sheriff, 97-98, 99, 102; knighted, 116; Lord Mayor, 132; Convention, 188 n.; 1740-1741 mayoralty elections, 197 n., 201, 202 n.

Beachcroft, Sir Robert, alderman, 22; death, 32; as Lord Mayor, 77

Beecher, Sir Edward, alderman, 22; sheriff, 32, 50, 64; knighted, 33; supports Conyers, 81; Lord Mayor, 120 n.; death, 136

Bellamy, Sir Edward (Joseph), alderman, 81; suggested for sheriff by Newcastle, 94; elected, 95-97; knighted, 115; Lord Mayor, 164; 1740 mayoralty election, 197 n., 199 n.; 1741 parliamentary election, 205-206, 207 n.